⸻ About This Book

Why This Topic Is Important

Talent is king! The war for talent! Talent is everything! These headlines tell the story. Having the proper talent in critical jobs is the key to organizational success. Also, during the last decade, talent retention has become a serious and perplexing problem for all types of organizations. Managing talent retention and keeping talent departure below target and industry norms is one of the most challenging issues facing businesses. From all indications, the issue will compound in the future, even as economic conditions change. Employee retention will continue to be an important issue for most job groups in the next decade.

Unwanted talent departure continues to be one of the most unappreciated and undervalued issues facing business leaders. This stems from several important assumptions and conclusions about turnover:

1. All stakeholders involved in the issue, including human resource executives, underestimate the true cost of employee turnover.

2. The causes of turnover are not adequately identified in most organizations.

3. The solutions to reduce turnover are sometimes mismatched with the cause of turnover and do not generate the desired results.

4. Many of the preventive measures for turnover are either overkill or they often miss the mark altogether.

5. A process to measure the success of retention solutions and place a monetary value on managing retention does not exist in most organizations.

These assumptions and conclusions create the need for a book to address these issues.

What You Can Achieve with This Book

Based on proven strategies, this is a practical book to provide direction to managers and specialists who are concerned about talent retention. First, it shows how to accurately cost the departure of talent providing examples and actual data from dozens of organizations. Second, it presents effective ways to identify the causes of turnover so that the problems can be quickly identified and rectified. Third, it shows how to lower an excessive turnover rate by implementing carefully designed and selected solutions to match the cause of turnover. Fourth, it reveals how to keep the turnover in an acceptable range by implementing a variety of preventive measures, tracking leading indicators, and placing alerts along the way to signal when action is needed. Finally, it demonstrates how to actually place monetary value and ROI on the implementation of solutions to improve or maintain retention, in a forecasting and a follow-up mode. In summary, this is a practical, indispensable approach to show how the retention issue can be carefully managed and monitored so that appropriate levels of turnover can be controlled and appropriate solutions can be implemented.

The Audience for This Book

Several audiences will find this new publication appropriate. First, the executives and administrators, who are concerned about retaining critical talent, will find the book to be a practical necessary approach to manage this issue on a proactive basis. Second, the human resources managers and executives who must address retention issues on a routine basis will find the book to be an indispensable guide. This book provides practical and useful information to address the issue and manage it in a realistic, practical way.

Third, the various specialists involved in different types of HR practices such as recruiting and selection, learning and development, career management, job design, communications, compensation, reward systems, and employee relations will find this book helpful. These specialists, who design solutions to help prevent or reduce turnover, will discover extremely valuable information as they confront this critical issue in their organization.

Fourth, managers at all levels, who must live with the consequences of turnover, will find this book useful in helping them fully understand the key issues and problems and, more important, the cost of talent. It will show them, in bottom-line terms, what turnover is actually costing them and what they must do to improve it in the future.

Finally, the fifth target audience group is professors and students who are involved in human resource courses, and consultants who assist HR managers with this issue will find the book to be a leading edge approved to managing retention. This book will offer proven strategies to deal with what is perhaps the number one issue facing the human capital management field.

How This Book Is Different

Several books are available to address employee retention. Most books on this issue focus on retention solutions without showing how to match solutions to need. Some of them attempt to show the impact of turnover although they sometimes fall short of addressing the fully loaded costs. Other books show how to retain employees by focusing on human relations programs and practices to increase job satisfaction. Still others focus on how to recruit the best employees in an effort to minimize future turnover. While these are all important issues, there is no book that focuses on the turnover issue from all vantage points beginning with the impact, working toward solutions, and showing the actual value of those solutions as they are implemented. For the first time in a major book—in one volume—an indispensable tool is developed to deal with this nightmare issue.

How This Book Is Organized

The book presents a logical process of managing retention. Chapter 1 shows why talent is critical in today's organization. It explores the forces driving the importance of talent and presents a system approach to talent management.

Chapter 2, Why Talent Retention Is a Serious Problem, explains why retention continues to be a serious problem, even in times of economic ups and downs. It explores the negative impact of retention on both organizations and on individuals, including what's driving the persistent retention issue. This chapter also dispels some of the myths of turnover and explains why this should be tackled immediately as a strategic issue in organizations.

Chapter 3, An ROI Approach to Managing Retention, presents the overall approach for the book. In eight distinct steps, this chapter summarizes the recommended approach to retention, beginning with measuring and monitoring turnover and cycling through all the issues of determining causes, matching needs to solutions, forecasting solutions, measuring the success, and continuing to make adjustments. This process is offered as a more systematic, methodical approach to the retention issue.

Chapter 4, Measure and Monitor Turnover and Retention Data, is the first step of the strategic accountability approach. It outlines what types of retention and turnover data should be collected, when data should be collected, and how data should be reported to the senior team. Additional data beyond the overall turnover rates are described.

Chapter 5, Develop Fully Loaded Costs of Talent Departure, discusses how to calculate the total impact of turnover, including both direct and indirect costs. In most cases, the indirect costs exceed the direct costs and the techniques for efficiently capturing these are described. This chapter provides the appropriate data to show the executive team if turnover is having a dramatic and sometimes devastating impact on the organization.

Chapter 6, Diagnose Causes of Talent Departure, is one of the critical chapters that explore how to pinpoint the causes of turnover in the organization. It shows how to use questionnaires, surveys, interviews, focus groups, exit interview data, as well as other techniques to identify the actual causes of turnover. This is an often-overlooked step as organizations sometimes review general research data about employee needs and attempt to develop solutions without uncovering the specific causes within the organization.

Chapters 7, 8, 9, and 10 are a major part of this book. They show a variety of typical solutions that are implemented. Each chapter begins with a discussion around a cluster of typical needs uncovered in organizations and outlines specific solutions that have been implemented to meet those needs.

Chapter 7, Recruit Talent, focuses on the initial processes that bring employees to an organization. Focusing on needs and solutions, the chapter examines what attracts employees to an organization and weaves through the recruitment, selection, orientation, indoctrination, and job assignment issues to ensure that the employee fits into the organization and the job.

Chapter 8, Establish an Adequate Work Environment, presents the essentials necessary for an acceptable work environment in today's climate. It explores such issues as job satisfaction, culture, climate, diversity, work life balance, and many other critical issues that employers take for granted. These are the basics and a variety of solutions are presented to provide them.

Chapter 9, Create Equitable Pay and Performance Processes, deals with the economic and reward issues. This critical chapter identifies what employees seek in terms of pay and benefits and their need for adequate rewards and recognition on the job. It explores a variety of solutions economically matched to these needs. The need for non-economic rewards is also covered in this chapter.

Chapter 10, Build Motivation and Commitment, is perhaps the most important set of solutions. In addition to exploring the issues that cause employees to remain with the organization, this chapter explores solutions aimed at building commitment and growth. Organizational commitment, motivation systems, building trust, ethics, job growth, career advancement, and other key issues employees are demanding in the organization today are described.

Chapter 11, Match Solutions to Needs, shows how the solutions should be selected to focus directly on the specific needs of the employee within the organization. Given that there are many possible solutions, this chapter outlines practical ways to ensure that appropriate matches are made between the need and solution with care taken to ensure that mismatches and multiple solutions are avoided, and that the solutions can be developed quickly.

Chapter 12, Forecast ROI of Retention Solutions, is probably the most innovative approach to managing retention. In this unique chapter, special techniques are offered to show how the value of a potential solution can be forecast to determine the potential ROI before it is actually implemented. This approach provides executives with a profile of potential payoffs from several solutions, thus helping to ensure that the funds are not misallocated or wasted on low payoff opportunities or mismatched solutions.

Chapter 13, Calculate ROI of Retention Solutions, shows how the payoff of retention solutions can be developed. Using the ROI Methodology, this chapter shows how six types of data can be collected from any type of retention solution (reaction, learning, application, impact, ROI, and intangible data). The ROI Methodology provides the management team with the information necessary to determine the overall success of the solution.

Chapter 14, Make Adjustments and Continue, focuses on the heart of the retention process by showing how data from successful retention solutions can be utilized to ensure that the processes are working properly. It shows how results are communicated and actions are taken to continue to bring turnover down or keep turnover at an acceptable rate. This is the last step of the strategic accountability approach, and the cycle continues in a routine process from measuring turnover to making adjustments.

Chapter 15 presents a case study showing how a master's degree program was used to reduce the departure of high-potential communication specialists, the critical talent. The study features a unique design and implementation and an impressive ROI in this government agency.

Chapter 16 presents a case study detailing how skill-based compensation was used in a banking organization to tackle an excessive talent departure More specifically, the case study shows how the causes of turnover were clearly pinpointed and how the impact of the solution was developed, including measuring ROI.

Chapter 17 presents a case study on the use of coaching for new employees to reduce the turnover of technology employees in the first years of employment. The strategy of the case lies in the success in gaining support for the ROI approach in this global media company.

Collectively, the logical, progressive presentation of the chapters provides for an easy-to-understand book. We think you will find this unique publication to be a valuable reference and user's guide.

About Pfeiffer

Pfeiffer serves the professional development and hands-on resource needs of training and human resource practitioners and gives them products to do their jobs better. We deliver proven ideas and solutions from experts in HR development and HR management, and we offer effective and customizable tools to improve workplace performance. From novice to seasoned professional, Pfeiffer is the source you can trust to make yourself and your organization more successful.

Essential Knowledge Pfeiffer produces insightful, practical, and comprehensive materials on topics that matter the most to training and HR professionals. Our Essential Knowledge resources translate the expertise of seasoned professionals into practical, how-to guidance on critical workplace issues and problems. These resources are supported by case studies, worksheets, and job aids and are frequently supplemented with CD-ROMs, websites, and other means of making the content easier to read, understand, and use.

Essential Tools Pfeiffer's Essential Tools resources save time and expense by offering proven, ready-to-use materials—including exercises, activities, games, instruments, and assessments—for use during a training or team-learning event. These resources are frequently offered in looseleaf or CD-ROM format to facilitate copying and customization of the material.

Pfeiffer also recognizes the remarkable power of new technologies in expanding the reach and effectiveness of training. While e-hype has often created whizbang solutions in search of a problem, we are dedicated to bringing convenience and enhancements to proven training solutions. All our e-tools comply with rigorous functionality standards. The most appropriate technology wrapped around essential content yields the perfect solution for today's on-the-go trainers and human resource professionals.

Pfeiffer
www.pfeiffer.com

Essential resources for training and HR professionals

Jack J. Phillips

Lisa Edwards

Managing Talent Retention

An ROI Approach

Pfeiffer
A Wiley Imprint
www.pfeiffer.com

Published by Pfeiffer
An Imprint of Wiley
989 Market Street, San Francisco, CA 94103-1741
www.pfeiffer.com

Readers should be aware that Internet websites offered as citations
and/or sources for further information may have changed or disappeared between the time this
was written and when it is read.
For additional copies/bulk purchases of this book in the U.S. please contact 800-274-4434.

Pfeiffer books and products are available through most bookstores. To contact Pfeiffer directly call
our Customer Care Department within the U.S. at 800-274-4434, outside the U.S. at 317-572-3985,
fax 317-572-4002, or visit www.pfeiffer.com.

Pfeiffer also publishes its books in a variety of electronic formats. Some content that appears in print
may not be available in electronic books.

Library of Congress Cataloging-in-Publication Data

Phillips, Jack J.
  Managing talent retention : an ROI approach / Jack J. Phillips, Lisa Edwards.
     p. cm.
  Includes index.
  ISBN 978-0-470-37595-2 (cloth)
1.   Employee retention. 2.   Labor turnover. I. Edwards, Lisa, 1963- II. Title.
  HF5549.5.R58P482 2009
  658.3'14—dc22

                                                                2008033073

Acquiring Editor: Matthew Davis   Editorial Assistant: Lindsay Morton
Marketing Manager: Brian Grimm   Editor: Rebecca Taff
Director of Development: Kathleen Dolan Davies   Manufacturing Supervisor: Becky Morgan
Production Editor: Michael Kay

Printed in the United States of America
Printing   10 9 8 7 6 5 4 3 2 1

Contents

~~~ List of Figures, Tables, and Exhibits

Figures

Tables

Exhibits

—ww— Acknowledgements

I would like to thank the many clients I have had the pleasure of working with over the past fifteen years. When we provide consulting services to organizations all over the world, our principle contact is the human resources executive. On every occasion we have learned from these executives. To this important group of clients I extend a personal thanks for what they have taught me over the years. They are truly a very capable and impressive group.

Special thanks go to our staff at the ROI Institute, who provided excellent support to make this book a reality. Thanks to Karen Wright, who coordinated this book and made the final push required to send the book to the publisher.

We are constantly indebted to Jossey-Bass and Pfeiffer for their continued support of our work. Matt Davis has been very patient through this process, allowing us to push deadlines as we continued to capture additional content. Matt is a very professional, highly respected, and productive editor. Thanks, Matt.

It has been a pleasure to work with Lisa Edwards on this project. Lisa is an admired and effective CLO in the business. Much of this book represents her experience and her tolerance for working with me. Thanks, Lisa, for a great coproduction.

And finally, thanks go to my partner, spouse, and special friend Patti, CEO of the ROI Institute. Although Patti is not one of the listed authors, she provided much insight, input, and some final editing to make this book a reality. She always contributes significantly to our work, and has done a marvelous job of pushing the ROI Institute to the forefront of the assessment, measurement, and evaluation field. To Patti, we owe you much, and we'll continue to owe you much more. Thanks.

Jack J. Phillips
July 2008

First, I would like to thank Jack Phillips for the many opportunities he has provided to me—and, especially for the opportunity to co-author this work with him. I have learned so much from Jack over the years and am sincerely privileged and honored for each of the experiences. Thank you, Jack, for your continued encouragement and generosity of time, wisdom and opportunity.

Karen Wright at the ROI Institute has been a pleasure to work with and instrumental to the success of this project. Karen kept all the trains running with her consistent, timely, and enthusiastic support and coordination. Thank you, Karen.

Many thanks go to Jossey-Bass and Pfeiffer for their support of this work and for their patience and professionalism throughout the project. Thank you for your interest in this project and for making it come to life!

Finally—thank you, Mom, for believing in me and for patiently nudging me forward, year after year.

Lisa Edwards
July 2008

CHAPTER ONE

Talent Management

The Key to Organizational Success

T alent management is one of the most important strategic objectives of organizations today. From every viewpoint, talent is essential and is often regarded as a key strategy in maintaining a competitive advantage. Talent management is needed for success, efficiency, and consistency. A systems approach is advocated, beginning with attracting talent and ending with removing talent. This approach brings a host of challenges:

1. A successful talent management process identifies critical jobs in the organization and finds ways to that ensure current and backup incumbents are top performers. Sometimes, people who are in critical jobs are not the best performers, and the best performers are not in critical jobs.

2. A successful talent management system is a clear process for identifying and developing high potentials. Many organizations carefully review and manage a small segment of their talent as high potentials. Other companies do not clearly segment out this group or provide preferential development or treatment. Either

way, identifying top performers and fostering their development provides higher chances for performance and retention.

3. A successful talent management process plans for organizational transitions. Some companies have extensive succession plans for several layers of management; others only create plans for the top leaders in the company. To avoid disruption in business performance, it is critical to plan for departures of talent or, in the words of McDonald's Corporation, backups in case someone "gets hit by the bun truck."

4. A successful talent management system addresses movement of talent and the holes this can leave in the organization. Talent management occurs when movement of talent happens regularly and has minimal impact on the business. If an employee's skills can be better utilized in another function, talent should be moved to those functions. Unfortunately, managers become territorial and fear shortages in their departments. It is necessary to plan for these gaps and create a culture in which talent belongs to the organization, not to a specific group. When managed appropriately, there will be no serious gaps or shortages because the talent management system is so robust that it can fill the openings quite quickly.

5. A successful talent management system creates talent pools. Formal rotation programs have flourished to simulate the concept of a centralized pool of talent. These programs enable a person, new graduate, or existing employee to work for different managers in different functions during their rotation assignments. Finance, for example, is a function that uses this model quite frequently with their new MBA graduates. A program is created that exposes the employee to financial accounting, financing strategy, financial analysis, and, sometimes, tax/treasury. At the end of the formal program, the employee can select a function or decide which manager or group they want to work with. This provides the employee with exposure to different functions and develops their skills.

6. A successful talent management system must report on the outcomes. Providing data to management about the number of employees with international experience, the number of leaders

with marketing education, or the percentage of employees with advanced degrees can provide critical information for business planning. Boards have an increasing interest in understanding the talent within a company as well as strategies for acquisition, development, and retention. Additionally, the success of talent management programs must be reported to senior executives.

WHY TALENT IS CRITICAL TO SUCCESS

Talent is considered the most critical source of success in an organization and no executive will argue this point. How did it get this way? How critical is it now? How critical will it be in the future? There are several major reasons why talent is so important and will be even more critical in the future. Each is briefly described here.

Stock Market Mystery

When considering the value and importance of talent, executives need look no further than the stock market. Investors place a tremendous value on human capital in organizations. For example, consider Google, Inc.—a global technology leader focused on improving the ways people connect with information. Based in Mountain View, California, Google is a Fortune 500 company traded on the NASDAQ stock market. Google is a very profitable company with revenues of $16.6 billion in 2007, and a net income of $4.2 billion (Annual Report, 2008).

Google reported total assets on its balance sheet of $25 billion and include not only the current assets of cash, marketable securities, accounts receivable, and inventories, but property, plants, equipment, and even goodwill. However, the market value is much higher. At mid-year the market value was $105 billion. In essence, the tangible assets represent only 23.8 percent of the market value. Investors see something in Google that has a value much greater than the assets listed on the balance sheet. This "hidden value," as it is sometimes called, is the intangible assets, which now represent major portions of the value of organizations, particularly those in knowledge industries, such as Google. It is helpful to understand what comprises the intangible assets; human capital is certainly a big part of it.

The Best Idea Will Fail Without Proper Talent and Execution

Talent management is fundamentally about ensuring that the right people are positioned in the right places and utilized to the fullest potential for optimal success of the organization. Top business leaders clearly understand their talent pools. They work hard to identify the key players who have critical relationships with customers and suppliers, and then work even harder to nurture and keep those key resources.

A number of business leaders have asserted that coming up with the best talent for their companies is the most important task they have to perform. Some, like former GE Chairman Jack Welch and Honeywell International's Larry Bossidy, spent a significant amount of time searching for the best talent within their own employee pools, hoping to build leadership that way. Both Welch and Bossidy have frequently said that all the great strategies in the world will have little effect on a company unless the right people are chosen to execute those strategies. Steve Miller, the most successful turnaround CEO, clearly connects talent and execution. This master of execution rescued Federal-Modul, Waste Management, Reliance Group, Aetna, Bethlehem Steel, and Delphi, among others. One of his first tasks as a new CEO was to find the critical talent who could exercise the plans to save the company (Miller, 2008).

Leaders understand this and put a premium on keeping the talent they need for growth. They do what is necessary to ensure that key people are secure and do not leave because of low morale, thus preventing a defection domino effect.

Human Capital Is the Last Major Source of Competitive Advantage

Today's organizations have access to the key success factors. Financial resources are available to almost any organization with a viable business model. Financial capital froze even during economic downtimes. One company no longer has an advantage over another to access the financial capital needed to run a business. Access to technology is equal; a company can readily adapt technology to a given situation or business model. It is difficult to have a technology advantage in an information technology society.

Businesses also have access to customers—even if there is a dominant player in the market. Newspapers are laced with stories of small organizations taking on larger ones and succeeding. Having entry and access to a customer database is not necessarily a competitive advantage. What makes the difference, clearly, is the human capital—the talent—of an organization. With relatively equal access to all the other resources, it is logical to conclude that the human resources are where a strategic advantage can be developed.

The Great Places to Work

Probably nothing about the importance of talent is more visible than the list of organizations selected as the 100 Best Companies to Work For. This list is published each year in *Fortune* magazine and has become the bellwether for focusing on the importance of talent. Although other publications have spinoffs and other countries have similar lists in local publications, this is the premier list that U.S. organizations strive to make. The most important factor in selecting companies for this list is what the employees themselves have to say about their workplace. For a typical list, at least 350 randomly selected employees from each candidate company fill out an employee-produced survey created by The Great Place to Work Institute, San Francisco. The annual list presents each company in rank, along with:

- Total employment, detailed by the percent of minorities and women;
- Annual job growth (percent);
- Number of jobs created in the past year;
- Number of applicants;
- Voluntary turnover rate;
- Number of hours of training per year;
- Average annual pay, detailed by professional and hourly; and
- Revenues.

These lists are alive with tales of how the employers focus on building a great place to work and building employee respect, dignity, and capability. These firms are successful in the market. A typical

These twenty-one companies have appeared on our list every year since its 1998 inception:

A.G. Edwards	Publix Super Markets
Cisco Systems	Recreational Equipment
FedEx	SAS Institute
First Horizon National	Synovus
Four Seasons Hotels	TD Industries
Goldman Sachs	Timberland
J.M. Smucker	Valassis
Marriott International	W.L. Gore
MBNA	Wegmans Food Markets
Microsoft	Whole Food Markets
Nordstrom	

Exhibit 1.1.   Hall of Fame Great Places to Work

list includes well-known and successful companies such as American Express, Cisco Systems, FedEx, Genentech, Eli Lilly, Marriott International, General Mills, Merck, Microsoft, Procter & Gamble, Qualcomm, and others. Inclusion in the list has become so sought after by organizations that they change many of their practices and philosophies in an attempt to make this list. Exhibit 1.1 shows the companies that have made the list every year since its inception in 1998.

This list underscores the importance of talent and how much emphasis companies place on it. It shows how diversity, job growth, turnover, and learning make a significant difference in the organization. For the most part, these organizations are investing heavily—far exceeding those on any other list. Investment, in their mind, translates into payoff.

Most Admired and Successful Companies

Two other important lists are *Fortune*'s America's Most Admired Companies and The World's Most Admired Companies. These lists are unique because the ranking is determined by peer groups. To develop the list, the Hay Group starts with the ten largest companies (by revenue) in sixty-four industries, including foreign firms with U.S. operations. Then they ask 15,000 executives, directors, and security analysts to rate the companies in their own industries with eight criteria, using a scale of 1 to 10. The respondents select the ten companies they admire most in any industry. From a talent perspective, it is interesting that three of the eight key attributes focused directly on talent: employee talent, quality of management, and innovation. The other five are indirectly related. The key point is that investors and business people admire companies who are placing important emphasis on the human capital aspects of their business.

Perhaps the most publicized list is the grouping of superstars. As there are superstars in almost every area in life, so there are superstar organizations—those perceived as being extraordinarily successful, based on major accomplishments. We all know them by reputation, success, and contribution. The literature is laced with showplace examples of these extraordinary companies including SAS, Qualcomm, SAP, GE, Southwest Airlines, Honda, and USAA, to name a few. One common denominator for the superstar organization is recognizing the people factor—the talent. Executives at superstar organizations always give recognition to the people who have created the outstanding performance.

Most executives not only declare that their people are the most important assets, but make statements like "We could not have done it without the people." Some will argue that the success of an organization can only be defined in terms of employees. Success cannot be generated in any way without successful people, not only at the top, but at all levels. People *are* the most important asset and no organization has been successful without them.

The Cost of Competent Talent

Successful talent acquisition and management is expensive. The total investment in talent is the total HR department expenses plus salaries and benefits of all other employees. All of the direct employee-related costs are included in the human capital measure. In essence, this includes every function that exists in the chain of talent acquisition and management. Attracting, selecting, developing, motivating, compensating, and managing talent are accounted for in this total cost. Because the traditional HR department expenses do not include salaries of other functions, this measure has the effect of showing the total cost. It should be reported as a percent of operating costs, or revenue, or on a per-employee basis to show realistic comparisons with other organizations.

Executives in some organizations realize the magnitude of these expenses and have a desire to manage them efficiently. Although the costs do not include the costs for office spaces and support expenses, they are still very significant, often two to three times the annual pay. In many—if not most—industries, the cost of talent is the largest operating expense category. Recruiting fully competent employees avoids some of the cost of initial training, development, and on-the-job learning, although the salary and benefits may be higher than those of less-skilled employees. Because talent is so expensive, it must be managed carefully and systematically.

The Cost of Talent Departures

When talent leaves, the costs are high. Executives see the direct cost of recruiting, selection, and initial training, but may not understand other impacts. The total cost of turnover is not calculated routinely in organizations. When the cost is estimated, it is often underestimated. Also, estimations of the total cost are not communicated throughout the organization, leaving the management team unaware of the potential costs. If turnover is a problem, the costs are always significant. In some cases, the actual impact can be devastating and can result in the organization's demise.

The total cost of turnover involves both the direct and indirect costs. There are many different costs, some of which are never known with certainty but can be estimated. When the total costs are calculated, it is often expressed as a percent of annual pay for a particular job group, and these costs are significant.

There is healthy turnover in any organization; people who retire, work in non-profit organizations, or go back to school. The area of most concern in managing talent is when top performers or critical employees depart their jobs. The challenge is to manage this turnover successfully and on-board new employees quickly. In an ideal scenario, talent sources are available so there are no gaps in organizational performance or product road maps.

Summary

It may be helpful to summarize this information, which clearly details the critical role of talent in the organization. Exhibit 1.2 shows ten reasons why talent is critical to success, most of which are briefly discussed in this section. The remainder of this chapter describes

1. We cannot be successful without talent.
2. Talent adds to the market value.
3. Talent executes the ideas.
4. Talent is the last source of competitive advantage.
5. Great workplaces attract and retain talent.
6. The most successful and admired companies have great talent.
7. The cost of competent talent is high.
8. The cost of turnover of talent is high.
9. The competitive environment has created a retention crisis.
10. Retention can be managed.

Exhibit 1.2.   Ten Reasons Why Talent Is Critical to Success

how organizations provide the focus, attention, and care needed to for this strategic issue.

A SYSTEM FOR TALENT MANAGEMENT

The most effective way to tackle talent management is to use a systems approach, ensuring that the different elements and pieces of the process are working in concert to acquire integrate talent into the system. Several issues support the need for this system.

Disconnected Efforts

The traditional way to deal with this issue is to have the responsibility assigned to various groups that traditionally cut across functional lines. Recruiting, learning and development, reward systems, and associate relations are the traditional functional groups. Several problems may surface with this approach. First, in this traditional style, talent management is in a reactive mode—reacting to critical issues, problems, and talent shortages. There are few early signs to signal an impending problem. Also, because individuals involved are not tightly integrated, with open communication, inefficiencies abound in the processes, often creating duplications and delays throughout the system. Consequently, this is a very expensive approach to the problem; one that fails to generate the success needed, leaving voids, omissions, and delays. The results can be disastrous for an organization in need of talent, attempting to grow. Most of all, the traditional approach creates confusion—not only in the roles and responsibilities, but designating who is in charge. This confusion has been minimized by a systems approach.

A SYSTEMS APPROACH

Figure 1.1 shows the traditional model for a talent management process where the focus is on acquiring and retaining talent. Today, more issues must be addressed and integrated as suggested in the systems approach to talent management presented in Figure 1.2. It includes the major issues of planning, acquiring, developing, managing, and retaining employees. These are often subdivided into responsibility areas, as outlined in the figure. Traditionally, many of these have been under different sections. This is a system that must work together in close coordination and integration, ideally under the direction of a central person whose key responsibility is talent management—perhaps a chief talent officer (CTO). When in place, the benefits are tremendous from the client's perspective. First, it presents consistent attention throughout the process. If these

Figure 1.1.   Traditional Talent Management Process
Source: Deloitte Research, 2004

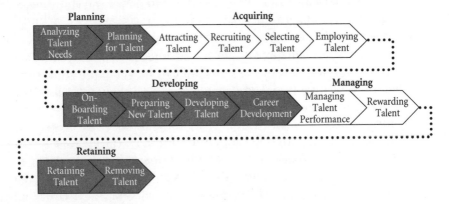

Figure 1.2.   Talent Management System

issues are integrated, it creates a smooth transition. Problems can be spotted quickly and adjustments made. Second, talent acquisition can be more effective, ensuring that adequate talent is recruited and integrated in the system as well as the appropriate quality and quantities are secured. Finally, there is a value add as costs are reduced when the process is more efficient and duplications are avoided. The systems approach is not only rationale and logical, but it is the economic way to address this important issue.

Defining the Critical Talent

Before describing the mechanics of talent management, it is helpful to define the critical talent in the organization. The critical talent are the employees who drive a major part of the company's business performance and generate above-average value for customers and shareholders. Typically, the critical talent possesses highly developed skills and deep knowledge. They don't just "do their jobs," but go above and beyond to contribute to the organization's success. They are in roles where they can make a difference—a big difference. Surprisingly, these are not always the high-tech or highest paid employees, but often the backbone employees who are seldom mentioned in the annual report. Take FedEx, for example, the world's largest overnight package delivery firm. One report suggested that the couriers might be more critical to the operation than the pilots who fly the packages through the night. The couriers have direct contact with the customers and must make continual decisions that impact efficiency and the effectiveness of the supply chain such as how to reconfigure a route and how long to wait for a customer's packages (Deloitte Research, 2004).

Critical talent can vary considerably by industry and organization. At Bristol Meyers Squibb they may include the scientists and clinicians who discover and develop pharmaceuticals that fuel the company's growth. At British Petroleum they may include the geologists and petroleum engineers who find and extract oil. At Boeing, it may be the machinists who perform precision operations to develop parts for airplanes using Six Sigma standards. At Wal-Mart it may be the inventory managers who ensure that the right goods are in the right store at the right time. Recruiting wars often erupt when there's a shortage of critical talent, leading to much inefficiency, cost, and disruptions along the talent management system.

Competencies: A Starting Point

In recent years, there has been a tremendous focus on the use of competencies, with some experts indicating that attracting talent can only be achieved if it is focused on identifying competencies and using them throughout the process. Competency models are fundamental to human capital management systems. Too many organizations use different languages when describing recruiting standards, training requirements, and promotional criteria. The problem is exacerbated when these organizations operate in different cultures and countries. By utilizing an agreed-upon competency model, the organization can communicate via a common language that describes performance from one unit to the next (Berger & Berger, 2004).

As shown in Figure 1.3, competencies drive the entire talent management system. Competencies relate planning, recruiting, and selecting talent at the beginning of the process. Preparing and developing talent focuses on the same competencies; managing, rewarding, and motivating employees also focus on these competencies. The competencies for a particular job—even similar jobs—can vary. A competency is a reliably measurable, relatively enduring characteristic (or combination thereof) of a person, community, or organization that causes or statistically predicts a criterion or level of performance. Competency characteristics are knowledge, behavioral skills,

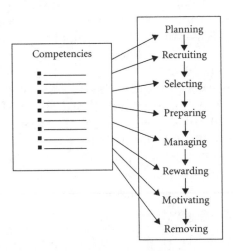

Figure 1.3.   Competencies and the Talent Management System

competency processing (IQ), personality trait, values, motives, and occasionally other perceptional capabilities (Spencer, 2004).

An example of competencies is shown in Table 1.1. While these can be typical competencies for organizations, they are not necessarily for *every* organization. They have to be specific in terms of what is important to an organization and the skills, knowledge, and value systems needed. Competencies can be evaluated through interviews and previous work experiences. Once on the job, competencies are often observable and translate directly into success or lack of success.

The key challenge is to determine, to the extent possible, the competencies needed for talent in specific divisions, groups, functions, or even job categories and use them to drive the talent management system.

The CTO's Role

Traditionally, the responsibility for talent management has not been assigned to a single executive.. Today, this has changed and in many organizations. a chief talent officer CTO is now responsible for all of the system, including recruiting, performance management, and managing layoffs. The chief talent officer ensures that the proper talent is selected, properly developed, and managed. The CTO has the opportunity to change the mindset of the organization and can have a key impact on lowering recruiting costs and offering employees new growth and opportunities that may not have been visible before.

PLANNING

Planning is perhaps the area that has been most neglected in many talent management systems. The objective of planning is to have an orderly process for acquiring the appropriate types of employees to meet the needs of the organization, given the constraints of market forces and the available labor supply. Three areas are often addressed, sometimes by separate individuals or units within the talent management system.

Analyzing Talent Needs

Several factors will determine the need for talent, as defined earlier. First, the growth of the organization often translates into the largest

Competency	Competency Definition
Action Orientation	Targets and achieves results, overcomes obstacles, accepts responsibility, establishes standards and responsibilities, creates a results-oriented environment, and follows through on actions.
Communication	Communicates well both verbally and in writing. Effectively conveys and shares information and ideas with others. Listens carefully and understands various viewpoints. Presents ideas clearly and concisely and understands relevant detail in presented information.
Creativity/Innovation	Generates novel ideas and develops or improves existing and new systems that challenge the status quo, takes risks, and encourages innovation.
Critical Judgment	Possesses the ability to define issues and focus on achieving workable solutions. Consistently does the right thing by performing with reliability.
Customer Orientation	Listens to customers, builds customer confidence, increases customer satisfaction, ensures commitments are met, sets appropriate customer expectations, and responds to customer needs.
Interpersonal Skill	Effectively and productively engages with others and establishes trust, credibility, and confidence with others.
Leadership	Motivates, empowers, inspires, collaborates with, and encourages others. Develops a culture where employees feel ownership in what they do and continually improve the business. Builds consensus when appropriate. Focuses team members on common goals.
Teamwork	Knows when and how to attract, develop, reward, and utilize teams to optimize results. Acts to build trust, inspire enthusiasm, encourage others, and help resolve conflicts and develop consensus in creating high-performance teams.
Technical/ Functional Expertise	Demonstrates strong technical/functional proficiencies and knowledge in areas of expertise. Shows knowledge of company business and proficiency in the strategic and financial processes, including P&L planning processes and their implications for the company.

Table 1.1.   Sample Competencies

Source: Berger and Berger, 2004

component of talent requirements. The CTO must be aware of the organization's strategy, both short- and long-term. Needs are sometimes driven by shifts in products and services, acquisitions, mergers, and routine growth through expansion. Whatever the reasons, this action translates into a specific number of individuals in different job categories.

Second, replacement needs create openings as employees leave the organization. If the turnover is excessive, replacement needs become significant. If there is low turnover, replacement needs are minimal. In the context of managing retention, only the avoidable turnover is considered. However, when replacements are needed, all types of turnover must be considered, including those individuals who retire, leave due to disability, or transfer to other regional areas. Just the retirement issue is a critical problem for many organizations. NASA, for example, faces a tremendous loss of talent as much of the science and engineering capability will be retiring in the next few years. This situation will have a tremendous impact on the talent management system to ensure that the proper talent is recruited and prepared for their assignments.

A third area that translates directly into needs is the changes in skills and competencies. As technology advances, markets change, and products shift, a different set of skills and competencies is sometimes needed, either in addition to or beyond those currently in the organization. These three areas generate needs that must be translated into specific numbers forecasted, in both short- and long-term scenarios.

Since the majority of needs must be filled from the available labor market, a market analysis is critical. When examining the labor market, several issues must be taken into consideration. First is the supply of labor in the recruiting area. This is a critical issue for some organizations because of labor shortages. This may require the relocation of facilities to ensure a better source of labor. For example, many automobile companies based outside the United States are developing plants in record numbers in the southern part of the United States. For example, Toyota, Honda, Mercedes Benz, and Hyundai have all developed major plants in the state of Alabama, making this state the automobile capital of the south. A major part of the attraction is the available labor supply—in both quality and quantity—as well as a strong work ethic.

Planning for Talent

After the numbers have been developed and the market is analyzed, the plans are developed, generating a schedule of the number that will be acquired at what times, from what sources, and—sometimes—by job group. If it becomes apparent that the market will not be able to supply the required resources, the shortages must be addressed and alternatives developed. For example, due to the difficulty of recruiting fully trained nurses, hospitals have created their own nursing schools, sometimes in conjunction with a university, at other times on their own. This is a classic case of attempting to regulate supply versus demand; taking control of the situation and creating the supply. This situation creates an important issue that must be part of the talent planning—that of scenario planning. Because all forecasts contain error and there are many events that can have a significant effect on the sources, including success, different scenarios should be developed, including worst-case conditions. This process provides insight into what can, should, and perhaps must be done to ensure that available talent is on board when needed.

ACQUIRING

Acquiring talent has four key issues: attracting (in essence, creating a talent magnet); recruiting (getting them into the organization); selecting (making the selection decision); and employing (actually putting them on the payroll). Each of these is an important step, often performed by different individuals.

Attracting Talent

Attracting talent is a long-term issue. The attraction of a place to work covers several issues, but two very important ones relate to the issue of developing a talent magnet. One issue is being an employer of choice, representing a great place to work. The second is the overall reputation, or employment brand, of the organization. Employers of choice have several things in common. They recognize and organize a work/life balance program that meets needs across the business; have professional and personal development opportunities for all; possess the ability to make a contribution to the firm tied to personal responsibility; enjoy a friendly and culturally rich environment, and operate a business that is responsible to the community as a whole. In the United States, employer-of-choice issues are developed by a variety of organizations and publications. The most common is the one developed by *Fortune* magazine and reflected as The 100 Best Companies to Work For and was described earlier in the chapter.

Organizations are working harder to polish their images in the eyes of prospective talent. Some have staff who do little but keep the firm's name in front of both faculty and students and promote their "employer brand." For example, GE focuses on over thirty universities where it actively promotes itself as an employer. PriceWaterhouseCoopers (PWC) targets about two hundred universities and gives a partner responsibility for each. PWC says that each of these partners spends up to two hundred hours a year building relationships on campus.

The reputation is based on several factors. Harris Interactive and the Reputation Institute published a corporate reputation poll based on the views of almost thirty thousand respondents. They developed six categories to rank reputation:

- Emotional appeal;
- Products and services;
- Workplace environment;
- Social responsibility;
- Vision and leadership; and
- Financial performance.

The reputations, particularly for those issues about a place to work, are often evolved and developed over time and have to be driven by senior leadership. A few scandals, ethical concerns, or ineffective leadership can spoil an otherwise superb reputation. Many companies work very hard to ensure that their image, from a talent attraction perspective, is superb. In essence, they are attempting to brand their organization as a great place to work as well as a great place to invest. Sears perfected this sentiment in their overall strategy to create a compelling place to shop, a compelling place to invest, and a compelling place to work, putting the customers, shareholders, and employees on equal footing.

Recruiting Talent

Recruiting has changed significantly in the last decade; not only the methods, but the overall approach. Exhibit 1.3 shows how the recruiting strategies have shifted from the old to the new. The new recruiting strategies are reflecting a comprehensive process involving many organizations with long-term focus.

Exhibit 1.4 shows the shift in the methods of recruiting. Although the traditional methods are still being used, newer methods are being adopted, particularly those involving web resources and networking. Monitoring current events in specific areas to understand where the talent may be located or what may be driving available talent is an effective tactic. Embracing employees so that they not only become referrals for others, but serve as talent scouts is another useful

Traditional Selection Methods	Non-Traditional Selection Methods
Resumes	Behavioral interviews
Background checks	Job simulation
Reference checks	Pre-employment training
Testing	Assessment center
Physical exams	Work samples
Drug testing	Referral profile
Interviews	

Exhibit 1.3.   Shifts in Selection Methods

Traditional Recruiting Methods	Non-Traditional Recruiting Methods
Job service agencies	Web resources
Recruiting ads	Open houses
Professional recruiters	Receptions at conferences
Campus recruiting	Information seminars
Internships	Diverse profile candidates
Employment support groups	Military recruiting
Community recruiting	Employee talent scouts
Job fairs	Networking
Walk-in applicants	Employee referrals
Trade and professional associations	Monitoring current events
Employment hotline	Pre-employment programs

Exhibit 1.4.   Shift in Recruiting Methods

approach. Because of the scarcity and competition for quality talent, a talent war is being waged in certain industries. Non-traditional recruiting methods are often needed to capture the interest of the passive prospect. Recruiting has become so subtle that some organizations, such as Cisco Systems, have a philosophy of not hiring people who are actually looking for a job.

Selecting Talent

Recruiting brings the prospects for consideration. Next comes one of the most critical talent decisions—the employment decision and how it is made, who makes it, when it is made, or whether or not it is accepted. Although the selection is only one component in the talent management system, the selection must be consistent. It is at this stage that the most scrutiny comes in terms of being fair and equitable. An inconsistent selection process is doomed to be challenged and may be difficult to defend. A systematic process is followed for each selection so that no one is subject to disparate treatment and represent an adverse impact. Figure 1.4 shows the selection system for a commercial banking officer for a large banking firm in the United States. The figure shows steps in the process and where the applicant can be rejected. Because there are so many components in a typical selection process, it has to be organized very carefully so that the selection time is minimized.

Just as the recruiting methods have changed, so have the selection methods. Exhibit 1.5 shows the non-traditional selection methods now being utilized to make a better employment decision. Executives are anxious to ensure a good fit for the employee before the ultimate selection is made. After it is made, it becomes expensive, time consuming, and disruptive to make adjustments or changes.

Employing Talent

Employing talent is the processing and administrative steps, but still important. Timing and convenience are the concerns as new talent joins the organization. All payroll tax forms and employee benefits forms are completed. An organized system is the key to handling these steps efficiently, effectively, and with as little frustration as possible. Two important problems areas must be avoided: administrative

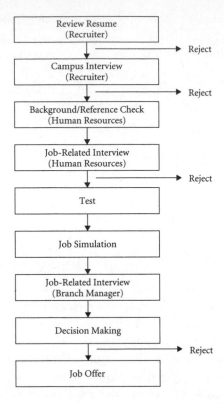

Figure 1.4.   Selection System for Commercial Banking Officer

delays in the processing and unpleasant surprises, particularly those that can create a negative impression.

DEVELOPING TALENT

After the talent is on-board, the learning and development process begins with on-boarding, initial training and learning for the job, and development to refine processes and improve capability as well as preparing individuals for other job positions.

On-Boarding New Talent

Initial indoctrination and orientation (or on-boarding, as it is some-times called) creates lasting impressions. It is important for new talent to have a positive first day on the job and an outstanding first

Old Recruiting Strategies	New Recruiting Strategies
Grow all your own talent	Recruit talent at all levels
Recruit only for vacant positions	Search for talent all the time
Go to a few traditional sources	Tap many diverse sources of talent
Recruiting is limited to a few individuals	Every employee is a recruiter
Advertise to job hunters	Find ways to reach passive candidates
Specify a compensation range and stay within it	Break the compensation rules to find the candidates you want
Recruiting is about screening	Recruiting is about selling as well as screening
Hire as needed with no overall plan	Develop a recruiting strategy for each type of talent
Keep a low profile except during employment growth	Create and brand an employer of choice

Exhibit 1.5.   Shifting Strategies of Recruiting
Adapted and updated from Ed Michaels, Helen Handfield-Jones, and Beth Axelrod.
The War for Talent. Boston, MA: Harvard Business School Press, 2001.

week. In some job situations, where employees have an opportunity to move quickly to another job with little investment, an unpleasant experience in the first week of work may result in an early turnover, that is, departures in the first month of employment. When this number is excessive, 10 percent, for example, this is an indication that either the selection was improper or that something happened in the early days of employment to change the person's opinion.

On-boarding helps the individual align with the organization, its values, mission, philosophy, policies, and practices. Employees must understand the rules, practices, policies—even the unwritten ones—so that initial success can be ensured. It is important to avoid frustrating experiences, missteps, miscues, and unpleasant surprises. At the same time, this is the best opportunity to secure the employee commitment to the organization. Both the motivation and the potential for engagement are extremely high. Both the efficiency and effectiveness of handling the orientation are important.

Preparing New Talent

Regardless of the level of talent, a certain amount of preparing for the job is necessary. For some it may be significant, as in preparing for skills or applications unique to the job. For most, it will be a matter of adjusting to the situation and learning specific practices, technology, and procedures. If the competencies are already in place, significant skill building will not be needed. If these competencies do not exist, significant training may be required.

Developing Talent

A variety of learning and development programs must be available to continue to improve performance, refine skills, learn new techniques and adjust to changing technology. A variety of development methods used with specific emphasis on the non-traditional ones.

Career Development

Career development focuses on preparation for the next job or series of jobs. Because today's employees are interested in all types of career movement and development opportunities, several approaches are utilized and explored. Succession planning is part of this as well as other types of replacement planning.

MANAGING TALENT

With talent in place and performing, the next challenge is to ensure that performance improves as employees are highly motivated and thoroughly utilized. Managing talent involves new responsibilities to the CTO: managing the performance and rewarding talent appropriately. In most cases, these functions have previously been performed by the compensation section, but now part, if not all, of this responsibility has shifted to the CTO.

Managing Talent Performance

To ensure that performance is discussed, recognized, rewarded, and understood appropriately, many organizations are focusing renewed efforts on performance management systems. The old approach was through the traditional performance review conducted quarterly, semi-annually, or annually, which was usually a one-way conversation from a manager to an employee. All parties hated the process. Managers hated to do it because there was the potential for conflict and they did not have the skills or the confidence to do it properly; employees hated it because it did not meet their needs and often left them confused, frustrated, and sometimes angry. The human resources staff hated it because it never seemed to be conducted properly, effectively, or consistently.

CTOs are attempting to make this process less painful by automating the system. For example, a typical approach to performance management is to develop briefing sessions and perhaps even e-learning modules that show how the process should work and the benefits of conducting these types of discussions. Discussions are often more frequent and there is a meeting between the employee and the manager to discuss performance improvement and set goals that align with organizational goals. These goals are entered into an online system, posted for constant review, follow-up, and adjustment. As progress is made, the status is updated. Performance data are available to others who need to keep track of key issues and see how well the system is working overall. Progress is monitored and the feedback is obtained in a variety of follow-up discussions. This approach brings constant overview, feasible goals, challenging assignments, alternative delivery, saves time, and provides excellent documentation. Figure 1.5 shows the performance management system at a large financial services firm. An important challenge for the CTO is to track and manage this type of process so that it becomes a motivational tool to drive performance instead of a headache that creates confusion.

Figure 1.5.   Performance Management System Example

Rewarding Talent

Rewarding performance, accomplishments, and milestones are very important. If used appropriately, recognition is one of the most effective motivators and one of the best ways is to tie bonuses and incentives directly to performance. Non-monetary rewards can often be just as motivational. The development of these programs is beyond the scope of this book and can be found in many other references.

When providing recognition, both the substance and the style must be considered. Substance is the value of the reward or recognition from the perspective of the person receiving it. If that person places no value on the reward, it will have very little motivational effect. The style is the manner in which the recognition is provided, including how, when, and where. The style relates to the sincerity of the communication and is just as important as the substance.

RETAINING TALENT

Keeping talent on-board is perhaps one of the most critical challenges for the CTO, representing one of the newest responsibilities. This principle involves managing the retention process and managing layoffs—now a CTO responsibility in some organizations. Much of this book focuses on the issues of retaining talent.

FINAL THOUGHTS

Talent management is fast becoming a critical strategic objective for growing organizations. This responsibility represents an excellent opportunity to create value. The importance of hiring competent talent is evident in any direction. Talent is king—now and in the future. It is the last source of competitive advantage.

Although several managers have always had the responsibility portions of talent management, only recently chief talent officer (CTOs) have evolved with the responsibilities for all talent management functions such as acquiring, managing, and retaining employees. These are key responsibilities that can make an enormous difference and add significant value. A complete talent management system with a single individual in charge—the CTO—is the trend. In this chapter we explored the various elements in the complete system and how the pieces fit together to offer an organized, effective, and successful talent acquisition and management process.

References

Annual Report, 2007. (2008). Mountain View, CA: Google, Inc.

Berger, L., & Berger, D.R. (2004). *The talent management handbook: Creating organizational excellence by identifying, developing, and promoting your best people.* New York: McGraw-Hill.

Deloitte Research. (2004). *It's 2008: Do you know where your talent is? Why acquisition and retention strategies don't work.* New York: Deloitte Development LLC.

Miller, S. (2008). *The turnaround kid: What I learned rescuing America's most troubled companies.* New York: HarperCollins.

Spencer, L.M., Jr. (2004). How competencies create economic value. In L. Berger & D.R. Berger (Eds.), *The talent management handbook: Creating organizational excellence by identifying, developing, and promoting your best people* (p. 64). New York: McGraw-Hill.

CHAPTER TWO

Why Talent Retention Is a Serious Problem

T alent retention is not a new issue. It is relevant today, and its importance will be even greater in the future. Some analysts believe that there may be twenty million jobs unfilled by the end of 2012. Others are projecting a shortfall of up to thirty million employees. For those individuals who believe that this issue may fade with slight economic downturns, consider this scenario. A blue-chip manufacturer announces 53,000 layoffs worldwide, a leading financial institution plans to shed 8,000 jobs, and a big-three automobile maker cuts 1,200 positions in a single plant. Given this situation, it appears that turnover might not be a problem. Digging a little deeper underscores the issue; the manufacturer in question was Boeing, the bank was CitiGroup, and the automobile maker was General Motors. These headlines aren't even from yesterday's paper—they're from the end of 1998, when the economy was at the height of a boom and employee turnover commanded everyone's attention (Bernasek, 2001).

Managing retention is a constant challenge for any organization. The awareness of the issue has heightened in the last decade, and, from all indications, the problem will be more serious in future decades. This brief chapter explores the seriousness of the issue and examines some of the major reasons for turnover and its consequences. It also dispels some of the myths about turnover and sets the stage for the remainder of the book.

DEFINITIONS

It is important to understand the basic distinctions between retention, turnover, and other related topics. These distinctions among these definitions will help clarify the concepts in this book and establish the appropriate framework.

Retention is the percent of employees remaining in the organization. High levels of retention are desired in most job groups.

Turnover, the opposite of retention, refers to the percent of employees leaving the organization for whatever reason(s). "Avoidable" turnover is distinguished from "unavoidable" so that the proper emphasis can be placed on the avoidable portion.

Turnover rate refers to the rate of individuals leaving. Several formulas are discussed in this chapter and in Chapter 4.

Tenure is the length of time an individual is employed by the organization and is usually related to the concept of employee loyalty. A loyal employee usually remains with an organization for a long period of time. In many organizations it is desirable to have long-tenured employees, although this situation taken to extreme can also *create* problems.

Experience levels are often defined as the months/years of experience in a particular job or functional area of the organization. Average levels of experience are critical issues in some job categories and knowledge industries.

Talent refers to the employees in critical jobs in an organization—and those jobs are not usually the managers and executives. Critical jobs are important to the success of the organization. Employees in those jobs can make a significant difference in organizational performance.

RETENTION IS A CRITICAL ISSUE

Recent publicity underscores the critical issues surrounding retention. The topic has reached widespread visibility through countless articles and books bringing the issue to the attention of managers and specialists. Retention articles are regularly included and sometimes on the cover of magazines such as *Fortune, Forbes, BusinessWeek,* and *The Harvard Business Review*. Publications in specific fields, such as *CFO* and *CIO*, devote substantial coverage to this topic. Books describing the competition for talent and suggested solutions are readily available. Workshops and seminars are regularly conducted on the issue of retention and turnover. It has become a mainstream topic in business and professional literature.

The concept of employer-of-choice has intensified in the last decade as "employer of choice" becomes a talent magnet. Employees want to work for the best employers. Organizations strive to be the "best company to work for" because that translates directly into lower rates of turnover and enhances the attraction of talent. Fueled, in part, by the book *The 100 Best Companies to Work for in America* (Levering &Moskowitz, 1993), many companies attempt to build the type of organization that can be included in, or at least meet the standards for inclusion into, these impressive lists, such as *Fortune* magazine's "100 Best Companies to Work for in America" and *BusinessWeek*'s "Employers of Choice." Making these lists often leads to this recognition in print ads, recruiting literature, and other communications.

Becoming an employer-of-choice is important to acquire the best talent, motivate talent to improve performance, keep talent engaged, and develop talent so they can grow and contribute skills.

Perhaps the most impressive development is the elevation of talent retention to the strategic levels of the organization. Consider the case of MicroStrategy, an information systems company whose software enables businesses to fine-tune their decision making and add very healthy profits. With a market capitalization of $25 billion, MicroStrategy was known for recruiting the best and the brightest for its workforce of more than two thousand and for sparing no expense to lure top talent. For example, it spent $5 million each year to conduct team-building exercises on a cruise ship in the Caribbean. Retention was an important part of strategy.

Unfortunately for MicroStrategy, the retention strategy suffered due to financial difficulties. The company had to disclose that, because of accounting problems, it would have to restate earnings for several previous years. In a single day, the company's stock lost 60 percent of its market value, and over several months, plunged from over $300 a share to below $30 a share. For the first time, the company was forced to rescind job offers and lay off 10 percent of its workforce while, at the same time, attempting to keep its key employees. In essence, its retention strategy shifted from attracting fresh new talent to hanging onto valued employees in the face of a financial blow. In both situations, retention was a key strategy driven by top executives.

Although it is always important, the talent retention issue becomes even more important when the economy faces a temporary decline. Most experts and executives who offer strategies to deal with a downturn in business, provide three rules not to forget:

1. Avoid the lay-off of key talent at all costs.
2. Keep recruiting, ensuring that talent channels are open.
3. Maintain talent development programs.

These rules focus on the long view, recognizing the importance of recruiting quality talent during a downturn while continuing to invest in their development.

The importance of talent, described in the previous chapter, has caused executives to focus on ways to retain talent. Now, talent retention has captured the attention of the business, financial, and executive communities. It is a strategic issue that now commands the focus, time, and resources it deserves. In many organizations, executives are creating integrated talent retention policies using internal and external data to shape focused retention solutions. In some organizations, the responsibility for coordinating this effort rests with a chief talent officer.

Negative Impact of Talent Departure on the Organization

Although every manager and team member is aware of problems associated with turnover, a review of its major consequences puts talent retention in the proper perspective. Eleven categories frame the major negative consequences. Chapter 5 provides more detail on the financial impact of turnover.

High financial cost.   Talent departure has a huge economic impact on the organization, both in direct and indirect costs. Translating turnover into numbers that executives understand is essential because they need to appreciate the true costs. Sometimes the cost impact alone causes it to become a critical strategic issue forcing some into bankruptcy in extreme cases. The performance of companies has been inhibited by high turnover rates.

Survival is an issue.   In a tight labor market where the success of the company depends on having talent employees with critical skills, recruiting and retaining the appropriate talent can determine the success or failure of the organization.

Exit problems and issues.   With increased litigation at the workplace, many organizations spend significant time and resources addressing the issues of disgruntled, departing employees. Some individuals find the need to involve the legal system, leaving the organization with the challenge of dealing with an even bigger problem. Even employees who leave voluntarily can cost the company time and money.

Productivity losses and workflow interruptions.   In most talent departures, a person who exits abruptly leaves a productivity gap. This void not only causes problems for the specific job performed by the departing employee, but also for others on the same team and within the flow of work.

Service quality.   With so much emphasis on providing excellent service to external as well as internal customers, high turnover has a tremendous negative impact on the quality of customer service. Turnover of front-line employees is often regarded as the most serious threat to providing excellent external customer service.

Loss of expertise.   Particularly in knowledge industries, a departing employee may have the critical skills needed for working with specific software, completing a step in an important process, or carrying out a task for a project. Sometimes, an entire product line may suffer because of a departure. A lost employee may be impossible to replace—at least in the short term.

Loss of business opportunities. Turnover may result in a shortage of staff for a project or leave the remaining staff unprepared to take advantage of a new business opportunity. Existing projects or contracts may be lost or late because a key player is no longer available.

Administrative problems. In most organizations, turnover creates a burdensome amount of administrative effort, not only in additional paperwork, but also in time spent confronting and addressing turnover-related issues. This takes precious time away from more important, productive responsibilities.

Disruption of social and communication networks. In every organization there is an informal network. Talent departure has a way of disrupting the communication and socialization patterns critical to the maintenance of teamwork and a productive work environment.

Job satisfaction of remaining employees. The disruptive nature of turnover is amplified when other employees are forced to take on the workload of departing colleagues or address problems associated with the departure. Remaining team members can be distracted by their concern and curiosity about why employees are leaving.

Image of the organization. High turnover creates the negative image of a company with a revolving door. Once this image has been established in the job marketplace, it's difficult to change—especially in the recruiting channels.

These are very significant, negative consequences. With this much impact and pain, excessive talent departure should command the attention of everyone in the organization.

Negative Impact of Talent Departure on Individuals

This book primarily focuses on what organizations are doing (and should do) to manage talent retention because of the negative impact of talent departure on the organization. At the same time, it is important to remember that turnover can have a negative impact on the individual, particularly if a person is leaving because of problems that could have been prevented. If the departure is involuntary, there are the usual issues about performance that could have been avoided. In addition, even a voluntary turnover because of issues that could have been avoided, creates a variety of negative consequences.

Loss of employee benefits or job seniority. Some employee benefits are tied to tenure. Starting a new job almost always resets the clock, with the employee losing the vested interest in benefits at the previous organization.

Stress associated with the transition and change. In every job change, anxiety, and stress associated with the transition will intensify, even if it's a desired transition. Job changes represent one of life's important stressors.

Financial difficulties. If a person leaves a job without having immediate employment, the transition can create a financial setback. Even in voluntary turnover, there may be a short break in employment.

Loss of social network. For many employees, the workplace is their primary social network; for some, their *only* social life. Giving that up and moving to another organization often destroys that network, along with the emotional support from the network.

Relocating costs. Although many organizations pay relocation costs, some do not. In almost every relocation situation, un-reimbursed personal expenses are involved, as well as a tremendous amount of time and effort.

Wasted efforts and uncompleted projects. Particularly in knowledge industries, where employees work on developing and completing projects, a departure may mean wasted effort. This often leaves the employee feeling as if the entire time on the project was wasted.

Career problems. A situation in which the departure is a result of a performance issue can be devastating for the individual's career and can take a tremendous toll on self-esteem. Also, frequent job changes can be difficult to explain to potential future employers.

With the significant negative impact of turnover—on both organizations and individuals—it is clear why turnover is a critical issue.

DRIVERS OF THE TALENT RETENTION CRISIS

What has caused the retention crisis? Major changes have occurred in organizations—both internally and externally—making this issue more critical today than in previous years. Unfortunately, these changes will only make the crisis worse in the future.

External Drivers

Externally, several factors are driving the talent retention crisis.

Economic growth. Almost all industrialized nations, and many emerging countries, have experienced long economic expansions. As economies grow, job growth will continue. In almost all segments of the economy, economic expansions translate directly into new jobs, which in turn creates new opportunities for employees to leave current employment.

Slower growth of job seekers. Despite economic growth, the number of job seekers is not increasing as quickly as job growth. In the United States, the job-seeker growth rate is actually growing at a slower rate each year. Consequently, many organizations have the compounding problem of fewer job seekers and more jobs created.

Unemployment rate at low levels. Low unemployment rates lead to increased turnover because more jobs are available. The unemployment rate in the United States continues to hover around a very low rate, from a high of 7.5 percent in 1992 to the 4 to 5 percent range in recent years. Many economists agree that whenever the actual unemployment rate falls in the 5 percent range or lower, it spells serious problems for employers seeking to fill job vacancies. Other developed nations are experiencing similar low unemployment levels, particularly in Europe and Asia Pacific companies.

Shortage of special skills. Compounding the situation is the short supply of talent skills, particularly in high-tech occupations, health care, and other critical areas. The news is often flooded with situations in which the number of candidates for jobs falls far short of the demand. This involves every spectrum from high-tech specialists, engineers, and scientists, where employment opportunities have outpaced the supply, to entry-level positions, such as those in the fast-food industry, where jobs go begging. This represents tremendous challenges for the future.

Entrepreneurship. In recent years, there has been tremendous growth in small businesses, particularly those created by individuals leaving large organizations and taking their expertise with them. In the United States, Baby Boomers are taking early retirement to start up their own businesses, sometimes in direct competition with the companies they left. A global entrepreneur boom has developed, with the United States ranked number 2 (behind South Korea and slightly ahead of Brazil) in the share of workers in new organizations.

Job changes for more favorable climates. In recent decades, a significant number of jobs shifted to areas where the weather is considered to be more favorable. In the United States, this is particularly noticeable in the western states, the coastal areas, the southern states, and other areas where year-round climates are milder. As people migrate, turnover is created. This change has little to do with a specific organization—just the location of the jobs themselves.

From all indications, most of the problems outlined above are largely out of the employer's control and are only going to get worse. The difference in the job growth rate and the workforce growth rate will cause the United States to have a shortfall in the future as birth rates are lower and Baby Boomers are retiring early. Unfortunately, many of the retiring boomers are in critical jobs, the talent that must be retained or replaced.

Internal Drivers

Internal changes in organizations operate in concert with the external influences to drive excessive talent departure. Internal issues include structural changes within the organization as well as changes in employees' attitudes about work and their employers. Here are the internal drivers that have a tremendous impact on turnover.

Lack of company loyalty. Perhaps one of the most frustrating issues is the growing lack of company loyalty. Many organizations show that much-needed loyalty has deteriorated in recent years. Some contend that allegiance is virtually non-existent in most American companies. Many years ago employees appreciated their jobs and would strive to stay with an organization for a long time. There was a sense of pride in working for the same company for forty years. Studies continue to indicate that loyalty is not only low, but continues to decline in recent times. Ironically, the research shows that employees want to remain with an organization for longer periods of time, creating an opportunity for the organizations to tackle this issue.

The desire to have challenging and useful work. Employees want creative, challenging, and useful work, a desire that has been evolving for many years. They want to be engaged. For many employees, their jobs are their "identities"—who they are. They have a need to use their minds and make a significant contribution. If they cannot achieve this within the framework of the current job, they will find one where they can. Engagement surveys capture these issues very well.

The need for autonomy, flexibility, and independence. Employees are becoming more accustomed to having the autonomy and flexibility to organize and control their work and work environment. Telecommuting is making it easier to work at home. This need is attracting many employees to organizations offering a flexible structure.

The need to have rewards based on performance. More employees are seeking appropriate reward systems that reflect individual contribution and individual performance. If rewards are not in direct proportion to achievement, employees often will find jobs at organizations where they will be rewarded accordingly.

The need to be recognized for participation, accomplishments, and contributions. In addition to monetary rewards, employees want credit for what they do and what they have accomplished.

Periodic feedback and recognition has been an important part of the motivational research for years. Employees seek workplaces where they can be acknowledged in a more systematic, routine fashion.

The desire for all types of benefits. Employees expect compensation in all forms. Some employees will go to the extreme to seek an organization with a particular benefit that is critical to their needs. Companies have had to adjust their programs and offer all types of perks, sometimes bordering on the absurd.

The need to learn new skills. Perhaps the most recent development is employees' desire to acquire new skills and skill sets. Employees want to learn new technology, processes, and projects and develop all types of skills, particularly in the technical area. Employees view skills acquisition—not seniority—as providing them with job security. Consequently, they seek organizations willing to invest in them. The availability of generous tuition payments, ample job-related training, and continuous development opportunities can be strong attractions.

Career growth in all directions. Along with obtaining new skills, employees want the opportunity to advance within an organization as they grow and develop these skills. Some advancement is upward and other movement is lateral, such as growth of specialized skills, but if employees can't advance inside the company, they will move to another one.

The desire to be on the leading edge. Employees are interested in organizations with a strong reputation, considered to be on the leading edge of technology or product development, or the best at what they do. These high-profile organizations—admired by many others and often the best in their field—are natural attractions for individuals wanting to be associated with the best. If their current situation does not provide it, they may move to one that does.

The desire for competitive compensation. Increased salary schedules have probably been the most visible and discussed internal change in organizations. Compensation levels have grown significantly, sometimes outstripping other economic indicators. Employees want more money, with more disposable income. They also view their income level as an indication of their worth to the organization and their field.

The need for a caring, supportive environment. Some employees place a high level of importance on working in a caring, supportive environment. Gone are the days when they're willing to tolerate harsh attitudes, continuous conflict, and unappreciative bosses. If they don't have the nurturing environment they want, they will move to another organization where they can find it.

Need for work/life balance. Many employees are seeking a job in which they can establish a balance between their work and personal lives. Fewer employees are willing to work an excessive number of hours, cope with unusual working conditions, or tolerate highly stressful and demanding situations. They want time for more involvement in family activities and social networks—as well as time for religious commitments. They seek organizations that will provide the appropriate work/life balance.

In some cases, the internal issues are affecting turnover rates more than the external drivers, but collectively, the internal issues and external shifts provide a tremendous challenge for organizations to manage employee retention.

TALENT RETENTION MYTHS

This chapter would not be complete without discussing some of the myths about talent retention. At one time or another, these myths surface in an organization and often inhibit efforts to manage talent retention in a proactive way.

Talent departure costs are not too high. When talent departure is excessive, costs are very high—both direct and indirect. This problem is often misunderstood; more precisely, the senior management team does not have a full appreciation for the high cost of excessive turnover. It is expensive and will be more costly in the future.

Talent departure is just a cost of doing business. Some managers accept turnover, even in excessive numbers, as an acceptable cost—just a cost of doing business in the organization. Accepting this philosophy is analogous to accepting high accident rates in the construction industry as a cost for doing business. The best construction firms have low accident rates and low accident costs. This myth must be dispelled! If excessive talent departure can be avoided, prevented, or controlled, the cost of doing business can be much lower.

Turnover is good; at least it has many positive consequences. While some turnover can be a good thing, excessive turnover is not. (On the extreme, zero turnover is not desirable.) When the benefits of turnover outweigh the negative consequences, the scale tips quickly to the need for preventive measures. The key issue is to define what is considered excessive turnover and avoid it.

Turnover is an industry problem. Executives in some industries with unusually high turnover rates accept it as an industry problem. For example, the retail sales industry has an average turnover rate of over 100 percent, and fast food even higher. Within this context, some organizations are able to achieve very low rates with proper attention to retention. It is a serious mistake to accept high turnover, believing nothing can be done about it.

Talent departure is an HR problem. Pointing fingers at the human resources executive or HR staff is unproductive in today's environment. Turnover is an organizational issue that must be addressed with leadership from the senior executive team. The human resource function can have a tremendous impact on retention, but, for the most part, they provide the administrative support for measuring, monitoring, analyzing, and reducing excessive turnover rates.

The manager's role is minimal. Individual managers, in particular the first-level managers, actually have a critical role in turnover reduction. Most of the causes of turnover and subsequent retention solution strategies involve managers in some way. The adage "employees join organizations and leave managers" underscores the importance of the managers' role. Their influence is crucial and they often underestimate their role and influence in the process.

Talent departure is out of our control. Executives sometimes accept an unusually high turnover rate, assuming that it's all externally driven, therefore out of their control. That's just not the case. Most of the effective retention solutions are internally driven. In some organizations in geographical areas or industries where it's very difficult to attract employee, turnover is still low. A high turnover rate doesn't have to be accepted as the norm.

Throwing money at the problem will solve it. While talent retention strategies cost money, continuing to throw money at the problem can cause two other problems. First, the expense sometimes outweighs the cost of turnover, resulting in a negative return on investment. Second, excessive spending can make the entire process ineffective because there are too many solutions, with too many activities in place at the same time. To combat this situation, it is necessary to take the ROI approach, where only those solutions that can produce the most results are tackled.

Turnover is a tactical issue only. The implementation of talent retention solutions will require a series of tactical steps. However, turnover is not only a tactical issue, it is also a strategic issue. Retention requires a commitment from the entire senior management team and must be addressed as a part of strategy. Only then will the tactical issues become a routine and supported step in the process. Technology and tools are now available to address getting and keeping talent, but if HR is not actively engaged in the planning process and does not receive corporate commitment from the top, the supply of talented employees will almost certainly be limited to ad hoc clusters of programs and boom and bust cycles of hiring and reductions that waste talent and inevitably cost more.

PAYOFFS OF TALENT RETENTION SOLUTIONS

Although it may appear obvious, it is helpful to recap the payoff of managing retention. Specific strategies aimed at overcoming the causes of turnover and implementing solutions to reduce turnover have important payoffs for organizations. Some studies have shown that the payoff for reducing turnover by 10 percent is greater than that of increasing productivity by 10 percent or reducing the actual inventories by 10 percent. Other studies have indicated that just reducing the turnover from industry average to the top 10 percent can increase profits by as much as 50 percent (Fitz-enz, 2008).

Turnover can have a devastating impact on an organization. Consider the situation between CVS and Walgreens pharmacies. CVS experienced serious problems with a shortage of pharmacists, 650 to 750 a day. A Merrill Lynch analyst blamed the company's less-than-expected financial performance on the shortage and a failure to manage retention. CVS shareholders filed a class-action suit alleging that it failed to tell shareholders that it was unable to successfully manage the retention issue.

Because of the tremendous cost of turnover (both direct and indirect), any efforts to lower turnover have a tremendous payoff, particularly when the value of the turnover reduction is compared with the cost of the solution. In turnover reduction studies, the actual return on investment can be as high as 1,000 percent (Phillips, 1997, 2001, 2005, 2008). This is achieved when comparing the actual monetary benefits from turnover reduction solutions to the actual cost of the solution.

One of the most visible payoffs of employee retention occurs in the operations areas and with the front-line staff. Lower turnover translates into fewer operational problems, fewer delays, increased customer service, smoother flow of work, and improved quality of transactions. Organizations routinely report operational improvements as the most important payoff of managing retention (Phillips, 2002).

Because of the negative consequences of turnover to the organization as well as the individual, there are many intangible benefits associated with turnover reduction solutions. Intangible measures are defined as measures not converted to monetary values. Typical payoffs include improved job satisfaction, organizational commitment, customer satisfaction, and teamwork, as well as reduced conflicts, stress, and bottlenecks. In some situations, these measures are more important than the monetary benefits.

FINAL THOUGHTS

This chapter sets the stage for this book by exploring the serious nature of talent retention in organizations. In recent years, managing retention has become a critically important topic that commands the attention of top executives and has become a part of the organization's strategy. The consequences of excessive turnover are significant and costly—both from the perspective of the organization and employee. External and internal drivers of the increased turnover are examined in this chapter, and the myths of turnover are presented in an attempt to dispel them. Finally, specific definitions and acceptable rates are defined and the payoff of the process is briefly discussed. The remainder of this book will examine, in detail, the recommended and needed approach for managing talent retention for the organizations.

References

Bernasek, A. (2001, March 5). Help wanted, really. *Fortune*, 118.

Fitz-enz, J. (2008). *The ROI of human capital* (2nd ed.). New York: AMACOM.

Levering, R., & Moskowitz, M. (1993). *The 100 best companies to work for in America*. New York: Bantam Doubleday Dell.

Phillips, J.J. (Ed.). (1997). *Measuring return on investment, volume 2*. Alexandria, VA: American Society for Training and Development.

Phillips, J.J., & Phillips, P.P. (2005). *ROI at work*. Alexandra, VA: American Society for Training and Development.

Phillips, P.P. (Ed.). (2002). *Retaining your best employees*. Alexandria, VA: American Society for Training and Development.

Phillips, P.P. (Ed.), & Phillips, J.J. (Series Ed.). (2001). *Measuring return on investment, volume 3*. Alexandria, VA: American Society for Training and Development.

Phillips P.P., & Phillips, J.J. (2008). *ROI in action casebook*. San Francisco, CA: Pfeiffer.

CHAPTER THREE

An ROI Approach to Managing Retention

Some organizations do a superb job of managing talent retention, whereas others fail miserably. The issues are not always externally driven, but often lie within the organization—sometimes in the approach to the problem. Finding a new approach requires shifting paradigms, changing perceptions, and throwing out old habits. A more rigorous, analytical, and strategic approach to addressing internal issues is needed.

In the previous chapter we underscored the seriousness of talent departures. In this chapter we describe the recommended approach to address talent retention, the basis for this book. Several issues pertaining to managing talent retention as a strategic initiative are explored. Eight distinct steps provide the basis for the ROI approach and bring the appropriate focus on accountability to the retention issue. We briefly explain the rationale for the approach and the steps involved. More detail around certain steps is contained in later chapters.

PROBLEMS WITH EXISTING APPROACHES

Old and outdated approaches to managing retention have created six distinct problems. How many of these sound familiar?

Proactive vs. Reactive (What Problem?)

Many organizations react to the retention issue—waiting until a problem surfaces, often developing enormous incentive packages to entice key employees to "stay with the ship." In these situations, the turnover issue results in severe stresses and financial impact in the organization before steps are taken to resolve it. The pressure is on—a solution must be implemented, now!

A proactive approach is needed to prevent the issue from ever surfacing. This is often easier said than done. Almost every manager will agree that talent departure should be prevented before it becomes a problem. Unfortunately, many external environmental factors exacerbate the turnover issue. The HR staff and management team are not fully prepared for these issues, and the results are sometimes disastrous. A continuous improvement process cycle is needed so that the focus is always on improving the current situation. This will help manage the talent retention issue.

Developing Too Many Preventive Programs (If We Try This, and This, and This, We Can Prevent the Problem in the Future)

Just as the reactive approach can be a problem, implementing too many preventive programs can also be a problem. In an effort to be proactive, many organizations implement preventive programs with a "try it and see" mentality without understanding the real impact turnover has on the organization. The philosophy is this: If enough programs are implemented, eventually one of them will help maintain staffing at the appropriate level, eliminating unnecessary turnover. Without the appropriate accountability applied to the program, the results of the program's implementation may never be known. Meanwhile, far too much money is spent. The organization's landscape is littered with overspending in an attempt to prevent the turnover problem from occurring. While prevention is important, some method to forecast the value of preventive programs must be in place. Forecasting value provides some assurance that the program will generate enough monetary benefit to offset the costs.

Searching for Solutions (Hey, They Have a Great Program Over at the Hard Rock Café!)

Many HR managers and staff members are continually searching for a solution, trying to find a program that has worked for another location. When workshops and conferences are offered about retention strategies, HR staff flock to sessions, taking copious notes, and feverishly attempting to apply newly discovered techniques or programs to their organization. Many times this approach results in failure. Searching for a solution without the proper analysis of the problem leaves the management team wondering whether there *is* a solution in their situation. An up-front evaluation is needed to identify the specific causes of turnover.

Too Many Solutions (I Never Met a Solution I Didn't Like!)

Even when employee retention is identified as a problem, far too many organizations, even some of the successful ones, base their approach to the issue on an excessive number of strategies. Turnover is a complex issue with many influences. There are probably five hundred specific solutions that could be implemented. The published literature on retention doesn't help—often offering countless solutions. One publication offers 154 solutions to "keep good people"(Herman, 1999). Implementing, or at least, attempting to implement, too many solutions can create disastrous results. The organization is burdened with an excessive number of new programs, projects, initiatives, plans, policies, and techniques. This can result in costly efforts with minimal, if any, results to show for them, while at the same time leaving staff members confused and managers perplexed. The objective is to tackle only the most critical turnover solutions, using precious organizational resources wisely to develop the most effective approach.

Mismatches Between Need and Solution (We Blew It on This One!)

Too often, a solution that doesn't actually address the need/problem is implemented. Perhaps there is insufficient information to provide a clear understanding of the solution required. Perhaps the wrong solution is selected or improperly implemented, resulting in a lack of added value. The solution may not be addressing the need as anticipated. It maybe have been the wrong solution. Whatever the case, these mistakes can be avoided by clearly matching the solutions to the needs.

Lack of Payoff (What Results?)

When an expensive solution is implemented, taking precious time and resources, a familiar scenario often surfaces. The management team wonders whether it made a difference. Did it add enough value to offset the costs of its implementation? Could a different, less expensive solution have similar results? Is the turnover rate still unacceptable? The solution might have successfully prevented further turnover deterioration or it could have left turnover unchanged, poised for further deterioration. The problem lies in not knowing. A process is needed to measure the results of a solution from a balanced perspective, collecting different types of data (tangible and intangible) so that management can clearly see the impact of major retention strategies.

The problems with these six approaches, and the rationale for preventing them, form the basis for the approach presented in this chapter.

NEEDED: AN ROI APPROACH

The ROI approach, outlined in Figure 3.1, brings accountability to the talent retention issue in eight steps.

The ROI approach has five very important advantages. These are:

It considers the retention issue to be an important part of strategy. The executive team is very involved in the retention issue. With many firms, retention has become a strategic issue

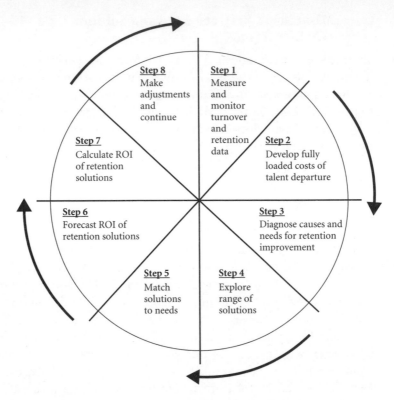

Step 8
Make adjustments and continue

Step 1
Measure and monitor turnover and retention data

Step 7
Calculate ROI of retention solutions

Step 2
Develop fully loaded costs of talent departure

Step 6
Forecast ROI of retention solutions

Step 3
Diagnose causes and needs for retention improvement

Step 5
Match solutions to needs

Step 4
Explore range of solutions

Figure 3.1. ROI Approach to Managing Talent Retention

because it makes the difference between financial mediocrity and excellence. It is a critical issue that deserves proper attention and management throughout the process.

The retention issues are measured with bottom-line results including ROI. Accountability is built in throughout the process so that those involved can fully understand the cost of the problem, cost of the solutions, potential impact of the solutions, and the actual impact of the solutions—all in monetary terms including ROI. This level of accountability is often missing in other approaches to retention analysis.

The approach moves logically from one issue to another. A series of steps, not necessary to manage the process, is followed with this approach. Each step has options and possibilities, but needs to be addressed in some way for the process to be successful.

The approach is a discipline and a methodology. With this approach, it's easy to stay on track because each of the different issues has to be addressed before moving on to another issue. The approach brings structure and organization to the retention issue, rather than shooting from the hip or implementing solutions without analysis.

It is a continuous cycle of improvement. Starting with a problem ultimately leads to a reduction in turnover. The process continues until turnover is at the desired level.

Ultimately, the approach positions the organization in a preventative stance working to maintain the appropriate level of staffing and reducing the risk of turnover. Each segment of the ROI approach is briefly discussed in the remainder of the chapter.

1. Measure and Monitor Turnover and Retention Data

Specific issues need to be addressed to properly monitor and measure turnover. Six key issues are explored within this area.

APPROPRIATE DEFINITION OF TURNOVER. For many organizations, turnover is voluntary; for others, it results from resignations and terminations based on unsatisfactory performance. Perhaps the cleanest definition to use is "avoidable turnover." A few organizations actually call this type of turnover "regrets"; employees left (voluntarily) or had to leave (involuntarily). It's important for the definition to match the definition in benchmarking studies, industry reports, or trade publications. While this seems simple, problems can easily develop because of the different classifications of turnover. Most professionals would agree that deaths, disabilities, and retirement should not be included in the turnover rate. However, in an organization where early retirement is an option, this could be an issue that deserves consideration. The important point is to select the proper definition and use it appropriately to compare with others.

TURNOVER RATES BY VARIOUS DEMOGRAPHICS. A variety of demographics could be reported, showing the regions, divisions, branches, plants as well as gender, age, and personal characteristics of the individual employees. Reporting by using too many demographics may confuse the issue. It is important to report demographics that appear to account for differences, thus enabling patterns to be developed and analyzed.

REPORT BY CRITICAL JOB GROUPS. A job group may be important for benchmarking comparisons. Also, certain jobs are more critical than others, particularly in technology industries. Employee groups that design, develop, or deliver products and services are essential to the lifeblood of the organization, requiring special skills that are often in short supply. These individuals have to be monitored and tracked separately, if possible.

REPORT TURNOVER WITH COSTS. While actual turnover rates and percentages are reported either monthly or yearly, additional reporting of actual costs can be more effective. Since the various components of the cost of turnover appear in different cost statements, it is important to bring the total cost of turnover to the attention of the senior management team, revealing the true impact that talent departure is having in the organization. The fully loaded cost of turnover should be developed, even if it is only an estimate. Cost formulas should be used to detail the cost of the turnover. Senior managers should reach an agreement on the assumptions, formulas, methods, and comparison values used to develop the cost of turnover, which is usually expressed as a percentage of annual salary. This agreement is not difficult to achieve. For example, most senior managers may agree that it costs 1.5 times the annual pay for the departure of a sales representative (relationship manager, client partner, etc.). To determine the actual cost of each turnover, simply multiply the annual pay for that individual by 1.5. More than likely, this approach will attract the senior team's attention and, subsequently, their support for implementing talent retention solutions.

COMPARE DATA WITH BENCHMARKING TARGETS. It's important to compare turnover data in three or four ways.

1. A comparison within the industry is recommended. Trade associations often have turnover data or access to benchmark

studies for the industry. This comparison shows how the organization stacks up with others in similar situations.

2. If possible, a custom-designed benchmark project should be developed in which the organization is compared to best-practice firms. This approach has the advantage of using benchmarking studies identified with best-practice organizations. This comparison involves a more select group.

3. A comparison with history is critical. Trending is important: Is employee retention going up, going down, or stable? Comparisons to last year, the year before, or last quarter are all-important considerations.

4. A comparison with expectations, particularly from the division manager, senior team, or plant manager is essential. What is expected? What is tolerated? What should the rate be? These comparisons provide an excellent opportunity to have a dialogue with the senior team and understand when a measure is not working adequately from their perspective.

DEVELOP TRIGGER POINTS FOR ACTION. When using benchmark data and other comparisons, trigger points for action must be developed. When should an alarm sound? Is it a rising trend or a sudden spurt? Is the measure going up when it should go down? Each of these could signal action necessary to begin exploring causes and creating solutions.

2. Develop Fully Loaded Costs of Talent Departure

The impact cost of turnover is one of the most underestimated and undervalued costs in the organization. It is often misunderstood because it does not reflect the actual costs of a turnover statistic and it is not regularly reported to the management team, who then are not aware of the actual cost. In addition, it can be alarming to management when fully loaded costs are calculated for the organization for an entire year. In one technology-based organization, the full costs for turnover were estimated to be almost $2 billion, in a firm with revenues in the $20 billion category. This is frightening when you consider the total impact on the organization. Essentially, 10 percent of revenue are needed to cover the costs for talent replacement.

In some turnover cost studies, only the costs for recruiting, selection, and training are considered. These are easily calculated

Exit costs	Lost productivity
Recruiting costs	Quality problems
Employment cost	Customer dissatisfaction
Orientation/on-boarding cost	Loss of expertise/knowledge
Job-related training cost	Management time for turnover
Compensation while training	Temporary replacement costs

Exhibit 3.1.   Recommended Categories for Accumulating Turnover Costs

and, consequently, inappropriately reported as the total cost of turnover. In reality, other costs should be included to generate a fully loaded cost profile. Exhibit 3.1 provides a more comprehensive listing that includes twelve categories.

Exit costs—the cost of employees leaving the organization, including termination expenses, severance arrangements, or even litigation connected to the departure. This category could be significant when the departure is involuntary.

Recruiting costs—the cost to attract candidates to the organization, sometimes involving external resources and sign-on bonuses. In recent years, this category has increased significantly.

Employment cost—the cost of selecting the candidate and completing all the necessary steps to hire an employee.

Orientation/on-boarding cost—the costs for the social adjustment processes (that is, initial orientation and socialization). This usually involves several days (sometimes weeks/months) to get someone fully adjusted to the organization and its culture.

Job-related training cost—the total cost of the training needed to elevate the new employee to the level of productivity of the previous employee. In some situations, this is extensive; for others, it may be minimal.

Compensation while training—the costs of the time for training, including the salaries, adjusted for employee benefits. This is a significant expense as employees are receiving compensation but not providing services to the organization.

Lost productivity—the cost of productivity lost because of disruption of service due to turnover. Almost every departure translates into something not being accomplished. Productivity loss is an elusive figure but represents a tremendous cost.

Quality problems—the cost of errors, mistakes, and bottlenecks that can develop during the learning process. The cost of lost quality can be a significant issue in turnover.

Customer dissatisfaction—the cost of dissatisfaction of internal or external customers. Having new, unprepared employees on the job causes disappointments and concerns from customers—and sometimes a customer defection.

Loss of expertise/knowledge—the cost to replace lost expertise. In many knowledge industries, this highly variable cost can be extremely significant when a departing employee possesses a high level of expertise.

Management time for turnover—the cost of the actual administrative time devoted to turnover problems. Supervisors, team leaders, and managers are involved in different steps of the replacement processes. This is valuable time that translates directly into cost.

Temporary replacement costs—the direct cost of temporary employees. In some situations, temporary replacements have to be used while another employee is being prepared for the job.

In summary, a complete cost profile is recommended, covering all the different categories above. Because this is such a critical issue, Chapter 5 is devoted to calculating the fully loaded cost of turnover for a specific job group.

3. Diagnose Causes and Needs for Retention Improvement

Determining the cause of turnover is a critical and illusive issue. Some causes may be obvious, while others can be extremely elusive. Collecting appropriate data is often a challenge because of the potential for bias and inaccuracies that surface during the data collection process. Several diagnostic processes are available. Exhibit 3.2 shows an initial list of diagnostic tools available to use with turnover

- Diagnostic tools
- Demographic analysis
- Diagnostic instruments
- Focus groups
- Probing interviews
- Job satisfaction surveys
- Organizational commitment surveys
- Exit interviews
- Exit surveys
- Nominal group technique
- Brainstorming
- Cause-and-effect diagram
- Force field analysis
- Mind mapping
- Affinity diagrams
- And the list continues

Exhibit 3.2.   Tools to Diagnose Turnover Problems

analysis, beginning with analyzing trends and patterns in particular groups and demographic categories to pinpoint the problem area. The tools range from a survey to a focus group to uncover the causes of turnover. Because of this critical issue, an entire chapter is devoted to this process.

4. Explore a Range of Solutions

Organizations are very creative in their approach to the turnover problem, resulting in hundreds of excellent solutions. Confusion may develop because there are so many potential solutions to a problem. The critical issue is to ensure that the solution is feasible for the organization. Because of this, four chapters are devoted to these most important solutions:

Chapter 7: Recruit Talent

Chapter 8: Establish an Appropriate Work Environment

Chapter 9: Create Equitable Pay and Performance Processes

Chapter 10: Build Motivation and Commitment

The entire middle section of this book focuses on the range of potential solutions.

5. Match Solutions to Needs

This step goes hand-in-hand with forecasting the value of solutions presented next. The development of the two issues should be parallel because the solutions selected for implementation are assumed to meet specific needs, making the forecast of the anticipated value imperative. When attempting to match solutions to need, five key issues are considered:

1. *Avoid mismatches.* The solution selected for implementation must specifically address the need that has been identified. More importantly, this process will ensure that the need has been identified in enough detail to make the solution most obvious.

2. *Discourage multiple solutions.* Adopting too many solutions is probably worse than taking on too few. It's important to focus on those key solutions that will add the most value. Consequently, the forecasting step should be developed simultaneously with the selection of solutions. Realistically, an organization can tackle only a few solutions because each solution requires the time and effort of many individuals—sometimes all employees. Taking on too many creates an air of confusion and takes precious time and energy away from other important issues.

3. *Select a solution for a maximum return.* Understanding the payoff of a solution will help guide the selection process. The discipline of this step is simple: implement a solution only if the perceived return is acceptable. This is critical in developing a few solutions that will provide the best return.

4. *Verify the match early.* Accumulating data expeditiously from appropriate individuals can "red flag" a problem. If a cause has been clearly identified, a solution can swiftly address the need. Feedback data, collected simultaneously with implementation, provides data to make quick adjustments.

5. *Check the progress of each solution.* Periodic progress reports provide data to ensure a solution is adding the appropriate value. Sometimes this requires collecting continuous feedback

from appropriate stakeholders using a variety of data, both tangible and intangible. The key issue for stakeholders is: Is it working for them and providing the desired results?

6. Forecast ROI of the Retention Solutions

Developing a forecast for the value of a solution allows the team to establish priorities, work with a minimum number of solutions, and focus on solutions with the greatest return on investment. A difficult, challenging, and, sometimes risky issue, forecasting is expert estimation of what a solution should contribute. When forecasting, it is imperative to accumulate as much data as possible to build credibility around the process. The payoff value can be developed if the percentage of expected turnover reduction can be related to it. For example, if the number-one cause of turnover is actually addressed with a solution, what percentage of the turnover would actually be eliminated? Sometimes, employees can provide input for this issue as data are collected to identify the causes of turnover. This step may require several "what if" decisions with employees while making various assumptions about the data. Also, this step may involve building on previous experiences to the extent possible. In some cases, the experience of other organizations can be helpful.

Ideally, the forecast should contain an expected return-on-investment (ROI) value. However, a more realistic approach is to offer a range of possible ROI values, given certain assumptions, removing some of the risk of making a precise estimation (Phillips & Phillips, 2007). This step is perhaps one of the most difficult, but necessary, parts of the process. Because of the difficulty, Chapter 12 is included to forecast values for solutions.

7. Calculate ROI of Retention Solutions

Another often-neglected step is the actual calculation of the impact of a turnover reduction strategy. This step is often omitted because it appears to be an add-on process. If accumulating solutions is the measure of success of turnover reduction or prevention, the impact to those solutions may seem to have no value. From a senior executive's point of view, accountability is not complete until impact and ROI data have been collected, at least for major solutions. The ROI process described in this book generates six types of data about the success of a turnover-reduction strategy:

1. Reaction to and satisfaction with the solution
2. Skill and knowledge acquisition
3. Application and implementation progress
4. Business impact improvement
5. Return on investment, expressed as a financial ROI formula
6. Intangible measures, not converted to monetary values.

This strategy also includes a technique to isolate the effects of the retention solution.

The ROI process has achieved widespread applications for the evaluation of all types of programs and solutions. It involves a series of steps collecting the six types of data at different time frames and processing the data in a logical, rationale approach, as shown in Figure 3.2 (Phillips & Phillips, 2007). This ROI process is comprehensive and accurate and can provide assessment of the impact of any turnover-reduction strategy. However, because of the time and effort required, the process should not be applied to every turnover-reduction program. Only those solutions considered to be expensive, time-consuming, high profile, and closely attached to the goals of the organizations should be considered for this type of analysis. Because of its importance, Chapter 13 is devoted to the calculation of ROI for turnover-reduction strategies.

8. Make Adjustments and Continue

The extensive set of data collected from the ROI process will provide information to make adjustments and changes in turnover-reduction strategies. The information reveals success of the turnover-reduction solution at all levels from reaction to ROI. It also examines barriers to success, identifying specifically what kept the solution from being effective or prevented it from becoming more effective. It also identifies the processes in place that enable or support a turnover-reduction solution. All of the information provides a framework for adjusting and/or repositioning the solution so that it can be revised, discontinued, or amplified. The next step in the process goes back to the

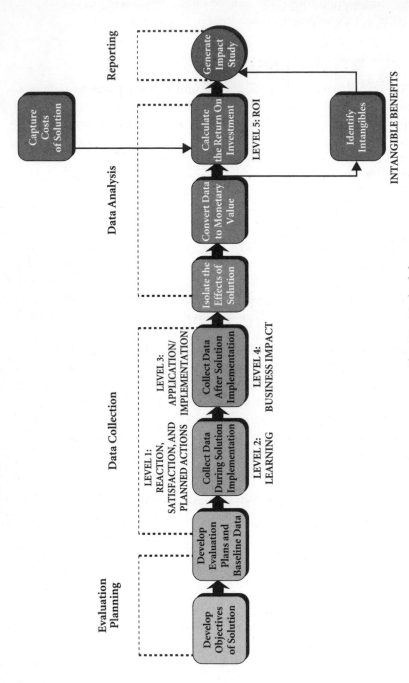

Figure 3.2.   The ROI Methodology

beginning—monitoring the data to ensure that turnover continues to meet our expectations—and the cycle continues.

FINAL THOUGHTS

In this chapter we explored a unique and necessary way to manage retention—implementing a strategic accountability approach. The approach has many inherent advantages and is highly recommended when there is concern with preventing turnover or reducing turnover from its current level. It is comprehensive, disciplined, and focuses on results throughout the process as retention is tackled in a productive and efficient way.

References

Herman, R. (1999). *Keeping good employees.* Winchester, VA: Oakhill Press.

Phillips, J.J., & Phillips, P.P. (2007). *Show me the money: How to measure the ROI on people, projects, and programs.* San Francisco, CA: Berrett-Koehler.

Phillips, P.P. (Ed.). (2002). *Retaining your best employees.* Alexandria, VA: ASTD.

CHAPTER FOUR

Measure and Monitor Turnover and Retention Data

T his chapter is the first step of the ROI approach to managing retention and logically begins with measuring and monitoring turnover. This simple step is not as easy as it may seem. Determining the precise definition of turnover is critical and other measures, such as intention to leave and turnover costs, should be considered a part of the measurement strategy. Also, while the organization's turnover rates are critical, they must be considered in the context of the economic climate and expectations of the senior team. A comprehensive approach to measuring and monitoring enhances the likelihood that the retention issue will be understood and proper action taken.

DEFINITIONS

When discussing turnover and what is considered to be an appropriate rate of turnover, several issues must be addressed. First is the misconception that a very low turnover rate (near zero) is the most acceptable. It is virtually impossible and undesirable to achieve a continuous zero turnover rate in an organization. Extremely low turnover rates can be dysfunctional as well as unhealthy, particularly when new thinking and fresh ideas are needed. Also, extremely low turnover rates for extended periods of time can add tremendous costs as incumbent employees reach higher salaries. The electric utility industry has been addressing this problem for decades. In recent years, the industry has gradually forced employees out, often with huge severance packages, simply because turnover rates were not high enough. In the early 1990s, many telecom companies, particularly the baby bells in the United States, faced this same situation. This pattern has evolved in other major organizations as well, including General Motors, General Electric, and IBM. In some cases, turnover is injected into the system as management policy. For years, General Electric has had a policy of terminating the bottom 10 percent of their employees, the lowest performers. Obviously, this adds to the annual turnover rate.

Another issue concerns the definition of the word "talent" or employee in the retention issue. For the purposes of this book, talent refers to *the employees in critical jobs and high-potential employees.*

Defining the acceptable rate of turnover is another concern. After the specific type of turnover is defined, the economic climate considered, the expectations detailed, and capabilities considered, a turnover rate above a certain level becomes excessive and will trigger action. More importantly, monitoring leading indicators to the actual turnover rate is better. Turnover may be defined in many ways and five different types of turnover calculations are described here. The employee-of-choice definition utilizes the first, third, and fifth category (Fitz-enz & Davison, 2002).

Total Turnover Rate

The definition of total turnover is the total number of employees leaving the organization during a month divided by the average number of employees during that month. Some calculations use the number of employees at mid-month in the denominator. However, this can be slightly misleading because of the surge of employees who leave at the end of the month (many professional employees prefer to leave at the end of the month). This category includes all the reasons for an employee's departure, regardless of the performance of the employee or unavoidable situations that created the departure. In reality, this value has little practical meaning because there are so many unavoidable reasons for turnover. Also, the value includes functional turnover, where a certain number of employees are purposely removed from the organization. Still, it does provide the absolute value, showing the total departure rate of talent in the organization.

Voluntary vs. Involuntary

Voluntary turnover usually refers to those employees who initiate their departure from the organization. It is defined as the number of employees voluntarily leaving during the month divided by the average number of employees during the month (or number at mid-month). At first glance, this appears to be the appropriate definition. However, a question often arises as to whether or not a departure is *actually* voluntary—the employee could be pressured into resigning. Also, the practical issue of voluntary versus involuntary coding may be a problem. An employee may actually leave voluntarily, but then the departure is coded as a performance termination, escaping the scrutiny of the volunteer issue.

Avoidable vs. Unavoidable

The next definition is based on the concept of avoidable turnover. This turnover rate is defined as the number of employee departures that are avoidable, divided by the average number of employees during the month (or number at mid-month). This calculation requires the analysis of turnovers that could have been avoided in some way. Figure 4.1 shows how the concept of avoidable turnover translates into specific types of departures. Obviously, the unavoidable turnover should not be considered as a controllable retention issue. For example, it is difficult to prevent an individual from leaving due to the relocation of a spouse, a home care issue, or a desire to care for children after a maternity leave. The avoidable categories include both voluntary and involuntary issues. In most situations, the focus of attention would be the voluntary, avoidable category, and most of this book is focused on this category. However, the other avoidable category, involuntary, deserves some attention. Terminations for substandard performance, layoffs, early retirement encouragement, and resignations in lieu of terminations could, for the most part, be prevented. Consequently, they should be included in the statistics.

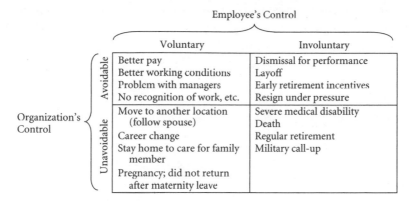

Figure 4.1.   Avoidable vs. Unavoidable Turnover

Source: Adapted from Griffeth and Hom, 2001

Dysfunctional vs. Functional

In previous definitions, the quality of the employee's performance is not taken into consideration. For talent management, the issue becomes critical when high-performing talent leave the organization versus those considered to be low performers. Some organizations intentionally weed out the low performers, creating turnover. On the other extreme, the departure of a high-performing individual can be a devastating blow to the organization. Figure 4.2 shows the concept of functional versus dysfunctional turnover (Hom & Griffeth,

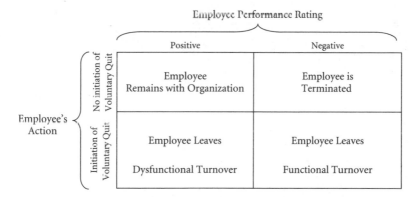

Figure 4.2.   Dysfunctional vs. Functional Turnover

Source: Adapted from Hom and Griffeth, 1995

1995). Employees with a negative rating are either terminated for substandard performance or quit because they see the inevitable consequences of their performance. This is called functional turnover. When an employee leaves after receiving a positive rating, it is considered dysfunctional turnover and should be the primary focus of attention for the organization.

Cisco Systems, which has a reputation for attracting and keeping the best talent, uses the above approach to turnover. According to the vice president of human resources at Cisco, two questions are addressed when analyzing turnover data: Are the low performers being moved out of the organization to create a better team? Of the volunteer turnover, how many of those are high performers? Both issues are critical to retain the best employees in the organization.

Consequently, the definition of dysfunctional turnover is the ratio of the number of high-performing employees who leave during the month divided by the average number of employees during the month (or the number at mid-month). This turnover rate can be developed for actual performance levels. For example, consider an organization with five levels (or categories) of performance evaluation for employees, typical of most performance review systems. This could range from 1 for unacceptable performance to 5 for outstanding performance. If voluntary turnover is tracked along performance ratings, the percentage of high performers leaving can be quickly pinpointed. This essentially modifies the definition. Turnover at performance level 5 is the number of employees leaving the organization with a rating of 5 divided by the average number of employees during the month with a performance rating of 5 (or at mid-month). This is an excellent way to examine turnover and focus attention on the critical issue that many organizations today face—retaining high-performing employees.

Early Turnover

A critical time in an employee's tenure with an organization is usually with the first few days, weeks, and months of employment. It is during this period that mismatches are identified and frustrations intensify. An employee may decide to leave if other opportunities are available. This early turnover is often a function of improper selection systems, ineffective orientation systems, and inadequate socialization processes to adapt the employee to the organization.

To understand this issue completely, it is recommended that an early turnover measure be developed. This measure is defined as the number of employees leaving in the first sixty days of employment divided by the number of new employees hired in the same period. The time period for the length of employment could vary from a shorter time frame, thirty days for entry-level unskilled employees, to a longer period for technical and professional employees (ninety days). Monitoring and understanding this specific turnover rate provides an opportunity for early attention to an important issue.

SETTING RETENTION TARGETS

Collectively, the five measures listed above should be appropriate for monitoring turnover data. Two other issues of monitoring will be discussed later: intention to quit and turnover costs. Total, avoidable, and early turnover are the measures typically collected by employers of choice. A more appropriate measure may be dysfunctional turnover rate.

In addition to selecting the appropriate definition, it is important to set the targets or triggers for action. Triggers can be set at different levels, depending on when and where action is needed. The maximum acceptable rate for the turnover is often the first trigger. A value above this rate is unacceptable and triggers significant analysis and/or action. A value below that rate is accepted as minimum; however, organizations often set lower targets as desired or stretch goals. Some organizations striving to be employers of choice set their turnover rates at a value below the maximum acceptable rate. These organizations focus much attention on attracting and retaining employees. In still other situations, a few organizations desire to be the best at this issue. When considering their position in the industry and other best-practice firms, a lower rate is often set that is considered to be a best practice, world class, or a top 10 percent standard for the industry. This represents truly exceptional performance, achieved by only a few organizations. This becomes a stretch goal for the entire organization. Figure 4.3 illustrates these three trigger points that drive action. Specific actions to address the retention issue can occur when rates hit either target. Other labels may be used, such as satisfactory, above average, and exceptional. The important challenge is to achieve success at different target levels.

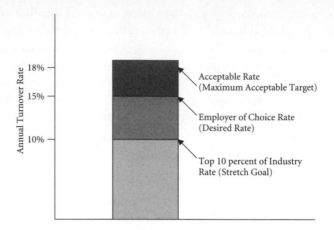

Figure 4.3.   Targets for Turnover Rate for Critical Talent

ECONOMIC CLIMATE AND NATIONAL DATA

One of the first places to start in a turnover and retention analysis is to examine the current economic situation. To a large degree, the economic climate will drive the availability of other opportunities and, thus, can inhibit or exacerbate the turnover issue. The economic climate also influences the talent retention rate that can be achieved, realistically. Several economic statistics should be monitored routinely to gain a sense of the state of the economy and the impact on the labor market. The following is a sample of the key indicators for the U.S. economy. Similar measures are available in other countries.

Gross Domestic Product

Change in the gross domestic product from the previous year or the previous month provide some indication of the state of the economy. These measures, available from the Bureau of Economic Analysis, indicate that the economy is growing, stagnant, or slowing down. This measure reflects the total amount of goods and services provided by a country in a given year.

Stock Market Changes

The stock market reflects a number of variables that can have an impact on employment and the labor market. Changes in stock market indices reflect corporate earnings, economic leading indicators, and the general business climate. In the United States, the Dow Jones Industrial Average, the New York Stock Exchange Composite Index, the NASDAQ, Standard and Poor's 500, and the Russell 500 Index are all measures that reflect the state of business from the private sector. Consistently advancing indices usually spell trouble for the labor market in the near future; declining indices may signal that the labor market will not be as tight.

Consumer Confident Index

This key index, released monthly by the Conference Board, measures consumer sentiment by surveying people about their confidence in the economy. Survey questions explore consumer job security and willingness to spend money.

Index of Leading Economic Indicators (LEI)

The Conference Board's LEI, regarded as a barometer of economic activity over three to six months, is designed to signal peaks and troughs in the business cycle. It is derived from ten leading indicators, four coincident indicators, and seven lagging indicators. Because it covers a wide scope of measures, from stock prices to building permits to interest rates, it presents a broad picture of the economy and helps to confirm suggestions of either recovery or recession. The index usually signals a change if it is positive or negative for three months in a row.

Help-Wanted Advertising Index

The Conference Board tracks help-wanted advertising volume monthly in fifty-one major newspapers across the country. Because ad volume has proven to be sensitive to labor market conditions, the index provides a gauge of change in the local, regional, and national supply of jobs. The index is released toward the end of every month for the previous month.

Weekly Hours Worked

Another important measure is the average weekly hours worked for all private, non-agricultural industries. Available from the Bureau of Labor Statistics, this information indicates how the workweek is developing. If it is increasing, it reflects a very tight labor market; if it's decreasing, a loosening market. The measures are presented in hours per week and generally hover under 40, but with some fluctuation.

Total Civilian Employment

Available from the Bureau of Labor Statistics, total civilian employment is the estimated total employment. An upward movement of this number means that there is much job growth occurring and that individuals are entering the labor market. More job growth usually translates into more opportunities, and thus turnover could increase. Declining or stable civilian employment indicates that jobs are becoming scarcer and that turnover may decrease.

Layoffs

In almost any type of economic climate, organizations announce layoffs of employees. Even in periods of high growth, layoffs occur as some industries are restructuring, merging, combining, or reinventing themselves. Consider, for example, the actual layoffs announced in the second quarter of 2001 in the United States during a time when most experts characterized the economy as slowing and in a recession. According to the Bureau of Labor Statistics, 350,000 employees were laid off. In the second quarter of 1998—during a period of high economic growth—employers laid off 402,000 workers. Layoffs are, of course, usually heavier in times of economic decline and the number of actual workers laid off for more than thirty days is an important number to track. Although it can be misleading, this number can be helpful in understanding the general economic climate.

Jobless Claims

Another figure from the Bureau of Labor Statistics is the number of individuals receiving jobless benefits (unemployment compensation) and the number of new claims filed during the week. These numbers reflect the impact of layoffs and employee migration, indicating that the individuals may be having a difficult time securing employment. When this rate is considered in conjunction with layoffs, it can begin to reflect how individuals are struggling to find jobs. For example, if there are high levels of job layoffs, but relatively low levels of jobless benefit claims, there is an indication that individuals are able to find jobs quickly. In recent years, the economy experienced high productivity, growth, and labor shortage at the same time.

Unemployment Rate

Perhaps the most critical measure is the annual unemployment rate. This rate has a tremendous importance to organizations as they attempt to address the retention issue. Some economists argue that full employment occurs when the economy experiences 6 percent unemployment rate. At that rate, the labor market is loose enough that employers can find suitable candidates and the jobs are not so plentiful that employees with high mobility are being enticed to move frequently. During the late 1990s and early 2000s, the economy experienced low levels of unemployment, including rates around the 4 to 5 percent mark.

National Turnover Data

Some organizations publish national turnover data reflecting annual turnover rates for all organizations using projections based on small samples. The Bureau of National Affairs, for example, publishes monthly turnover rates as a percentage of average workforce by number of employees, industry, region, and overall for all organizations. Employment organizations and professional groups attempt to publish data for the industry as a whole. The Society for Human Resource Management publishes annual turnover data based on a small sample, reflecting the actual turnover by organizations, grouped by the number and type of employees.

Collectively, these measures provide a sense of the overall climate, primarily on a national basis. While the data presented here reflects the economic indicators and labor data in the United States, similar types of data are available in industrialized and emerging nations. It is important for the management team (and the retention management team) to have an adequate understanding of the current economic climate and, more importantly, changes in the climate, particularly from those measures considered to be leading edge and related to retention and turnover.

BENCHMARKING TURNOVER

While meaningful by itself, turnover data collected by the organization need to have some basis of comparison. It's helpful to compare
the data with a variety of types of organizations and groups. Five
possibilities emerge.

National Reports

Some organizations have developed national turnover studies that
attempt to benchmark employee turnover. Different types of organizations that collect the turnover data use techniques to ensure
that the data is accurate, fair, and useable. While the firms involved
in these studies may not reflect best practices, they do provide a
measure that is important to understanding the actual turnover rates
by particular industry segments. Participating organizations pay for
their involvement and often take the responsibility more seriously
and provide more accurate data. These measures are often more
accurate than government data and voluntary data provided through
a professional organization.

Industry Associations

Because retention is sometimes a critical issue within an industry,
many trade and industry groups have begun to track turnover
data—collecting it directly from the members and reporting it
back to them. For example, the National Restaurant Association,
concerned about high turnover rates in their industry, publishes
reports, studies, and data concerning the turnover in that industry.
The Direct Marketing Association publishers information about
turnover in call centers. Industry reporting provides benchmarks,
which are necessary to compare with other operations in similar
situations.

Occupational or Field Data

In some situations, the professional society or organization reflecting
a professional field will collect turnover data. This is particularly true
in the professional and technical areas. For example, the Institute
of Electrical and Electronics Engineers collects data about the engineering shortages in the electrical and information science fields and
publishes it regularly in their bulletins and other communication.

Regional or Local Data

A little closer to home, some cities, states, and regions collect turnover data in the local area. Business and economic development authorities, chambers of commerce, metropolitan development boards, and even chapters of the Society for Human Resource Management are great sources for regional and local turnover data—sometimes even by industry. This brings turnover down to the local employment scene, where it becomes an important issue. It reflects the actual applicant pool for the organization, which is sometimes more relevant than national data.

Customized Benchmarking Study

Perhaps the most accurate way to obtain comparison data is to develop a custom designed benchmarking study. While this seems to be an expensive and time-consuming process, it may be worth the effort if retention and turnover are considered to be critical issues and appropriate comparison data are a major part of the process. Figure 4.4 shows the basis steps to develop a benchmarking project. As the figure underscores, the process is cyclical; collecting data, reacting to it, and continuing to collect more data.

Step One: Develop definition of turnover. This will ensure that the specific measure that is most critical to the organization can be captured. This approach is particularly helpful when national data sources do not reflect an appropriate definition of turnover.

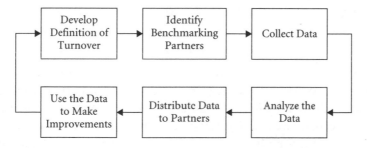

Figure 4.4.   Building a Customized Benchmarking Project

Step Two: Identify benchmarking partners. Perhaps the most critical part of the process, this step means finding the desired group for comparison. The group may be competitors, non-competitors in the same industry, or organizations in the same geographic locations competing for the same employees. The group may include organizations in the United States, multinational organizations, or organizations based in other countries. The important point is to define those organizations for which it makes the most sense to compare. Often, comparison organizations are those with best practices, although the concept of best practices can be elusive.

Step Three: Collect data. The most economical and credible method is to use a survey, followed with a telephone interview. As the data-collection process begins, it is important for the partners to fully understand definitions, data desired, the confidentiality of data, and the use of the data. Response rate should not be a problem because partners make a commitment to provide data when they agree to participate.

Step Four: Analyze the data. The data should be summarized by individual firms (identified by a code) and for all partners. Having access to the data provides an incentive for partners to share information. Most human resource executives will participate in benchmarking projects if they can find value in the project.

Step Five: Distribute data to partners. Prompt, on-schedule distribution is critical to providing current data. The data should be reported in a variety of ways that can be helpful to the partners.

Step Six: Use the data to make improvements. The benchmarking data should be used as a basis for setting targets and triggering actions for improvements.

While this approach takes time, it has several advantages. It will be more valuable than other national or regional data that is available because it uses only the most desired organizations for comparison. Also, the data are more accurate because the quality is controlled by the organization initiating the survey. Additional information on developing a benchmarking project can be found in Phillips (1997).

MONITORING TURNOVER AND RETENTION DATA

Monitoring turnover and retention data is the next step to measure the organization's current performance. Trends and patterns can be observed and addressed when action is needed; however, before monitoring, it is essential that definitions be clearly developed and data-collection systems put in place. There are two general categories of internal turnover data for analysis: organizational and individual.

Organizational Data

When collecting organizational talent departure data, eight break-downs are suggested:

1. Organization-wide;

2. Different divisions, particularly if the divisions are vastly different or represent companies within the organization;

3. Geographic regions, if the organization is national;

4. Functional units, such as sales, marketing, manufacturing, engineering, or research and development;

5. Major departments, such as design, sales support, and supply chain management;

6. Work units such as call centers and technical support;

7. Occupational groups, such as nursing, engineers, software specialists, or other critical talent categories; and

8. Specific jobs, such as customer service reps, mechanics, or x-ray technicians.

These breakdowns show where the turnover is occurring, which is important for understanding problems as well as successes.

Individual Data

In addition to showing where turnover is occurring by location, other demographic data can be helpful in understanding the causes of turnover. The recommended groupings are:

1. Tenure or the length of service of departing employees (or tenure of remaining employees);

2. Age breakdown of employees (or age of remaining employees);

3. Gender of departing employees (or gender of remaining employees);

4. Race and national origin of departing employees (or origin of remaining employees);

5. Educational levels of departing employees (or education of remaining employees); and

6. Family status (married, single, single head of household, having children, etc.) of departing employee (or family status of remaining employees).

These breakdowns are important to see how the workforce is changing and where the turnover rates are highest. The measures in parentheses reflect the status of remaining employees. Together, they provide useful tools for analyzing particular issues, understanding the causes, and ultimately developing solutions. Figure 4.5 shows how tenure is used to spot problem areas. Breaking points can usually be outlined in three areas: a new employee crisis, promotion crisis, and

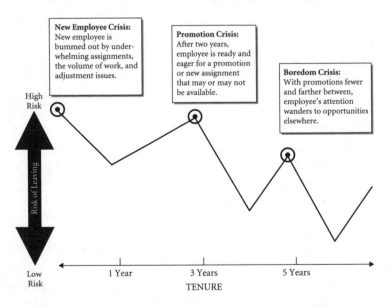

Figure 4.5.   How Talent Departure Relates to Tenure

boredom crisis (Branch, 1998). Monitoring turnover by tenure can keep the focus on breaking points, taking action as needed. Also, by projecting tenure data, it is possible to predict when these issues may come into play.

By creatively breaking down the data (which can readily be accomplished with today's human resource information systems), it is possible to conduct the first step of analysis. Trends and patterns readily appear and the potential causes of turnover quickly emerge from the data. For example, high levels of turnover with single mothers may indicate childcare issues. This issue will be revisited in Chapter 6 (diagnosis) because it is the first step in understanding where turnover is occurring and with which groups and at what time.

ADDITIONAL MONITORING

In addition to monitoring turnover data and comparing it with a variety of benchmark sources, it is helpful to consider two additional measures. The first is a leading-edge indicator of turnover and the second highlights the impact of turnover.

Intention to Leave

Researchers often attempt to identify leading-edge indicators of turnover. Historically, job satisfaction has been the best measure. Low rates of job satisfaction would usually translate into turnover. While this relationship still holds up in many circumstances, there are several situations in which satisfied employees are leaving for a variety of other reasons, so satisfaction data alone is not necessarily a valid leading-edge indicator. It seem that organization commitment may be a better indicator, as it measures the degree to which an employee identifies with, connects to, and supports the organization. Employee engagement is often also a better indicator of turnover. Engagement reflects the degree to which an employee feels involved and an important part of the organization. Organization commitment and engagement data are not always readily available. However, the most important linkage may be with the employee's *intention* to leave.

Intent to leave is measured by asking survey respondents, usually in the annual employee survey, how strongly they agree or disagree with this statement: "I intend to look for a new job in the next year."

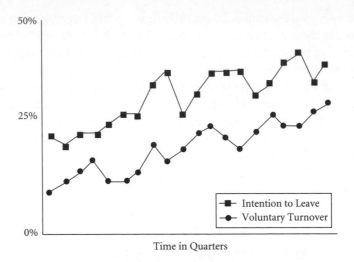

**Figure 4.6.   The Correlation Between Intention to Leave
and Actual Departure**
Source: Adapted from The Conference Board, 1999

The answers have a significant correlation with actual turnover, as shown in Figure 4.6. This measure is easy to collect in a traditional employee survey, even if the survey focuses on job satisfaction. However, it is critical for the data to be collected anonymously and treated confidentially.

Turnover Costs

It is important to develop a fully loaded cost for employee turnover and report it to executives. Too often, executives do not have a grasp of the total impact of turnover on their own organizations. The fully loaded turnover costs should be developed using the cost categories and procedures described in the next chapter. Turnover costs should be routinely reported also. This can be as easy using a multiple of employee compensation, or it can be more difficult. The value varies with the job. For example, for software designers, turnover cost may be as much as three times annual compensation; for sales reps, it could be one and a half times annual compensation; for fast-food employees in a restaurant chain, the value could be half the annual compensation.

After an agreement on the measure is reached, the costs should be routinely reported along with turnover data for each particular job group to show the management team the full impact of turnover. Unfortunately, turnover is sometimes ignored because the true costs are not known. However, hundreds of cost studies have been developed that provide a better picture of the cost of turnover. Approximate costs are sufficient; the important point is to determine the approximate amount early in the process and to use a standard reporting mechanism to share them with management.

DISTRIBUTION OF INFORMATION

Turnover data must be distributed to the management team and other interested parties so that appropriate action can be taken. Three time periods are recommended: monthly, quarterly, and annually. The monthly report should contain current turnover performance and turnover costs. The quarterly report should be more comprehensive and stimulate action and build support for retention solutions. Six specific areas should be addressed in these reports:

1. *A description of the current employment climate.* Use national data, including economic and labor information, to describe the current state of affairs. This is a perfect lead-in to current performance.

2. *Current turnover or retention data.* Sliced in a variety of ways the data should focus on the very critical issues. The retention counter-measure may be appropriate.

3. *Turnover costs.* At the current level of turnover performance, present the fully loaded costs of turnover by unit, department, region, or division. This will grab the attention of any executive.

4. *Benchmark data.* Present side-by-side comparisons with a benchmarking source.

5. *Issues and trends.* Highlight the economic climate, current performance, and comparative scenarios, as well as specific issues and trends that deserve recognition or attention. This shows the need to make adjustments and improvements, if necessary.

Reporting Options

Topic / Presentation	Monthly in a Report	Quarterly in a Summary	Annually in a Meeting
1. Current economic climate		X	X
2. Turnover (or retention) data in all categories	X	X	X
3. Turnover costs	X	X	X
4. Benchmark data		X	X
5. Issues and trends		X	X
6. Planned actions		X	X
7. Success with solutions			X
8. Leading indicators			X

Figure 4.7.   Recommended Reporting Options

6. *Planned actions.* Detail recommended action as a result of the trends and issues. The specific actions required may vary, but it is important to translate measurement into action.

The annual review should also show *success with solutions* and *leading indicators*, such as the intention to leave, job satisfaction, and organizational commitment data. Figure 4.7 gives a profile of information that should be considered in three reporting formats. Collectively, these issues should be addressed. The important point is to focus attention on this critical issue.

RESPONSIBILITY

Historically, the talent retention issue has been perceived to be a human resources problem. That perception is rapidly changing. Most management teams readily accept retention as a strategic issue and recognize it as their responsibility. As part of a retention strategy, it may be helpful to clarify the responsibility for retention and turnover. While the human resource staff, under the direction of the chief talent officer, must collect and assimilate data, perform appropriate analyses, and make comparisons, it must also create action items, coordinate and implement solutions, and show the value of solutions. The management team, however, is ultimately responsible for making it all work, and they often need to be reminded of their critical role. Because of this emphasis, turnover data must be included with the managers' operating data as part of the operations report. It becomes a routine part of the managers' performance indicators.

An important test of the shift in responsibility occurs when senior executives are actively exploring and examining the retention issue. The answers to several questions define the extent of the shift: Who reports on the retention issue? Who describes the steps taken when turnover is unacceptable in certain job groups? Who accepts the responsibility? If the senior team is addressing these issues in executive meetings, they have accepted retention as their responsibility. If all of the comments and questions are deferred to the chief talent officer or top HR executive, the shift has not occurred.

Responsibility for retention is a critical issue—one that seems obvious given the role and influence of top managers. However, in practice, the shift in responsibility does not take place as often as it should. While chief talent officers must accept responsibility from every aspect in their control, ultimately, the responsibility and accountability must rest with the operating departments because so many of the issues and causes of employee turnover *originate* in operating departments. When managers clearly see that it is their responsibility, they will become more involved with the process, initiating solutions and taking a more aggressive role to ensure that the solutions are successful.

FINAL THOUGHTS

This chapter is the starting point of the ROI approach to managing retention. Properly measuring and monitoring turnover is essential to bring the appropriate attention to the issue and take constructive action. Understanding the employment climate is fundamental to developing an understanding of retention. Also, having acceptable targets, based on precise definitions of turnover that are meaningful to the organization, helps bring the process clearly into focus. A variety of ways to collect and categorize retention and turnover data were described in the chapter. These are all aimed at bringing the proper resources and attention to this critical issue so that action is taken and the senior management team accepts responsibility for managing retention.

References

Branch, S. (1998, November 9). You hired 'em. But can you keep 'em? *Fortune,* p. 248.

Corporate Executive Board. (1999). *Salient findings on the career decisions of high value employees.* Washington, DC: The Conference Board.

Fitz-enz, J., & Davison, B. (2002). *How to measure human resources management* (3rd ed.). New York: McGraw-Hill.

Griffeth, R.W., & Hom, P.W. (2001). *Retaining valued employees.* Thousand Oaks, CA: Sage.

Hom, P.W., & Griffeth, R.W. (1995). *Employee turnover.* Cincinnati, OH: South-Western.

CHAPTER FIVE

Develop Fully Loaded Costs of Talent Departure

~~~

In this chapter we explore the financial impact of turnover, outlining specific costs that should be captured and economical ways in which they can be developed. One of the important challenges addressed in this chapter is to decide which costs can be developed from cost statements and which costs will have to be estimated. Some costs are hidden and, consequently, never counted. The conservative philosophy is utilized to account for all costs—direct and indirect. Several checklists and guidelines are included.

IMPORTANCE OF COSTS

A Silicon Valley high-tech company specializing in the delivery of total enterprise solutions signed a $30 million contract to install and maintain a new, state-of-the-art business enterprise software solution. Not long into the project, the lead manager unexpectedly resigned. He was the master engineer experienced in the design and installation of the product as well as the initial the reason the client signed the contract. Recruitment of a new project leader dragged on and on. It was difficult to find an individual with sufficient skills to complete the job on schedule. As can be expected, the promised delivery date came and went, forcing the client to cancel the contract. An enterprising reporter picked up the story and published it in the local business journal. A Wall Street analyst who was interested in the company's performance read the story. Wall Street immediately downgraded the company's rating, which led to a sharp plunge in its stock price. As employees' option prices eroded, the company suffered from a flood of other talent departures, which further damaged customer relationships and prolonged other time-sensitive projects.

As this story illustrates, the cost of unwanted and avoidable departure of talent can be catastrophic. While most managers are aware of the destructive nature of the loss of a valued employee, few managers actually understand the true cost of turnover. The problem revolves around three important issues.

1. The costs are not contained to any one location or one report.

2. The costs are not routinely reported to managers.

3. Most of the costs are actually hidden. They are difficult to develop.

These obstacles have caused many organizations to place a less-than-desired emphasis on developing and reporting the actual costs.

The following situation underscores the apparent lack of understanding about the true cost of turnover. Cisco Systems' business strategy was affected by a serious slowdown in the company's sales figures. The company reported that it would write off $2 billion in excess inventory and lay off 8,500 full-time and temporary employees. Five thousand of those employees had been hired between November and March of that same year. (Thrum, 2001) Some analysts estimated that the cost to bring the 8,500 employees on board could total $1 billion. The write-off did not include the $1 billion sunk costs involved in the acquisition and development of those employees. According to *The Wall Street Journal*, Mr. Chambers and other Cisco executives ignored or misread crucial warning signs. The sales forecasts were too ambitious, overstating Cisco's backlog after misleading information was provided by its internal order network. Still, the company continued to aggressively expand, even after business slowed in some of their divisions. If Cisco's chief executive had a full understanding of the actual costs and the devastating consequences of turnover, the decision to acquire all those employees may have been very different. The more that CEOs understand the full impact of costs, the more likely that the decision to increase or decrease staff size will be considered more carefully.

Monitoring the costs is an essential step in managing retention. Observing costs as they occur makes it easier to bring issues to management's attention. Cost monitoring not only reveals direct expenditures, but makes the impact of turnover and its consequences clear. Also, monitoring costs on an ongoing basis is much easier, more accurate, and more efficient than trying to reconstruct events.

From any viewpoint, turnover is a costly process and should commands the appropriate attention. This chapter provides all the information needed to develop a fully loaded cost of turnover.

HOW TO DEVELOP TURNOVER COSTS

The first step in monitoring turnover costs is to define and discuss several issues about a cost control system. The key issues are presented here.

Some Costs Are Difficult to Determine

The huge difference that often exists between the cost estimates from HR and the actual turnover cost lies in the indirect or hidden costs category. Where direct costs are usually in the cost accounting system, the hidden costs are almost never considered. However, they can be developed using assumptions and estimation processes.

CASE IN POINT

In one retail store chain with over four hundred locations, turnover was considered to be a major problem. The turnover rate for permanent employees was hovering around 100 percent. With 25,000 full-time, permanent employees and 50,000 part-time, seasonal employees, the company decided to find a more accurate value for the cost of turnover. To obtain an objective view, the firm engaged the services of an external consulting firm experienced in cost impact studies. Hidden costs were obtained as estimates, with input from a variety of credible individuals. The principal consultant obtained information directly from HR managers representing recruitment, employment, benefits, compensation, training, organization development, employee relations, and compliance. The managers were all asked to provide estimates of the annual, fully loaded cost of turnover for the 25,000 permanent employees. The estimates ranged from $2 million to $12 million. When the final costs were reported, the results were staggering. The total fully loaded cost of turnover was $180 million—greatly exceeding estimates. Incidentally, the HR staff did not question the credibility of the estimate, preferring to focus their attention on what they could do about the problem. Unfortunately, they never had the opportunity. The company was forced to file for Chapter 11 bankruptcy—turnover being one of the key issues leading to their demise.

If the organization had taken the time to develop the fully loaded cost of turnover and reported it routinely to senior management, there's a chance the bankruptcy could have been avoided.

Fully Loaded Costs

Using the approach to capturing the fully loaded costs of turnover described in this chapter, each cost is identified and put into a specific category. Where an estimate is required, the entry is adjusted later. The controller or chief financial officer should review and approve the data. The process should be able to withstand even the closest scrutiny, so organizations must ensure that all costs are included.

Reporting Total Costs

Costs are typically expressed as a percentage of the wages and salaries of the employees in a particular job group. This figure is usually determined after a detailed cost study is conducted. The percentage can be fixed for a group (for example, the sales force) or a specific job (for example, client relationship manager [CRM]). For example, if a cost study in another industry has concluded that the cost to replace a CRM averages 150 percent of pay, this amount can be a beginning point. If there is some concern about the cost being too high, perhaps a lower number would be appropriate, perhaps 120 percent or even 100 percent. After a figure has been determined, the turnover cost is then reported on statements along with the actual costs. In the retail store example above, 45 percent of the average sales associate's salary was included as a cost for each turnover. It is important to reach an acceptable figure without expending excessive time and resources.

THE DANGER OF REPORTING COSTS WITHOUT SOLUTIONS. It is sometimes risky to communicate the costs of talent turnover without presenting a retention solution or, at least, an action plan to develop a solution. Unfortunately in many cases, because some of the costs can be retrieved from the accounting systems, these are reported to management. Although they are not necessarily fully loaded, the costs are still staggering. The next obvious question from the senior management team is, "What can be done about it?" This often pressures the HR group or others to quickly find solutions, sometimes overreacting and throwing solutions and money at the problem before fully diagnosing it. A decision to report fully loaded costs should include a way to understand the causes of turnover and develop solutions to address the issue. The ROI approach presented in this book provides a framework to address this issue credibly.

DEVELOPING AND USING COST GUIDELINES. To find most turnover costs, it may be helpful to develop guidelines for the HR staff or (others who monitor and report costs), detailing the organization's philosophy and policy on costs. These guidelines should show which cost categories are included in turnover and how the data are captured, analyzed, and reported. Standards, unit costs, guiding principles, and generally accepted values should be included in these guidelines, which can range from a one-page brief in a smaller company to a fifty-page document in a large, complex organization. A simpler approach tends to be better. When completed, cost guidelines should be reviewed and approved by the finance and accounting staff. The final document provides direction to those who are collecting, monitoring, and reporting turnover costs. Turnover costs can be presented in a summary form or table, and the cost guidelines should be referenced in a footnote or attached as an appendix.

TYPICAL COST DATA. Fortunately, many detailed turnover cost studies have been published in the literature. Of all employee-related variables (turnover, absenteeism, sick leave, accidents, grievances, and complaints), turnover is studied more extensively because of

Job Type/Category	Turnover Cost Ranges as a Percent of Annual Wage/Salary
Entry Level—Hourly, Non-Skilled (such as Fast-Food Worker)	30 to 50
Service/Production Workers—Hourly (such as Courier)	40 to 70
Skilled Hourly (e.g., Machinist)	75 to 100
Clerical/Administrative (e.g., Scheduler)	50 to 80
Professional (e.g., Sales Representative, Nurse, Accountant)	75 to 125
Technical (e.g., Computer Technician)	100 to 150
Engineers (e.g., Chemical Engineer)	200 to 300
Specialists (e.g., Computer Software Designer)	200 to 400
Supervisors/Team Leaders (e.g., Section Supervisor)	100 to 150
Middle Managers (e.g., Department Manager)	125 to 200

Percentages are rounded to reflect the general range of costs from studies. Costs are fully loaded to include all of the costs of replacing an employee and bringing him or her to the level of productivity and efficiency of the former employee.

Exhibit 5.1.   Turnover Costs Summary

its significant impact on organizations. Consulting firms, industry associations, and business support groups routinely publish turnover cost studies, particularly where retention is a critical issue. Because so much is available in the literature, many organizations do not need to use their own resources to conduct a fully loaded cost study.

Exhibit 5.1 shows selected turnover cost data captured from dozens of impact studies arranged by job category, ranging from entry-level, non-skilled jobs to middle managers. The cost of turnover is shown as a percentage of base pay of the job group. The ranges are rounded off. The costs include exit cost of departing employees, recruiting, selection, orientation, initial training, wages and salaries while in training, lost productivity, quality problems, customer dissatisfaction, loss of expertise/knowledge, supervisor's time for turnover, and temporary replacement costs. The sources for these studies follow these general categories:

• Industry and trade magazines where the costs have been reported for a specific job within the industry;

- Practitioner publications in general management, human resource management, human resources development, and performance improvement;
- Academic and research journals where professors, consultants, and researchers publish the results of their work on retention;
- Independent studies conducted by organizations and not reported in the literature, but often available on a website or through membership arrangements. These are research-based groups supported by professional and management associations; and
- In addition, a few consulting firms develop and report on cost impact studies.

This list is not intended to be all-inclusive, but illustrates the availability of current studies and the tremendous cost associated with turnover. Unfortunately, finding a study in a specific field is sometimes difficult and can tax the search skills of even the most adept Internet browser.

COST MONITORING ISSUES

One of the most important tasks is to define the specific costs to be included in turnover. This involves the HR staff and usually management. In many instances, the finance and accounting staff may also have a need to approve the list.

Sources of Costs

The sources of costs vary in an organization. If there is one, the human capital management system can provide some of the cost data, particularly those items involving recruiting, selection, employment, employee processing, separation costs, and other expenses related to termination. Any learning management system in place should provide data for the training and orientation costs. Compensation and benefits records can provide detail regarding benefits for employees and the subsequent administrative costs. Beyond the HR records, much of the data will be housed in other parts of the organization. In some cases, sales, productivity, and quality records may reflect the impact of turnover, if the disruptions are clearly identified.

In other cases, the impact must be estimated using input from team leaders and managers in the areas where turnover is excessive.

Sometimes, managers who have to address turnover issues are the most credible sources of data, particularly when estimates are needed. For some hidden costs, it may be necessary to include input from other sections and functions, such as quality, process improvement, marketing, and the customer relations staff. Virtually any department or function adversely affected by turnover is a valid source.

The Timing of Turnover

The timing of turnover significantly affects the costs. For example, if a new employee leaves after only one week on the job, the total cost is low, depending almost totally on the costs involved in recruiting, selection, employment, orientation, and training during the initial week of employment. At the other extreme, a specialized, high-performance employee who remains on the job for five to ten years has probably made a contribution that offsets the cost of recruiting, training, and other transition activities. The greatest turnover cost occurs when a new employee leaves the organization just prior to becoming fully competent in the job. Up to that point, the organization has invested heavily in a variety of processes to bring the individual to the desired level of performance. This specific time can vary considerably—ranging from one week for employees with simplistic skills and repetitive functions to two years for specialized employees who need to understand the organization's specific processes, products, and capabilities. To develop costs for a specific job group, an average must be established. In most situations there is no way of knowing whether the next turnover would be expensive or not. Thus, you must come up with an average cost that reflects the impact of several turnovers.

The Employment Cycle

Another important way to develop turnover costs is to consider the cycle of an employee as he or she enters and exits an organization. Figure 5.1 shows the employment cycle of a six-month employee who left just after becoming fully competent on the job. The attraction/recruitment, selection, pre-employment training, and employment expenditures occur before the employee actually begins the work cycle. Orientation, socialization, and initial training are often downtime activities for the new employee and represent significant expenses because the employee is now receiving a salary. On-the-job learning and development represents a net loss to the organization as the employee is still learning the job, yet receiving a salary equivalent to that of a fully competent employee. It is not until the employee has reached the desired or optimum level of performance that compensation is in line with contribution. Additional maintenance costs are necessary to ensure that the individual is adapting to the organization. These costs are usually more significant for newer employees, compared with costs for those with longer service.

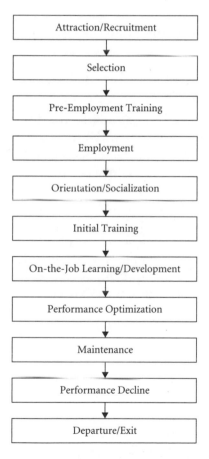

Figure 5.1.   Employment Cycle for a Six-Month Critical Employee

A decline in performance occurs whether the exit is involuntary or voluntary. Involuntary terminations occur when an employee's performance begins to deteriorate (for a variety of reasons) and the coaching, counseling, and discipline fail to salvage the employee. When employees are making a voluntary decision to exit and begin seeking other opportunities, there is also usually a performance decline. Employees are mentally checked out, often distracted, and a drop in performance may be intentional if the departure is because of a mismatch in the employee job placement or assignment. Either way, the employee incurs exit costs.

The cycle shown in the figure underscores the wide range of activities associated with the employment experience, but does not consider the other effects of turnover as unexpected vacancies result in disruptions and operational problems. In most settings, this disruption will continue until a replacement employee is fully competent.

Types of Costs

When considering costs for turnover, five different types of costs are usually captured. **Direct costs** are those directly charged to the turnover issue. For example, recruiting costs should be directly charged to turnover costs as a total cost divided by the number of recruits. At other times, **indirect HR costs**, not directly related to turnover, are allocated in some way to the total costs. For example, the overhead in the HR staff should be allocated to all HR functions and the overhead for the functions related to turnover are included in the turnover costs. For example, if 40 percent of the HR staff time is devoted to recruiting, employment, orientation, initial training, and separation, then 40 percent of the HR department overhead should be directly charged as overhead in costs of turnover.

Another category is **prorated HR costs**. For example, a new college graduate is recruited, and participates in six months of formal classroom training and a job rotation schedule. The initial development cost for that program should be prorated for the expected life cycle of the program and included in the turnover costs. The life cycle would be the time from the initial development of the program until a major revision is initiated. This is usually two or three years.

A fourth type of cost is **estimated costs**, usually from experts who have credibility with the cost item. For example, supervisors and team leaders can usually estimate the cost of an employee's abrupt departure, but such estimates for the inconvenience and disruption are very subjective and should be adjusted for error.

The final cost category is **linking costs**, those that are very difficult to convert to monetary value, but linked to measures that are more easily converted to monetary value. For example, turnover may be directly linked to customer dissatisfaction, which is linked to sales. The profit margin on sales provides an approximate value for the disruptive nature of the customer service function.

In summary, all five types of data should be considered and captured for a fully loaded cost profile. The values listed in Figure 5.1 contain the five types of measures.

Employee Benefits Factor

When an employee's time is required to address turnover, these costs must be represented. This means that the employee benefits factor should be included also. This number is used in other costing formulas and usually readily available. It represents the cost of all employee benefits expressed as a percentage of payroll. In some organizations this value is as high as 50 to 60 percent, while in others it may be as low as 25 to 30 percent. The average in the United States is almost 40 percent (*Nation's Business*, 2008).

CLASSIFYING COSTS

Because so much has been developed and written about turnover costs, various classification schemes are often devised. Figure 5.2 shows one classification scheme, which places turnover costs into two major categories. This shows turnover costs as being an iceberg, with the tip of the iceberg being the visible turnover costs (labeled "Green Money"). A major part of the iceberg under the water is the category called "Blue Money," the invisible cost of turnover (Ahlrichs, 2000). The iceberg concept is useful because it emphasizes how much of the cost is hidden or indirect.

More detail is needed to calculate all costs. Figure 5.3 shows the major cost categories presented in this book. Turnover costs have been divided into four major categories, three of which are relatively easy to develop. The first category is departure/exit costs, which includes those costs connected with leaving the organization,

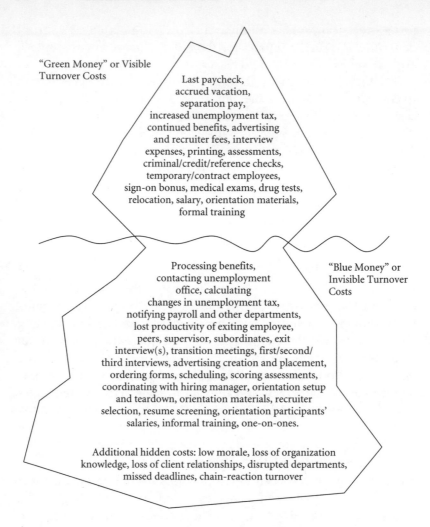

"Green Money" or Visible Turnover Costs

Last paycheck,
accrued vacation,
separation pay,
increased unemployment tax,
continued benefits, advertising
and recruiter fees, interview
expenses, printing, assessments,
criminal/credit/reference checks,
temporary/contract employees,
sign-on bonus, medical exams, drug tests,
relocation, salary, orientation materials,
formal training

Processing benefits,
contacting unemployment
office, calculating
changes in unemployment tax,
notifying payroll and other departments,
lost productivity of exiting employee,
peers, supervisor, subordinates, exit
interview(s), transition meetings, first/second/
third interviews, advertising creation and placement,
ordering forms, scheduling, scoring assessments,
coordinating with hiring manager, orientation setup
and teardown, orientation materials, recruiter
selection, resume screening, orientation participants'
salaries, informal training, one-on-ones.

Additional hidden costs: low morale, loss of organization
knowledge, loss of client relationships, disrupted departments,
missed deadlines, chain-reaction turnover

"Blue Money" or Invisible Turnover Costs

Figure 5.2.   Turnover Iceberg
Adapted from N.S. Ahlrichs, *Competing for Talent*. Palo Alto, CA:
Davies-Black, 2000

whether voluntary or involuntary. The concept of reducing turnover for involuntary departures is important if the exit could have been avoided. (This issue was explored in the previous chapter.) The second major cost is actually replacing the individual and includes recruitment, selection, employment, and the administrative overhead

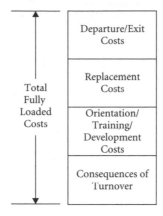

Figure 5.3. Major Cost Categories

associated with those issues. This is a very significant cost for most organizations. The third category is the initial orientation, socialization, training, and development costs. Included in this is any formal or informal preparation and training for the individual to assume the initial job and become fully competent. The fourth category, which may be the largest and most difficult to measure, is hidden costs—productivity and quality problems, disruption of service, loss of knowledge and expertise, and loss of client relationship, and so forth. Total fully loaded costs are not complete until all categories in the classification scheme have been developed, even if some have been estimated. Each of these major cost categories is described in more detail below.

Departure/Exit Costs

Exhibit 5.2 presents the details of the four major cost categories. Departure/exit costs, those incurred when an employee leaves for avoidable reasons, represent significant investment in time and direct expenditures. Eight cost items are included in this category.

Exit interview costs. This category involves all the costs for the exit interviews, including the downtime of the departing employee as well as the interviewer. Also included are the costs of the materials, processing, analysis, and reporting the data.

Departure/Exit Costs   _____
    Exit Interview Costs   _____
    Administration Time   _____
    Management Time   _____
    Benefits Termination/Continuation   _____
    Pay Continuation/Severance   _____
    Unemployment Tax   _____
    Legal Expenses (If Applicable)   _____
    Outplacement (If Applicable)   _____

Replacement Costs   _____
    Recruitment/Advertising   _____
    Recruitment Expenses   _____
    Recruitment Fees   _____
    Sign-Up Bonuses   _____
    Selection Interviews   _____
    Testing/Pre-Employment Examinations   _____
    Travel Expenses   _____
    Moving Expenses   _____
    Administrative Time (Not Covered Above)   _____
    Management Time (Not Covered Above)   _____

Orientation/Training Costs   _____
    Pre-Employment Training   _____
        Development   _____
        Delivery   _____
        Materials   _____
        Facilities   _____
        Travel (If applicable)   _____
        Overhead (Administration)   _____
    Orientation Program   _____
        Development   _____
        Delivery   _____
        Materials   _____
        Facilities   _____
        Travel (If applicable)   _____
        Overhead (Administration)   _____
    Initial Training   _____
        Development   _____
        Delivery   _____
        Materials   _____
        Facilities   _____
        Time off the Job   _____
        Travel (If appropriate)   _____
        Overhead (Administration)   _____
    Formal On-the-Job Learning   _____
        Development   _____
        Job Aids   _____

Exhibit 5.2.   Cost Accumulation Categories

Delivery   _____
Management Time   _____
Overhead (Administration)   _____

Consequences of Turnover   _____
  Work Disruption   _____
  Lost Productivity (or Replacement Costs)   _____
  Quality Problems   _____
  Customer Dissatisfaction   _____
  Management Time   _____
  Loss of Expertise/Knowledge   _____

Exhibit 5.2. (*continued*)

Administrative time. All the time associated with the entire issue of separation, departure, and exit should be included. Essentially, this category is the HR staff time for completing paperwork and addressing the issue.

Management time. This category is the time allocated by the management group, direct supervisors, and other managerial stakeholders to address the turnover issue. This includes not only their individual participation, but also the time spent in meetings discussing the issue. There will always be some management time involved in any departure, but some situations require more than others.

Benefits termination/continuation. The cost to continue benefits for a period of time must be included. Also, the cost to remove employees from benefit programs, or administer benefits in the future is included. Some benefit programs, such as a 401(k), may require company maintenance after an employee has terminated.

Paid continuation/severance. This category of costs can be significant, depending on policy. As part of company policy, there may be salary continuance—even with voluntary separations. Preventable, involuntary separations often result in much larger severance arrangements, sometimes consisting of packages extending over an entire year.

Unemployment insurance. The employer pays this tax to a state or local agency, enabling the departing employee to obtain unemployment benefits. This provides income while the employee is seeking new employment and is usually appropriate for those who involuntarily leave. In some states in the United States, these benefits are also available in cases of voluntary departures.

Legal expenses. Some departures, particularly involuntary terminations, may result in litigation for the company. There may also be situations in which a voluntary departure will generate legal expenses, for example, a sexual harassment complaint. It is important to note that only a few separations will actually involve legal action. To determine an average value, the total costs are spread out over the total number of departing employees.

Outplacement. For those employees leaving involuntarily, outplacement is sometimes included as part of a severance package. This includes counseling and support services to assist the employee in obtaining a new job. Again, this usually applies only to the involuntary terminations and will be applicable only to those avoidable situations.

The departure and exit costs are significant and often omitted from turnover cost analysis. As previously indicated, these expenses are incurred even in voluntary termination and should be included. In certain situations, this can be a critical part of the turnover issue, particularly if employees leave voluntarily because they are dissatisfied with the organization to the point at which they are considering litigation.

Replacement Costs

As Exhibit 5.2 illustrates, the recruitment costs are perhaps the most visible cost directly related to turnover, as new employees are recruited and employed to replace the departing employees. Ten major cost categories are contained in the replacement costs.

Recruiting/advertising. Expenditures directly related to attracting new employees are included. Image-building ads and materials, direct letters, and other communication tools are typical.

Recruitment expenses. This category includes direct expenses involved in recruiting, such as travel to visit job candidates, conducting job fairs, and expenses to inform applicants about the organization prior to the actual application process.

Recruitment fees and bonuses. One of the most significant expenditures for highly specialized employees and managers is the recruiting fees paid directly to third-party agencies. It is not uncommon for these fees to be equal to one year of the new employee's salary or more.

Employment bonuses. Bonuses may be paid to join the organization. Payments may include cash, expense allowances, vacation time, stock, stock options, or a new computer. Obviously, not all new employees enjoy such bonuses, but in many situations, specialized employees and managers are offered these items as an incentive to join the organization.

Selection interviews. This category includes the expenses associated with the interview process, including the interviewer's time, along with materials and/or other expenses directly related to the interview.

Testing/pre-employment examinations. This includes the cost of administering and analyzing any type of pre-employment test. Physical examinations, drug screening, and other pre-employment hurdles are included.

Travel expenses. All company-reimbursed travel expenses for the candidates to interview for the job and cycle through the pre-employment process are included. This includes airfare, ground transportation, lodging, meals and other direct expenses.

Moving expenses. All moving expenses are included in this category, including fees for any relocation firm. In a competitive recruiting situation, employees are sometimes offered relocation expenses, including the direct costs of moving. Most professional, technical, and managerial employees will have moving expenses.

Administrative time. The time for administrative staff support, including overhead, and other expenses allocated to the replacement functions are included here. To avoid duplication of cost, time allocated in any categories listed above should be factored out.

Management time. This category is the time managers spend on this process, from planning a recruitment strategy for a particular individual to conducting interviews and making the final job offer. If previous categories account for management time, it should be excluded from this category.

Overall, replacement costs are relatively easy to ascertain, but may require some adjustments to ensure that the costs assigned to a specific individual or type of employee can be easily determined.

Orientation and Training Costs

As shown in Exhibit 5.2, orientation and training costs include formal and informal pre- and post-employment training and development. These may represent the most extensive part of the training and development budget. For example, a major aircraft manufacturer may spend weeks training a new employee before the actual job assignment. A large banking organization recruits new college graduates for a variety of professional assignments. A six-month training program is typical prior to actually being assigned to the job. In each situation, training is significant and the fully loaded costs must be included in turnover costs.

Pre-employment training. Some organizations conduct pre-employment training as a screening tool. For example, a major automobile company in the southeastern United States has a special facility designed to train individuals to perform basic job functions. The pre-employment training becomes a screening tool and they use the results in the selection process, allowing only the best candidates to advance to employment. This approach is very advantageous for the employer because the candidate is not on the payroll and the training is conducted on the participant's own time. In some situations, local government provides pre-employment training to support businesses or as an incentive to lure a business to the area. In these cases, the fully loaded costs of the pre-employment should be included because the total cost is there, even if local taxpayers share it. Six major categories should be included when there's pre-employment training.

Development—The development of the training program should be considered on a per-participant basis. The estimated number of participants who will be involved in the program during its life cycle is divided into the cost of developing the program, yielding a development cost per participant. The life cycle is determined by estimating the time from the initial development (or last major revision) and the next major revision.

Delivery—The delivery costs are those costs directly allocated to the actual instruction or facilitation. Major items are the facilitator's time and direct coordination expenses. Meals or refreshment costs are also included.

Materials—The materials are the consumable items in the training, which includes reference guides, manuals, books, and other handout material used or retained by the participants. Equipment rental also would be included in this category.

Facilities—The cost of the facility for the training center is included, which is usually the total cost divided by the number of participants trained during the life of the facility (which would usually be quite long). If a designated on-site training room is utilized, the equivalent rental price would be appropriate.

Travel (if applicable)—This category includes the cost of travel for the instructor, or any other travel related to the actual training. Participant travel should be included if travel costs are reimbursed by the organization. Since participants are not employees, travel costs may not be an issue.

Overhead/administration—This category is the cost of administrative time not included previously, but allocated in some convenient way.

Orientation/socialization program costs. The costs for the orientation and socialization are both formal (e.g., training sessions and meetings) and informal (e.g., self-study materials and on-the-job coaching). The costs can be captured using the same six categories of pre-employment training plus time off the job:

Development—This category includes the cost to develop the program, which should be prorated on a per-person basis, using the expected life cycle of the program. The life cycle would be the expected duration of the program before a major revision is considered.

Delivery—The costs directly related to the delivery of the program are included. Examples are the time of the individual facilitating the program and any other direct expenses, such as equipment rental and meeting costs. Meals and refreshment costs should be included.

Materials—This category includes the costs for handouts, such as manuals, documents, books, annual reports, and other materials provided in orientation. These materials are designed to improve understanding of the organization their role in it.

Facilities—This is the cost for the room where the orientation occurs, whether it's a rented facility or an on-site conference room. To have the cost fully loaded, it's important to allocate cost for this space. The amount can be estimated by pricing a comparable meeting room at a local hotel. Facilities costs would also include any direct meeting room expenses.

Travel—In some cases, a new employee may travel to a different location for orientation and have these expenses reimbursed by the company. On other occasions, the person providing the orientation may travel for this presentation. Either way, the expenses should be included.

Time off the job—When employees are involved in off-the-job activities, the value of the time should be included. The cost is the estimated (or actual) wages or salaries, adjusted upward for the employee benefits factor.

Overhead/administration—The expenses not directly involved in the program, but allocated in some convenient way, would be included.

Initial training. Initial training has several major cost categories and varies considerably with the individual, type of job, and objective of the program. Six key areas are represented.

Development—This category is the cost for developing the training program, usually prorated by cost per participant. The estimated number of participants involved in the program during the life cycle is divided into the development cost to obtain the cost per new employee. The life cycle is determined by estimating the life of the program from its initial development to the next major revision.

Delivery—The cost of the instructor, direct coordination, and meeting room expenses, such as refreshments and meals are included.

Materials—This includes direct training materials, including workbooks, manuals, books, and other consumables used during the training and distributed to the participants.

Facilities—Direct cost of the meeting room should be included, even if part of the organization's facilities. In most situations, using the cost to rent a comparable training room at a nearby hotel will suffice.

Time off the job—This category may be very significant. It is the time for the participants to be involved off the job, including the direct wages or salaries for the time in training, adjusted for the employee benefits factor.

Travel (if appropriate)—Actual travel expenses for the new employees to attend training are included. This category also includes airfare, hotel, meals, ground transportation and other related travel costs.

Overhead/administration—The expenses not directly involved in the program, but allocated in some convenient way are included.

Formal on-the-job learning. In addition to formal classroom training, some employees receive formal on-the-job learning. The supervisor or team leader may coordinate this job-site learning. In some cases, a training coordinator for the local area may coordinate the learning. In other cases a coach or mentor may be involved. This training is important and often represents a significant expense. Five areas are usually involved.

Development—This category is the cost to develop the program, which should be prorated on a per-person basis, using the expected life cycle of the program. The life cycle would be the expected duration of the program before a major revision is considered.

Job aids—This category includes specific job aids developed to teach the job or parts of the job. The expense of this could be prorated over their potential use on the job until the job aid is redesigned.

Delivery—This category includes the actual time of the on-the-job coordinator, team leader, mentor, coach, or others who are actively involved in delivering the training.

Management time—Time of management group involved in job teaching or coaching—not counted in the above categories—should be included.

Overhead/administration—The expenses not directly involved in the program, but allocated in some way should be included.

Consequences of Turnover

Some argue that the most significant costs of turnover are those hidden costs that represent the consequences of unexpected employee departure. These costs underscore the importance of having a capable staff in the work setting at all times. In some cases—particularly in direct customer contact jobs—the costs can be staggering. Consider the customer service area in which employee turnover can adversely affect service delivery. As shown in Figure 5.4, two critical consequences affect customer service: (1) the staff shortage created by the often-sudden departure of employees and (2) the problems created when inexperienced employees are learning new skills to serve the customer. Either of these processes translates into unacceptable customer service, which leads to customer dissatisfaction and, ultimately, to a decline in sales. Customers do not buy as much as they did or no longer buy from the organization, convincing others to do the same or discouraging them from going there in the first place. This model has been supported and validated in many organizations and often called the "Service Profit Chain."

The specific cost categories in the area of customer service can be grouped into six categories.

Work disruption. This includes the actual costs associated with having the workplace disrupted due to staff shortages or inexperienced staff. This can range from being an inconvenience to the complete inability to deliver appropriate levels of service.

Lost productivity (or replacement costs). This category is the actual work lost because the previous employee is absent or the new employee is not quite up to speed. It is easy to envision this loss in a production or sales environment, but it exists in all types of jobs. An alternative to this cost would be the actual replacement costs if temporary labor were used until other employees are fully prepared for their jobs. Either way, this cost is significant and would have to be developed directly from estimates or the records in the organization.

Quality problems. This category is the cost for the errors, mistakes, rework, and rejects directly related to the turnover issue. In most cases, it is directly related to the new, inexperienced employee on the job.

Customer dissatisfaction. As discussed above, customer dissatisfaction can result in a significant loss of income. This amount will be an estimate from management in the area where employees are leaving. It's also possible to develop a chain of impact or linkage arrangement presented in Figure 5.4. Either way, an estimate has to be included, particularly for those employees directly involved in customer service.

Management time. This is the cost of time taken by management to address the turnover issue or focus on those problems arising

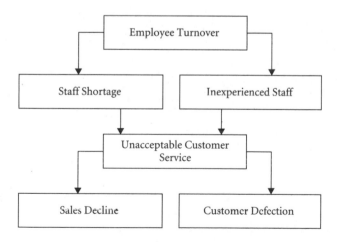

Figure 5.4.   Customer Service Consequences of Turnover

out of turnover. This figure would include any time not allocated previously, and would usually involve operational issues and problems stemming from staff shortages and inexperienced staff.

Loss of expertise/knowledge. In a knowledge industry, enormous cost is connected to replacing an individual who has accumulated a significant amount of expertise with the products, processes, and projects in the organization. In some cases, it may take years to recoup this investment. In this category, a rough estimate is generated to reflect the costs (or time) to develop the lost expertise.

Clearly, the customer service consequences of turnover are tremendous, representing one of the largest categories of turnover cost. This aspect is often discussed, but rarely calculated. But it is important to at least estimate the costs, as it is better than having no data at all. If estimates are used, use an error adjustment process like the one discussed in Chapter 13, Calculate ROI of Retention Solutions.

General Considerations

In summary, several important issues must be taken into consideration.

Collect cost, even if they're not required or immediately utilized. Too often, the HR staff neglects to accurately collect and report the turnover costs because they are not requested or no action is taken when they are presented to the senior management team. Cost control is an important management function and necessary to properly manage retention. Eventually, these costs will be requested by the senior team and utilized in their analysis of the issue. It's best to develop them before they're actually requested.

Costs may not be precise. As discussed in this chapter, costs will not always be exact. With so many hidden costs and cost allocation possibilities, it is difficult to develop a completely accurate picture of turnover costs. But lack of precision should not discourage the HR staff from attempting to monitor and collect these costs. A reasonably accurate cost estimate is better than no estimate. Senior executives who review cost data are aware of the tenuous nature of information being presented. They know that much of the data they work with on a daily basis is based on expert input and not actual calculations.

Use external studies. Fortunately, many external studies on the cost of turnover have been developed. It is best to use these studies to the extent possible. While it is helpful to develop the fully loaded cost for a particular key job group, it is also important to be mindful of the availability of resources. Most organizations cannot afford to develop their own detailed impact studies for all major job groups. Consequently, external cost studies should be used whenever possible.

Use a practical approach. The cost for ongoing monitoring of the costs of turnover is significant and may not be practical for many organizations. Using more estimates and external studies may be an option. The tradeoff of accuracy versus feasibility in maintaining a system must be weighed. Most categories of data presented here can be monitored and allocated directly to the cost of turnover. If major systems modifications are needed to develop more accurate data, the costs may exceed the utility of having these reporting systems. As an alternative, use other informal processes within the budget constrains of the organization.

Develop a standard. Unfortunately, external standards do not exist in terms of which cost should be included or how the cost should be defined and calculated. Until a standard is developed, a fully loaded cost profile should be used, with a conservative approach to making estimates and adjustments. The approach presented in this book can be used as a standard for reporting the fully loaded costs of turnover.

Use caution when reporting costs. As discussed earlier, it is important to communicate cost data carefully. The target audience should know when there are estimates. The actual methodology used should be detailed, including how estimates were obtained. The data should be compared to any external data as a benchmark, if possible. Costs should always be presented when there is a problem that should be rectified, but costs should be included with routine reports on turnover, not just when there's a serious problem.

FINAL THOUGHTS

The message is simple: Turnover is expensive—more expensive than most executives realize. The importance of costs and cost tracking cannot be over-emphasized. The various issues involved in accurately reporting, monitoring, and communicating costs are complex. In this chapter, we presented the different categories of cost in order to help you to develop more accurate, fully loaded costs of turnover (including indirect and hidden costs). We have also presented guidelines and general considerations for using these cost data.

References

Ahlrichs, N.S. (2000). *Competing for talent* (p. 12). Palo Alto, CA: Davies-Black.
Annual Employee Benefits Survey. (2008, January). *Nation's Business.*
Thrum, S. (2001, April 18). Behind Cisco's woes are some wounds of its own making. *The Wall Street Journal*, p. 1.

CHAPTER SIX

Diagnose Causes
of Talent Departure

In this chapter we address one of the most critical issues in managing retention: determining the exact cause of excessive talent departure. Too often, retention is focused on solutions and employee needs without uncovering the specific problems or issues in the organization. The consequences can be disastrous.

A variety of tools are needed to analyze the exact causes of talent departure so that potential solutions can be matched to particular causes. We begin with fundamental issues that must be addressed before tracking turnover. Analyzing turnover data is the first step to understanding where the problems are. However, additional analysis is needed to determine a particular cause. The diagnostic tools in this chapter include questionnaires, surveys, interviews, focus groups, and other analytical techniques. The chapter concludes with a process to determine the actual causes of turnover.

THE DILEMMA OF ANALYSIS

Analysis is often misplaced, misunderstood, and misrepresented. The process conjures up images of complex problems, confusing models, and a plethora of data with complicated statistical techniques. In reality, analysis needn't be so complicated—simple techniques may uncover the causes of turnover. When talent departure is excessive, organizations may not examine the reasons because:

1. *Employee needs appear to point to a solution.* When employee needs are examined, several potential solutions usually are suggested. However, these solutions may not be appropriate. For example, the fact that employees want supportive managers doesn't necessarily translate into a need for manager training. If employees characterize their managers as unfair, it doesn't mean that the managers need training. Maybe managers know how to treat employees fairly and with respect, but are not required or encouraged to do so.

2. *Solutions appear to be obvious.* For example, if the base pay of a critical employee group is lower than a competitor's pay for the same group, the obvious solution appears to be to increase the base pay. However, the principal reason for employee departures may not be pay. Low turnover rates can be achieved in organizations providing a lower than average salary. The actual causes for turnover must be thoroughly researched.

3. *Everyone has an opinion about the cause.* Almost everyone who wrestles with the retention issue will have an opinion about the causes of turnover. In a recent study of turnover causes in a manufacturing plant, multiple reasons for turnover were identified. The cause of turnover, as perceived by the plant manager, was completely different from the reasons offered by the supervisors, and still very different from the causes pinpointed by the individuals who were leaving. Because everyone has an opinion, it is tempting to go with the highest ranking input (that is, the plant manager).

4. *Analysis takes too much time and consumes too many resources.* But the consequences of no analysis can be even more expensive. If solutions are implemented without determining the actual cause, time and resources may be wasted—and the results can be more damaging than doing nothing at all. It is possible to complete an analysis within any organization's budget and time constraints. The key is to use the right tools.

5. *Analysis appears confusing.* Some analyses are simple, straightforward, and achieve excellent results. For instance, the nominal group technique described later in this chapter is a simple, inexpensive process that can often accurately determine the causes of turnover.

The challenges that prevent good analysis are apparent, but this critical step cannot be omitted.

FINDING THE CONNECTIONS AMONG EMPLOYEE NEEDS, CAUSES OF TURNOVER, AND SOLUTIONS

Before discussing any specific analysis techniques, it is helpful to review the relationships among the needs of employees, the causes of turnover, specific solutions offered, and the context in which employees often make the decision to leave. When employees have particular needs on the job, the challenge of the employer is to meet those needs in some way or face the consequences. If employees' needs are met, an employee stays. If a need is not met and is not considered important enough, an employee may decide to adjust or adapt to the situation rather than leave the organization.

A tremendous amount of research has been conducted about the relationship between employee needs and employee turnover. Perhaps the most analyzed connection is the relationship between job satisfaction and turnover. Job satisfaction involves a variety of issues, including the issues discussed later in this chapter. Studies show that job satisfaction has been declining in organizations since about 1995.

The second most analyzed group of factors are those labeled "organization commitment," where there is an attempt to understand the extent to which employees are committed, even emotionally attached, to the organization. Measures include the degree to which employees identify with the organization's mission, vision, and values; the extent to which employees have meaningful and challenging work; and the freedom to grow and develop within the organization. These two measures—*job satisfaction* and *organization commitment*—have been extensively researched in relation to turnover.

Other factors have been shown to drive retention as well. For example, the concept of *job alternatives* is an issue for retention.

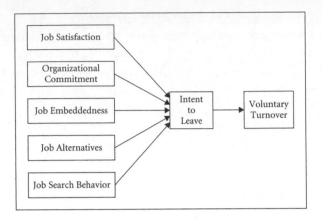

Figure 6.1.   Employee-Job Factors and Retention

When employees think that they can find a better job elsewhere within a short period of time, the likelihood of their leaving increases. *Job search behavio*r has an important connection to the actual intent to leave and departure. In recent years, additional research has been conducted on the extent to which employees feel attached to their positions or *job embeddedness.* Employees have a greater tendency to stay with an organization if their job is a good fit, they are comfortable with their work group, or if they feel that leaving would require a sacrifice.

Figure 6.1 shows the relationship of these issues to turnover. Job satisfaction, organization commitment, job embeddedness, job alternatives, and job search behavior all are linked to intent to leave and intent to leave is linked to voluntary turnover. While this relationship fails to hold up in every organization in every context, it provides a general understanding of the connection between these job-related factors and actual turnover in the organization.

Clearly, there are some very strong relationships between what employees need at work, their perceptions of their jobs, their perceptions of the job market, and their actions to seek jobs and voluntary turnover. While these provide some indication as to the reasons for turnover, they do not point to the reasons why employees intend to leave or are leaving a specific organization. In essence, these factors and their relationships form the overall framework in which to understand the complex nature of talent retention.

Key Questions for Employees

*1. Do I know what is expected of me at work?
*2. Do I have the materials and equipment I need to do my work right?
*3. At work, do I have the opportunity to do what I do best every day?
  4. In the last seven days, have I received recognition or praise for doing good work?
*5. Does my supervisor, or someone at work, seem to care about me as a person?
  6. Is there someone at work who encourages my development?
  7. At work, do my opinions seem to count?
  8. Does the mission/purpose of my company make me feel my job is important?
  9. Are my co-workers committed to doing quality work?
10. Do I have a best friend at work?
11. In the last six months, has someone at work talked to me about my progress?
12. This last year, have I had opportunities at work to learn and grow?

*Correlation with turnover

Exhibit 6.1. Key Questions for Employees, According to Gallup

Some research efforts take a more simplistic approach. The Gallup organization published a major study involving thousands of employees in which twelve questions were identified that would link to employee turnover in some way (Buckingham & Coffman, 1999). These questions, shown in Exhibit 6.1, are simple issues, but powerfully connected to turnover in many organizations. The research shows that questions 1, 2, 3, and 5 show the strongest direct relationship to turnover.

Still other research focuses on becoming an employer of choice. It is assumed that an employer of choice would be able to attract and retain employees more easily than those not considered to be employers of choice. Of course, the definition of an employer of choice depends on who is advocating the particular research study or publication. Exhibit 6.2 shows the shift that must take place in organizations to develop into employers of choice (Ahlrichs, 2000).

Still more confusing are the various reports that claim to have the secrets to reducing turnover, often presented as the solutions found in a particular organization or across several organizations. These reports are generated by consulting firms, research groups, industry groups, and professional organizations concerned with the retention issue.

It is important to note that these types of reports merely develop a framework for consideration and identify an initial point in analysis.

Then	Now
Lean and mean	Lean and nice
No time to train	Invest in training
Hire experienced people	Hire people who can learn
Career development is the employee's responsibility.	Career development is the responsibility of the organization and employee.
If you don't like it here, leave!	If you don't like it here, why?
You should be grateful just to have a job.	Thank you—your contribution matters!
Anyone off the street could do your job.	Only *you* will do!
(If someone gives notice) Don't let the door hit you on the way out.	(If someone gives notice) If you must leave us, we hope you will stay in touch and tell us why you're leaving.
It's not personal; it's just business.	It's all personal.

Exhibit 6.2.   Paradigm Shift to an Employer of Choice
Source: Adapted from Ahlrichs, 2000, p. 228

It is essential for any organization to drill down and determine the exact cause of its own turnover. Every organization is unique—the exact causes of turnover in one organization will not necessarily be duplicated in another. The remainder of this chapter is focused on the steps that need to be taken to determine the specific causes of turnover.

STARTING POINT: ANALYSIS OF TURNOVER DATA

The starting point is the examination of turnover records. This includes reporting data along different categories and around various job characteristics. For example, turnover occurring with single mothers under the age of twenty-five may indicate that there's a work/family balance issue and that on-site childcare could be a solution. As illustrated in Figure 6.2, however, the records merely indicate that there's a problem with a particular group; they do not necessarily identify the cause of the problem, nor define a solution.

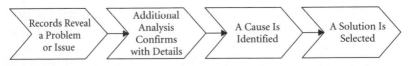

Figure 6.2.   Analysis of Records Leads to More Analysis

Key Questions	Example
Which major job group contains the most turnover?	(Professional)
Which specific job category contains the most turnover?	(Senior Client Partner)
Which specific function contains the most turnover?	(Sales and Marketing)
Which specific department contains the most turnover?	(Direct Sales)
Which specific area/region contains the most turnover?	(West Coast)
What is the timing of most turnover?	(Early Summer)
What is the tenure of most turnover?	(Less than six months)
What is the age of most employees who leave?	(25 to 30)
What is the educational level of most employees who leave?	(Master's Degree)
What is the sex of most employees who leave?	(Male)
What is the race or ethnic background of most employees who leave?	(Asian)
What is the marital status of most employees who leave?	(Single)
What is the family status of most employees who leave?	(Divorced Parent)

Exhibit 6.3. Key Questions Addressed Directly from Records

Additional analysis is needed to confirm or refute the data and identify a potential solution. This point is important because the first step of analysis is often where a solution is inappropriately applied.

Turnover data can be analyzed in many ways: by job group, region, variety of personal characteristics, or job status, among others. Data must be collected so that key questions such as those listed in Exhibit 6.3 can be answered. As you can see, many answers point to a problem area and potential causes.

Developing an appropriate database about turnover is critical. Many of the human capital management systems (HCMS) provide multiple options for capturing, dissecting, and analyzing data. Not only do they slice the data into the types of category shown in Figure 6.3, but they also show connections between the data and such factors as the relationship between turnover and salaries, expressed as a percent of the competitive rate. Another example is the relationship between job satisfaction and turnover. The analysis of the turnover data, presented in Chapter 4, serves as the beginning point of the analysis. Determining the cause(s) of turnover will require the use of additional techniques, many focused on the employees who are leaving or who may leave.

Sufficient resources must be devoted to analyzing turnover records, examining solutions, and plotting strategies to retain key employees. It is sometimes more important (and efficient) to go directly to employees and ask them what motivates them to stay with the organization, who might lure them away, and what would cause them to leave. The next few sections focus on some of the ways to ask employees these key questions.

QUESTIONNAIRES

A questionnaire is probably the most common and inexpensive instrument used to examine turnover. Questionnaires come in all sizes, ranging from brief reaction forms to detailed instruments. Questionnaires can be used to obtain all types of data, ranging from subjective information about employees' feelings to business impact data for use in an ROI analysis. It is important for questionnaires to be designed properly.

Types of Questions

Five basic types of questions are recommended, depending on the purpose of the questionnaire. Any or all of the following may be utilized:

Open-ended question—has an unlimited answer and should be followed by ample blank space for the response.

Checklist—offering a list of items, the respondent is asked to check the items that best apply to the situation.

Two-way question—has alternative responses, a yes/no, disagree or agree, or other possibilities.

Multiple-choice question—has several choices whereby the respondent is asked to select the one most applicable.

Ranking scales—requires the respondent to rank a list of items.

Questionnaire Design

An improperly designed or worded questionnaire is confusing, frustrating, and potentially embarrassing. Questionnaires should be simple and logical. The following steps will help ensure that a valid, reliable, and effective instrument is developed.

Determine the information needed. The first step is to determine the topics and issues to be addressed. Questions are developed later. It might be helpful to develop this information in outline form so that related questions can be grouped together.

Select the type(s) of questions. Determine whether open-ended questions, checklists, two-way questions, multiple-choice questions, or ranking scales are appropriate. Take into consideration the planned data analysis and variety of data to be collected.

Develop the questions. The questions should be simple and straightforward enough to avoid confusion or leading the respondent to a response. Terms or expressions unfamiliar to the respondent should be avoided. Develop the appropriate number and variety of questions consistent with the validity and reliability issues (Phillips & Stawarski, 2008).

Check the reading level. To ensure that the target audience can easily understand the questionnaire, it is helpful to assess the questionnaire's reading level. Most word processing software contains features that will evaluate the reading difficulty by grade level.

Address the anonymity issue. Questionnaires should be anonymous unless there are specific reasons for individuals to be identified. Because there is usually a link between anonymity and accuracy, respondents should feel free to respond openly without fear of reprisal. In situations in which the questionnaire must be completed by a captive audience or submitted directly to an individual, a neutral third party should collect and process the data, ensuring that participants' identities are not revealed. In cases in which the identity of respondents must be known (for example, to compare output data with the previous data or to verify the data), every effort should be made to protect the respondents' identities.

Design for ease of tabulation and analysis. Each potential question should be viewed in terms of data tabulation, data summary, and analysis. If possible, questions should be outlined and reviewed in mock-up form. This step helps avoid inadequate, cumbersome, and lengthy data analysis caused by improper wording or design.

Test the questions. After the questions are developed, they should be tested for understanding—ideally on a group of typical respondents. If this is not feasible, the questions should be tested on employees at approximately the same job level as the potential participants. Collect as much input and as many critical comments as possible. Revise the questions as necessary.

Prepare a data summary. A data summary sheet should be developed so that data can be tabulated quickly for quick analysis and meaningful presentation.

Develop the completed questionnaire. The questions should be finalized in a professional format with proper instructions. Now, the questionnaire is ready to be administered.

RETENTION SURVEYS

Attitude measurement is critical, whether measuring job satisfaction, organizational commitment, employee engagement, or a variety of other retention-related issues. However, it is impossible to measure an attitude precisely, because the input may not represent a respondent's true feelings. Also, attitudes tend to change with time, and several factors make up an individual's attitude. Even considering these issues, it *is* possible to obtain a reasonable assessment of employees' attitudes about work and the organization.

Continuous measurements are required to show changes in attitudes. Attitude surveys are not the only way to measure attitudes. Interviews and focus groups may be appropriate in some situations. These are discussed later.

Survey Design

The principles of attitude survey construction are similar to those of constructing a questionnaire. A few guidelines unique to the design of an attitude survey are presented below:

Involve appropriate management. The executives involved in this process must be committed to taking action based on survey results. Include management early in the process, before the survey is constructed. Address management concerns, issues, and suggestions and attempt to win commitment to using the data.

Determine precisely the attitudes that must be measured. While this may seem obvious, it is easy to stray into areas unrelated to the subject. "Let's check their attitude on this" is a familiar trap. While it may be interesting information, it should be omitted if not related to the purpose of the survey.

Keep survey statements as simple as possible. Participants need to understand the meaning of a statement or question. There should be little room for differing interpretations.

Ensure that responses are anonymous. Respondents must feel free to respond openly. The confidentiality of their responses is of the utmost importance. If data are collected that can identify a respondent, a neutral third party should collect and process the data.

Communicate the purpose of the survey. Respondents tend to cooperate better if they understand the purpose of the survey. When a survey is administered, an explanation of its purpose and what will be done with the information should be provided. Also, participants should be encouraged to provide correct and proper responses.

Identify survey comparisons. Attitudes by themselves are meaningless. They must be compared to expected results, to changes over time, or to the attitudes of other groups. A group of employees may be compared to all employees, a division, or a department. For purchased surveys, information may be available on a regional or national scale and in similar industries. In any case, specific comparisons should be planned before administering the survey.

Design for easy tabulation. In an attitude survey, yes/no or varying degrees of agreement and disagreement are the usual results. Uniform responses make it easier for tabulation and comparisons. On a scale of "strongly agree" to "strongly disagree," assign numbers. For instance, a 1 may represent strongly disagree and a 5 strongly agree. Some argue that a 5-point scale permits the respondent to select the midpoint range, not really making a choice. If this is a concern, an even-numbered scale is advisable.

Purchasing an Existing Survey

Many organizations purchase existing surveys to use in retention improvement. This can have several advantages. They can save time in development and pilot-testing. Most of the reputable companies producing and marketing surveys have designed them to be reliable and valid for retention. Also, external surveys make it easy to compare the results with others. Benchmarking and norm comparisons are possible.

The Timing and Focus of Retention Surveys

Surveys and questionnaires can be administered at a variety of different times. Table 6.1 shows the five most important time frames for conducting surveys. Probably most important would be the routine, annual surveys. These are preventative data-collection tools that indicate the status of employees and their perceptions of the organization and their jobs. The issues usually focus on job satisfaction and organization commitment.

Reaction surveys are used when major actions are undertaken or events have occurred that may influence talent retention. The reactions are necessary for preventing problems or evaluating the impact of a particular action. For example, if several major change processes have taken place due to a company merger, it may

Survey	Focus	Timing
Routine surveys to identify trends and issues	Prevention	Annually
Reaction surveys after major actions/events	Prevention, evaluation	Immediately after event
Surveys to analyze problems and seek causes	Diagnostic	Immediately after problem uncovered
Exit surveys as employees leave the organization	Diagnostic	Just before, or immediately following departure
Impact surveys to measure success of a retention solution	Evaluation	Three to six months after solution implementation

Table 6.1.   The Timing and Focus of Retention Surveys

be helpful to administer a survey soon after the integration has begun as an attempt to spot issues that influence retention before they become problems. If the company has experienced a significant change in its business, major customers, or other significant events, it may be helpful to understand the extent to which the event or action is affecting employees. As serious problems surface, surveys can help leaders develop more insight, pinpoint the exact causes, and develop potential solutions.

Perhaps the most important use of surveys is the exit interview. Although the term exit interview is used, it is often conducted by a survey and is usually taken on the employee's last day or immediately following departure.

Finally, impact surveys are an effective way to measure the success of a solution. When retention problems are addressed and improvement has occurred, it may be helpful to capture the reactions to the solution implementation. Surveys and questionnaires are very flexible and perhaps the most useful tool in turnover analysis.

Survey Content

The specific issues addressed in a survey can vary with the organization, structure, and situation. Exhibit 6.4 shows typical content issues for a retention survey. This is a list of twenty issues developed as a composite from several surveys conducted by employer-of-choice organizations, the Society for Human Resource Management, and other major consulting firms. The number of issues addressed in an organization may be less than this number. Remember that the content of the survey must be directly related to what are perceived to be the key issues, particularly those identified through an analysis of turnover records.

Improving the Response Rate for Questionnaires and Surveys

The items listed in the exhibit above represent a wide range of potential issues to explore in a questionnaire or survey. Obviously, asking too many questions could cause the response rate to be reduced significantly. This is a critical issue when the questionnaire is the only data-collection method being used. The following actions can be taken to increase the response rate.

Appreciation for work

Benefits and benefits package

Bonuses, pay for performance

Burnout/stress

Career development

Flexibility in work schedules

Job security

Leadership

Meaningful work

Opportunity to excel at work

Opportunity to learn skills/knowledge

Organization's values and mission

Recognition of individual contribution

Relationship with associates

Relationship with supervisor

Resources to perform work

Salaries and base pay

Viability of organization

Work expectations

Work/life balance

Exhibit 6.4.   Typical Content Issues for Retention Surveys

Provide advance communication. When feasible, employees should receive advance notice of the questionnaire or survey. This minimizes some of the resistance to the process, provides an opportunity to explain the circumstances in more detail, and positions the survey/questionnaire as an integral part of data collection.

Have an executive sign the introductory letter. For maximum effectiveness, the letter sent with the questionnaire or survey should be signed by the top executive or by the senior executive responsible for the division, region, or location. Employees may be more willing to respond to a senior executive than to a member of the HR staff.

Communicate the purpose. Respondents should understand the reason for the questionnaire. They should also know whether the survey is part of a systematic process or a special analysis tool.

Let them know they are part of the sample. If appropriate, employees should know that they are part of a carefully selected sample and that their input will be used to make decisions regarding a much larger target audience. This appeals to employees' sense of responsibility and often encourages them to provide data for the questionnaire.

Use anonymous input. Usually, the questionnaire or survey should not identify the employee. Using anonymous input will increase the response rate and the input will be more candid.

Explain who will see the data. It is important for employees to know who will see the data from the questionnaire. Confidentiality and anonymity should be clearly communicated, along with the steps being taken to ensure them. Employees should know whether senior executives will see the results of the analysis.

Describe the data-integration process. Employees should understand how results will be combined with other data, if appropriate. Often, the questionnaire is only one of the data-collection methods utilized. Employees should know how the data is weighed and integrated to provide the final report.

Keep the questionnaire as simple as possible. A simple questionnaire or survey may not always provide all the data necessary for analysis, but simplification should still be the goal as questions are developed and the questionnaire is finalized.

Simplify the response process. The survey should be designed for easy response. If appropriate, a self-addressed stamped envelope should be included, or offer the option to respond via e-mail. In some situations, a conveniently positioned response box provided near the work area is advisable.

Utilize local manager support. Management involvement at the local level is critical. Managers can distribute questionnaires, make reference to them in staff meetings, follow up to see whether they have been completed, and generally show support for completing the questionnaire. Later, they should be involved in the feedback of results and planning specific actions to address issues.

Consider using incentives. In some situations, an incentive is provided to enhance response. This approach may be helpful when a survey is new or commitment is low. A variety of different types of incentives can be offered. When employees return the questionnaire, they could receive a small gift, such as a T-shirt or mug. If identity of the employee is an issue, a neutral third party can provide the incentive.

An incentive could also be provided to make respondents feel guilty if they choose not to respond. One U.S. dollar (or other monetary equivalent) can be clipped to the questionnaire or a pen can be enclosed in the envelope. Respondents are asked to "take the dollar, buy a cup of coffee, and fill out the questionnaire" or "please use this pen to complete the questionnaire." For e-mail surveys or web-based surveys, a coupon can be included.

Use follow-up reminders. Follow-up reminders should be sent a week after the questionnaire/survey is received and repeated two weeks later. Of course, times could be adjusted depending on the questionnaire and the situation. In some situations, a third follow-up is recommended. The follow-up could also be sent via different media. For example, a questionnaire may be sent by regular mail, the first follow-up reminder provided by the immediate supervisor in a staff meeting, and the second reminder sent by e-mail.

Provide a copy of the results to the employees. Employees should always be given the opportunity to see the results, even if in an abbreviated form. More importantly, employees should be told that they will receive a copy of the study. This promise often increases the response rate, as people want to see the results of the entire group.

Collectively, these actions help boost response rates. Using all of these strategies can result in response rates in the 70- to 90 percent range, even with a lengthy questionnaire that might take thirty minutes to complete. Some companies report over 90 percent response rates.

INTERVIEWS AND FOCUS GROUPS
Interviews

Another helpful collection method is the interview, although it is not used as often as questionnaires or surveys. The HR staff, supervisors, or an outside third party can conduct interviews. Interviews can provide data that is not available in performance records or is difficult to obtain through written responses. Employees may be reluctant to provide input on a questionnaire, but will volunteer the information to a skillful interviewer who uses probing techniques to uncover changes in perceptions and attitudes.

Two basic types of interviews are structured and unstructured. Much like a questionnaire, the *structured* interview presents specific questions with little room to deviate from the desired responses. The *unstructured* interview is more flexible and can include probing for additional information. As important data are uncovered, a skilled interviewer can ask a few general questions that can lead to more detailed information.

Two major disadvantages of the interview are that it is time-consuming and there is little sense of anonymity. Also, interviewers must be trained to ensure that the process is consistent across respondents. The primary advantage is that the interview process ensures that a question is answered and that the interviewer understands the responses.

INTERVIEW GUIDELINES. The steps for interview design are similar to those for the design of the questionnaire or survey. A brief summary is outlined below:

Determine specific information needed. The topics, skills, issues, problems, and other needed information are identified.

Develop questions to be asked. Specific questions must be developed. Questions should be brief, precise, and designed for easy response.

Test the interview. The instrument should be tested on a small number of employees. The responses should be analyzed and the interview revised, if necessary.

Train the interviewers. The interviewer should have the appropriate skills, including active listening and the ability to ask probing questions, collect information, and summarize it in a meaningful form. If the employee is nervous during an interview and develops signs of anxiety, he or she should be made to feel at ease.

Provide clear instructions to the employee. The employee should understand the purpose of the interview and know how the information will be used. Expectations, conditions, and rules of the interview should be thoroughly discussed. For example, the employee should know whether answers will be kept confidential.

Administer the interviews according to a scheduled plan. As with other instruments, interviews need to be conducted according to a predetermined plan. The timing, location, and the person conducting the interview are all relevant issues. For an organization with a large number of employees, a "sampling" may be necessary to save time and reduce the cost of the analysis.

Focus Groups

A focus group is a small group discussion conducted by an experienced facilitator. It is designed to solicit qualitative judgments on a planned topic or issue. An extension of the interview, focus groups are particularly helpful when in-depth feedback is desired. Group members are all required to provide their input; individual input builds on group input.

A focus group strategy has several advantages. The basic premise is that when judgments are subjective, several individual judgments are better than one. Thus, the group process, in which participants often motivate one another, is an effective method for generating new ideas and hypotheses. It is inexpensive and can be quickly planned and conducted. Its flexibility makes it possible to explore a variety of retention-related issues.

FOCUS GROUP APPLICATIONS. Essentially, focus groups are most helpful when information is needed that cannot be collected adequately with simple, quantitative methods. For example, these separate issues can be addressed in the focus group setting:

- Identify the reasons for the exit of other colleagues;
- Identify the reasons why employees stay with the organization; and
- Identify the reasons why employees would leave the organization.

In one high-tech firm in Silicon Valley, there was some concern that a specific group of talented people was being targeted by "headhunters" and recruited by other firms. Recognizing the potential risk of losing these employees, the company formed focus groups and secured information on two major issues: What would keep employees from leaving and What would lure them away. As a group, they were able to provide insight into those two key questions.

FOCUS GROUP GUIDELINES. While there are no set rules on how to use focus groups for turnover issues, the following guidelines should be helpful:

Ensure that management supports the focus group process. Because this is a relatively new process, it may be unfamiliar to some management groups. Managers need to understand focus groups and their advantages. This should raise their level of confidence in the information obtained.

Plan topics, questions, and strategy carefully. As with any data collection, planning is the key. The specific topics, questions, and issues to be discussed must be carefully planned and sequenced. This enhances the comparison of results from one group to another and ensures that the group process is effective and remains focused.

Keep the group size small. While there is no magic group size, a range of six to twelve seems to be appropriate. A group has to be large enough to ensure different points of view, but small enough to provide every participant a chance to communicate freely and exchange comments.

Ensure that there is a representative sample of the target population. It is important for groups to be stratified appropriately so that participants represent the target population. The group should be homogeneous in experience, rank, and influence in the organization.

Insist on facilitators with appropriate expertise. The success of a focus group rests with the facilitator, who must be skilled in group process. Facilitators must know how to control aggressive members of the group and diffuse the input from those who want to dominate. Facilitators must also be able to create an environment in which participants feel comfortable offering comments freely and openly. Because of this, some organizations use external facilitators.

In summary, the focus group can be an inexpensive and quick way to determine the causes of turnover. For a complete analysis, focus group information should be combined with data from other instruments. A focus group also may be used in conjunction with other techniques described in the next section.

NOMINAL GROUP TECHNIQUE
Target Audience

Perhaps one of the most useful and productive tools to determine the causes of turnover is to use a group process called the nominal group technique. With this process, a group of employees are asked to provide information on why their colleagues are leaving the organization. The key issue is to focus on the reasons why *others* would leave and not why *they* would leave. This repositions the data collection from a potentially threatening to a non-threatening environment. The recommended audience is a representative sample of the target groups experiencing the highest turnover. The group size should be eight to twelve. A small number of samples would be appropriate for large target groups. The total sample size needed for statistical validity depends on several factors and can be accurately determined. However, this number may become expensive and unnecessary. One approach is to sample until trends and patterns begin to emerge. For example, in a target group with a thousand employees doing the sample job, five to ten samples would probably be sufficient. The key issue is to examine the results to confirm a pattern. Although the group process is inexpensive compared to some techniques, the issue may represent a balance of economics versus accuracy.

Facilitation

Normally, two facilitators are required for this process. Both should be trained to facilitate the nominal group technique. Both should be neutral to the organization (that is,, independent third parties) and removed from ownership of the issues that will be discussed. Employees must feel free to discuss issues; it is important for them to be assured of the confidentiality and anonymity of their input.

The setting should be comfortable with ample space for two flip-chart easels and a place to tape flip-chart paper on the wall. The process follows a series of steps, each of them very important.

1. *Explain the task.* As an introduction, the facilitator should explain the purpose of the meeting, stressing the importance of input from the group. The ground rules are covered, focusing on the mechanics of how they will provide information (that is, the requirements for everyone's input, limit of time for input, confidentiality of information shared, and plans for sharing results).

2. *Employees are asked to think of reasons why their colleagues have left or may leave the organization.* It is important for them to understand that the focus is on *others* and not on themselves. A misunderstanding on this issue can cause employees to overact or clam up. If the issue is handled properly, employees will actually reveal why *they* would leave and that's what is needed.

3. *Employees are asked to make a list of why they believe other employees are leaving.* At least five reasons are needed; however, more can be listed if desired. On blank pieces of paper, employees should include as much detail as possible so it is clear about each issue and how it relates to turnover.

4. *Lists are revealed, one item at a time, and captured on the flip chart.* Rotating through the group, employees reveal their first items. The second facilitator should capture the essence of each item on the flip chart, being as clear as possible. This may be

captured on a screen, if a decision support system is used. After everyone has had a turn, they go on to the second item, and so forth until all items are revealed. It is important that each item be captured accurately.

5. *As the lists are posted, the charts are taped to the wall.* The lists should be displayed so that all the participants have an opportunity to refer to them often, thinking through the issues as the process evolves.

6. *Merge items on the list only if the meanings are the same.* Clarification may be required from the individuals who offered the items. The combinations are helpful in terms of having a manageable list, but should not be forced for the sake of efficiency. If the issues are different, they should be listed that way. After this step, a smaller, merged, and integrated, list remains.

7. *Employees then list the five (or ten) most important reasons for turnover.* Using index cards, employees list the items—one on each card—using the wording on the flip charts. Employees are asked to focus on five (if the list is fairly short) or ten (if the list is longer). In this step, employees will have the opportunity to consider other issues in addition to their own items. The result is usually a blended list that reflects the input of the group.

8. *The employees are asked to arrange their cards in order of priority.* The most important causes of turnover (or anticipated turnover) should be listed as number 1. It must be stressed that the ranking is to be performed when considering the issue that is causing the most turnover, *not* the one that may be most important to the employee. This step helps downplay personal biases.

9. *Employees reveal their lists one at a time.* Rotating through the group, employees reveal their top-priority items first, followed by the second priority items, and so on. Points are assigned to each item as follows: the number 1 cause for turnover is assigned a value of 5 points, number 2 equals 4 points, number 3 equals 3 points, and so on. (If there are ten items on the list, the number 1 cause is assigned 10 points, number 2 receives 9 points, and so on.)

10. *Assign the points.* As the items are assigned point values, each number is written on the original flip-chart sheet (taped on the

wall) so that a total can be determined as the process is completed.

11. *Tally the points.* The points next to each item are totaled. The item with the most points is considered to be the number 1 reason for turnover by this group. The item with the second-highest number is the number 2 reason for turnover, and so on. As expected, the level of importance diminishes as the score diminishes.

12. *Post the top ten reasons for turnover.* The ten items with the highest numbers are the top ten reasons for turnover, from the point of view of those who are still with the organization.

Data Integration

The data can usually be integrated easily from one group to the next when the items are similar. In most situations, the issues are clearly identified and well known. The combined data can be placed in a spreadsheet to show the results of different groups and emerging patterns. A trend will usually be seen clearly as the issues causing turnover are identified.

The advantage of this process is significant. When facilitated properly, the data are objective, thorough, and thoughtful. The group members express their opinions about why others may leave the organization and why some left. Employees typically open up to the neutral third-party facilitators and ultimately reveal reasons why *they* would leave. This information is usually difficult to obtain due to the stigma attached to revealing why another employee would leave the organization. The process is very efficient and can be accomplished in a one- to two-hour time frame, depending on the size of the group and the number of reasons offered. If the group is confined to one geographic area, this can be an inexpensive process as well. The critical parts of this process are the trust that's established when employees realize that their names will not be attached to any of the information and the mechanics of the facilitation.

EXIT INTERVIEW (OR SURVEY)

One of the most utilized processes to uncover the causes of turnover is the exit interview, taken just before or after an employee leaves the organization. Exit interviews can be face-to-face interviews, a questionnaire, a brief survey, or even a focus group. An anonymous questionnaire, administered confidentially, usually gets the best results for the costs.

Issues

Although exiting employees would seem to be the best source of data to determine why employees are leaving, exit interviews are notoriously inaccurate and unreliable; however, they needn't be. When properly designed and implemented, they can provide excellent data to develop retention solutions. Three key issues represent challenges to conducting exit interviews.

> *The response rates.* Return rates may be very low. Departing employees don't feel obligated to provide data. The last thing they may want to do is help the organization after they have decided to leave.

> *The data may be incomplete and/or inaccurate.* Even when employees respond to the questions, their responses may not be complete or accurate. Since they are no longer attached to the organization, they may be unwilling to devote much time to this issue. Consequently, their responses are short, incomplete, and sporadic.

> *Data may be purposely biased.* For fear of retaliation or negative references, the employee may provide misleading input. An employee may indicate that working conditions were fine, but that he or she received an offer that could not be refused.

These issues pose critical challenges when conducting exit interviews.

Design

The issues with the design of this type of survey is similar to the design issues discussed earlier in this chapter. Several key issues are emphasized here:

> *Keep it simple.* Because of the above issues, the survey (or interview) should be brief and simple. Questions must be direct and designed for easy response.

Build trust. It is essential to establish trust with exiting employees so they will provide reliable feedback (or refrain from purposely exaggerating the feedback). This may be difficult in a climate where trust is nonexistent. A key issue is the explanation of how the information will be used and reported. If employees have seen no improvement from previous exit interviews, they won't trust the organization to do anything with future data. If they are aware of retaliation for those who have provided straightforward, candid responses, they will be reluctant to provide the same type of data. The individuals conducting the interview, or administering the survey, must convince the departing employee to trust them to use the data appropriately.

Ensure confidentiality and anonymity. Along with building trust are the steps taken to ensure that the data are collected anonymously, if possible, and kept confidential. Demographic data, while helpful in analysis, should be kept to a minimum because it may identify the departing employee. Using a third-party data collection source can help ensure anonymous input and demonstrate how the data are treated confidentially in reporting, use, and discussions. An indication of who will actually have access to the data is critical to help with the confidentiality issue.

Set the stage for input. The individuals providing data needs to know what's in it for them. This is a challenge with exit interviews because the respondent may have very little to gain personally and a lot to lose. As a first step in this process, it is helpful to inform the individual that his or her departure is regrettable and that the organization would like to keep in touch. This can be accomplished in several different ways. Some organizations establish alumni groups, planning periodic outings and activities. Others have alumni newsletters. An "open door" attitude lets them know they can return to the organization, assuming an opportunity comes up. This atmosphere might even encourage them to provide constructive criticism. Consider questions such as, "Would you like to make some changes in the organization? If you were to stay, what would you change?"

Consider an incentive. Incentives will motivate some individuals to provide responses, but the incentive should not be so large that it appears to be a reward for leaving. The types of incentives discussed earlier in this chapter may be sufficient, with slight modification. Some organizations will send a "departure gift" as a small token of their appreciation for providing information on the exit questionnaire. A gift in the $25 to $50 price range may appeal to some individuals. Most departing employees would feel guilty accepting the gift and not providing data.

Appeal to concern about colleagues. Another issue is appealing to their sense of responsibility for the left-behind colleagues. A typical question might be, "What can we do to improve working conditions for those you leave behind?" This provides departing employees with the opportunity to influence conditions for friends remaining in the organization.

Memo Posting

Some organizations have experimented with having employees post memos explaining why they are leaving. These memos could be posted on a bulletin board, the Internet, or a website designed for this purpose. Some organizations create blogs for departing employees. Whenever an employee leaves, he or she is allowed to (or asked to) place a memo on a bulletin board or write a blog. Employees explain (sometimes in excruciating detail) their decision to leave the organization.

Even those employees who are fired or laid off for economic reasons write these memos or blogs. This approach takes tremendous courage and outstanding leadership to allow people to write about why they are leaving. If this type of trust is established, nourished, and supported over time, it can be an amazing and rich source of data to determine why employees choose to leave.

Face-to-Face Interviews

Generally, face-to-face interviews are ineffective for obtaining candid information about why a person is leaving. Obviously, trust is a critical issue—an interview is not anonymous, and there may be much concern about who will see the data. Interviews may be appropriate in very trusting climates where the interviewer is a respected, trusted person. In other climates, the face-to-face interview is usually not worth the time it takes to conduct it, unless it is conducted by a trusted, third-party individual.

Timing

The exit interview data, whether obtained via a survey or face-to-face, should be collected as soon as possible after the decision has been made to leave the organization. It is quite common to mail questionnaires to home addresses, providing a stamped return envelope addressed to a third party. This removes the survey from the job environment and places some distance between the individual and the organization. The longer the wait, the less likely the individual can (or is willing to) recall all the issues that influenced the decision to leave. If feasible, it may be appropriate to administer the exit survey while the employee is still there. Otherwise, it should be sent as quickly as possible.

Using the Data

Exit interview data should be tabulated and summarized around key groups and issues. The data becomes an integral part of data collection for retention. Steps should be taken to ensure that data are in no way connected to an individual. For example, if a specific section has experienced only one departure in the last three months, it may be better not to include data from that person's exit interview. It is probably best to summarize and cut out parts of the information such as job title and area of the company. Data should be integrated by job type so that trends and patterns can emerge, particularly with changes over time. Some amount of voluntary turnover is always present; it only becomes a problem when it's excessive.

Post-Exit Interviews

Some organizations attempt to collect data six months after employees leave to determine the status of the employee and gain more insight into why he or she left. The results from post-exit interviews may be different from those of a traditional exit interview, underscoring flawed methodology in the exit-interview process. Many possible explanations for differences exist. One organization, Agilent Technologies, offers three reasons for differences:

1. Individuals are less emotional six months after resigning and, consequently, offer more accurate information.

2. The individuals have had time to compare their new situations to the jobs they left and can be more objective.

3. The individuals no longer have to worry about a good reference from the manager, thus avoiding intentional bias.

Admittedly, post-exit information is very difficult to obtain and the process can be quite involved. But, it may be worth the effort to attempt to collect this type of data. It will require use of multiple strategies to achieve a good response rate, utilizing essentially every technique described earlier in the chapter. In lieu of the post-exit interview process, it may be best to focus more attention on increasing the credibility and usefulness of the exit interview process itself, as it is more manageable.

IDEA GENERATION TOOLS

The tools discussed to this point in the chapter are the principal tools that will yield insight into the causes of turnover. However, additional tools are available that can help to determine the causes of turnover. Most of these tools come from the quality and process improvement field and have proven to be useful in resolving retention issues. Several important tools to generate ideas about the cause of turnover are presented in this section.

Brainstorming

Brainstorming is perhaps the most widely recognized technique to encourage creative thinking. It has become an important tool for generating the causes of organizational problems such as turnover. The process facilitation is similar to that for a focus group and those design issues and guidelines also apply to the brainstorming session. The goal is to generate as many ideas as possible with no restrictions. The groups are best kept small, usually in the six to twelve range. The group focuses on the actual problem — excessive turnover.

The individuals invited to participate should be those who best understand the excessive turnover problem and are in a position to know the causes and corresponding potential solutions. The group should have a complete understanding of the problems, issues, and challenges. Providing information in advance will help the individuals develop ideas prior to the meeting.

The ground rules for the process are fairly straightforward:

1. Individuals are encouraged to offer as many ideas as possible.
2. The ideas are not criticized by anyone, regardless of how they may be perceived.
3. All ideas are recorded.
4. All participants should have ample time to share their ideas.
5. Freewheeling is encouraged, even if the ideas seem to be off the wall.

When input ceases to be productive, a variety of techniques are available to stimulate additional creativity and ideas. Three are very helpful:

1. The participation is rotated through the group to enable one individual to build off the ideas of another. This also provides ample time for reflection from those who are not directly participating.
2. Using the concept of idea building, individuals are encouraged to add to or expand on previous ideas or to offer similar or even alternate issues as ideas.
3. Quiet periods can help people reflect and think through the problem, sifting through the data mentally and generating additional ideas. This period could last up to half an hour before it becomes pointless.

The data can be summarized in a variety of ways. Eliminating items, combining items, and reaching consensus on items are key steps in the process.

Cause-and-Effect Diagrams

The cause-and-effect diagram is very useful for repetitive issues. This process can be used to create what is sometimes called the fishbone

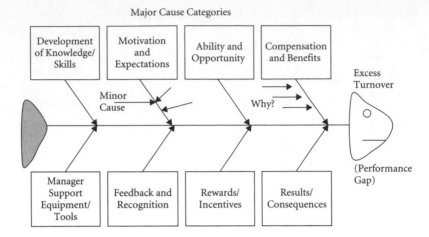

Figure 6.3.   Example of a Fishbone Diagram

diagram because of its appearance. The process follows the focus group and brainstorming formats, except the major categories of causes are identified first, with minor causes added. As shown in Figure 6.3, the diagram illustrates the problem (excessive turnover) along with the major causes—eight in this case. The minor-cause categories, which can be considerable, are provided by the group using idea-generating processes. Here, the focus is more specific and the group must be knowledgeable about the problem so that they can offer minor causes of the problem. The steps are very simple:

1. The groups are selected based on their capability to provide insight into the causes of turnover.

2. The groups are provided instructions and their role in the process is outlined.

3. The major cause categories are either identified or offered. They are offered if there is previous information to indicate the specific cause (from exit interviews or other data-collection methods).

4. After some discussion, the most likely causes are circled. This is only after each item is critically evaluated and the group has reached a consensus as to which causes are most relevant. This

process is more focused and, therefore, is more likely to establish help the group find the real cause for a problem.

5. With the major cause categories clearly identified and entered on the diagram, the group members are asked to indicate the minor causes related to each major cause category. These can be listed as minor causes, or sometimes just the "why" for the particular major cause category.

6. The fishbone diagram is then completed, showing the major and minor causes for the turnover problem.

OTHER TOOLS

A variety of other tools are available, primarily from the quality and performance improvement process, which can be used to analyze the cause of turnover. Listed here are five that might be helpful:

Force field analysis is a visual tool for analyzing the different elements that resist change (restraining forces), and those elements that wish for change (facilitating forces). This is a useful technique to drive improvement and retention by developing plans to overcome the restraining forces and make maximum use out of the facilitating forces.

Mind mapping is an unstructured cause-and-effect analysis tool primarily designed for taking notes and solving problems. The problem (excessive turnover) is written on the center of a piece of paper and members of the group offer their suggestions or ideas as to the causes. These causes are drawn from the center as legs or lines. Branches are added to a line as additional causes or sub-causes are generated. This is similar to the cause-and-effect process, but might be more helpful with those individuals familiar with the mind-mapping process.

Affinity diagrams are used to collect input from groups and organize it according to the natural relationships between items. This technique has a conceptual and logical simplicity that allows for a clear view of the largest and most complex problems. Basically, it is a way to structure and classify vague ideas. Consequently, it is helpful when there's a need to focus on a complex, multi-faceted problem, such as turnover.

Relationship diagrams are used when there is a need to build a map of the logical, sequential links among items that are interconnected and related to a central problem, such as turnover. It facilitates the solution of problems when causes interact by dividing a problem into its basic components and isolating the relationships. The basic logic behind this tool is the same as that behind the cause-and-effect diagram.

Tree-shaped diagrams systematically outline the complete spectrum, paths, and tests that must be carried out in order to achieve a particular goal, such as solving a turnover problem. The use of this tool changes some generalities into details by isolating the intermediate conditions that must be satisfied. The diagram leads to identification of the more appropriate procedures and methods to solve the problem.

These and other techniques may be helpful for analyzing causes and relationships between them and other causes. The important point is to use a tool that works best for the organization in a specific setting.

FINAL THOUGHTS

In this chapter we explored how to determine the causes of turnover, one of the most critical steps in managing retention. We began with an explanation of the relationship of turnover to major variables, such as job satisfaction and commitment and then discussed the process of analyzing the specific causes of turnover. Analyzing the records is the beginning point. Several tools, both quantitative and subjective, can be used to explore the actual causes. Questionnaires, surveys, interviews, and focus groups are the primary tools. Other tools were presented that may be helpful to understand the relationships between a turnover problem and various causes. The output of doing everything we suggested in this chapter is a list of the causes of turnover (arranged by priority), providing the organization with the top two or three (or four or five) causes to study. A later chapter will focus on how to match a specific cause to a possible solution.

References

Ahlrichs, N.S. (2000). *Competing for talent: Key recruitment and retention strategies for becoming an employer of choice.* Palo Alto, CA: Davies-Black.

Buckingham, M., & Coffman, C. (1999). *First, break all the rules.* New York: Simon & Schuster.

Phillips, P.P., & Stawarski, C.A. (2008). *Data collection: Planning for and collecting all types of data.* San Francisco, CA: Pfeiffer.

CHAPTER SEVEN

Recruit Talent

W hile previous chapters have dealt with a strategic approach to determining the cost and the exact cause of critical talent turnover, this chapter and the following three chapters focus on various solution sets. These solution sets are based on the needs of critical talent. Chapter 7 focuses on critical talent needs prior to, and at the time of, joining an organization. These corresponding solutions, which address these critical talent needs, provide suggestions on how employers can address turnover issues. Table 7.1 shows the first six categories along with the corresponding needs and solutions.

Great organizations understand that recruiting top talent for critical roles is instrumental to the success of the organization. Top talent has many employment opportunities available to them and are almost always employed in roles that already meet their needs at some level. Before they will leave their current employer, the new employer must offer greater value than what they currently receive. Moreover, current employers of critical talent must be keenly aware of the needs of their critical talent to avoid the possibility that their critical talent is lured away by another employer with a better value proposition. Top talent is attracted to an organization for many reasons, including

Category	Needs Solution	Recruiting Talent
1. Image and Brand	To be associated with an organization with a positive public image and great brand	Maintain a strong, positive public image and develop and employment brand
2. Stable or Strong Market and Financial Performance	To be assured of job stability and growth potential	Maintain or improve financial performance
3. Effective Recruitment Strategy	To be attracted to a specific organization that is a culture fit	Develop a recruitment strategy that attracts top talent that fits the organizational culture
4. Effective Selection and Attractive Offer	To be selected fairly and offered an attractive, compelling employment offer	Develop competitive packages that appeal to the right target audience
5. Job Fit and Career Advancement Opportunities	To be in a role that leverages talents, skills, and knowledge, and provides opportunity for growth and advancement	Place employees in a job that matches talents, skills, and knowledge and allows for growth
6. Orientation and On-Boarding	To adapt quickly to the job, team, and organization	Provide a formal orientation, socialization experience, and on-boarding process

Table 7.1. Needs and Organizational Solutions for Recruiting Critical Talent

the organization's image or brand, strong financial performance, an effective recruitment and selection process, and the job fit and career advancement opportunities. These factors influence the expectations of any new hire and impact whether that individual will fit into the organization and his or her role.

IMAGE AND BRAND

All organizations have an image in the employment marketplace, positive or negative. While image is only the public's perception of the organization, it carries great weight, as it can be the leading indicator of whether a company will survive in the future. Organizations that are committed to attracting the best talent develop an employment branding strategy that goes beyond public opinion. Employment branding is a more targeted approach to communicating the culture, success, and personality that distinguishes a company from its rivals. An effective employment brand leverages the strengths of the organization and attracts the right talent to the organization. A good employment branding strategy delivers its message through appropriate communication vehicles targeted at the group of employees the organization wishes to attract and includes:

1. Being discussed in relevant industry events and publications;

2. Landing on one of the best-places-to-work lists;

3. Frequently being referenced on best practice benchmarking lists and in research studies;

4. Improving management behaviors across the organization through rapid "what-works sharing" among managers;

5. Developing an industry-leading employee referral program; and

6. An eye-catching website that even attracts passive candidates.

   (Sullivan, 2005)

An effective brand connects to prospective employees in a way that is meaningful. For example, Royal Philips Electronics' brand message is, "technology that touches people's lives." Its employment brand message echoes that message and connects to prospective employees in a meaningful way with the message, "You can touch lives every day" (Overman, 2006).

Need for Positive Organizational Image and Brand

Current and prospective talent wants to be associated with an organization that possesses a positive public image and a strong, recognizable brand. An organization's image reflects not only on the organization as a whole, but also on the individual employees of the organization. Top talent concerned with their personal reputation as well as their future employability will choose organizations that have a positive image in the community and marketplace. Additionally, top talent feels a sense of pride and belonging when they believe they are contributing to, and creating a positive image of, an organization. An organization with a tarnished public image, for whatever reason, will be challenged to attract talented employees.

Key to attracting critical talent groups and top performers is to understand what is most important to these groups. In addition to being associated with a winning brand, educated and bright talent groups have additional concerns about the qualities of an organization. For example, in an effort to attract the most talented employees, some organizations are "going green" to improve their ability to attract innovative talent groups. Corporate social responsibility such as environmentalism is especially appealing to younger workers. According to a 2007 Harris Interactive survey conducted for Adecco, 33 percent of employees reported that they would prefer to work for an environmentally responsible organization (*Earth Day 2007*, 2007).

One organization that found a way to leverage environmentalism into improving its public image with a target talent group is GE. In 2006, GE partnered with mtvU, a 24-hour college network of MTV, to promote an environmental contest worth $25,000 in grant money to the winner of the contest. The purpose of the contest was to improve GE's image with potential college-age recruits, and the contest fulfilled that purpose. One hundred proposals were submitted, and GE considered the program a success in raising awareness of GE with college-age students, a key talent group for the company (Huff, 2007).

As environmentalism and social responsibility grow in awareness and importance to top talent groups, organizations that demonstrate social responsibility are likely to have an edge over the competition.

Employment Brand

In order to achieve the best organizational performance through their people, organizations must focus on attracting the talent most critical to the organization. More importantly, great organizations recognize the value in linking the customer-facing brand to the internal culture of the organization and work to attract and select individuals who reflect the external brand. For example, Starbucks actively recruits front-line employees who resemble the customer. "When customers walk into a Starbucks, we want them to see themselves behind the counter and feel a sense of affinity for the brand. To that end, we focus our recruiting efforts on special populations such as college-age adults, ethnically diverse populations, and seniors" says Genevieve Long, director of human resources for Starbucks (Long, 2008).

Nike is another organization that works hard to link the type of employees they hire to its brand. Nike's consumer-facing branding strategy is to use athletes in its commercials, and the organization links that strategy to their internal culture. Nike's mission statement sub-tagline is, "If you have a body you are an athlete" and at Nike that applies not only to its consumers, but to its employees. "Managers at Nike are expected to behave like coaches. We look for talent that is enthusiastic and passionate about goals and ideals so that they will fit Nike's core values of authenticity, commitment, innovation, and teamwork," says Jim Sutton, senior director of global talent development. As a result of appealing to a workforce that is focused on winning, competition, and is enthusiastic and energetic, Nike is better able to further its mission through its people (Sutton, 2008).

Developing an Employment Brand

Creating a strong employment brand begins by understanding the strengths of the organization and determining ways to leverage those assets. Just as brand marketing is only as good as the product or service behind it, an organization's employment brand is only as strong as the actual employment experience behind the brand.

To develop an effective and realistic employment brand message consider the following steps, as outlined by Peter D. Weddle, employment branding expert:

1. *First, ask the internal experts.* Facilitate several focus groups with the top performers in the organization who represent the most important job categories. These sessions should be uninhibited and truthful. Ideally, hire a third-party, professional facilitator to conduct the meetings. The objective is to obtain accurate information that helps uncovers why these individuals decided to join the organization and what keeps them there.

2. *Accurately describe what top performers say about the organization.* Use the information and insights captured in the focus groups to craft various versions of the brand message. Themes need to resemble the most important ideas communicated through the focus groups. The objective is to connect the experience of existing key talent with values that will resonate with target, prospective employees.

3. *Pilot branding messages with top performers.* Organize a follow-up session with top performers from the focus group session. Allow the group to consider and evaluate the possible branding messages. Ideally, the group will identify a message

that is most compelling; if not, consider taking input from the group and re-crafting the message.

4. *Communicate the branding message.* Avoid the common mistake of failing to utilize the employment brand statement in all communication vehicles. The branding message should be included on the recruitment website, all applications and forms, every posting and ad, and communicated verbally in phone screens, interviews, and offers.

(Weddle, 2003)

Creating the branding message is the first step in creating the employment brand. The brand should shape everything from recruiting strategy to employee rewards and recognition. In other words, to be lasting and effective, the employment brand message must reflect the total employment experience.

STABLE OR STRONG MARKET AND FINANCIAL PERFORMANCE

Top talent is interested in working in organizations that have strong positive images and are able to perform well in the marketplace. Successful financial performance is a means to and the end of a successful retention strategy. Without a successful financial performance, the organization ceases to exist and there is no need for employees. Strong performance in the marketplace includes financial performance as well as the organization's ability to attract and retain key talent.

Need for Stable or Strong Financial Performance

Top talent needs to ensure a positive future and, to that end, they need their organization to perform well in the marketplace. When an organization performs well in the marketplace, it ensures the employees that the organization will be able to continue to provide opportunities for them in the future. More importantly, successful market performance ensures top talent that their own names and reputations will be protected. Key to attracting top talent is to have a top-performing organization.

The dot-com years were known for creating high-risk, high-reward jobs, but today's employees are more interested in stable and predictable earnings that a financially stable and strong organization can ensure. Based on responses from over 225,000 employee responses, CLC Solutions has discovered the most important elements of a job offer to an employee and identified three key trends in employee preferences. They discovered that manager quality is still important. They also found that:

1. Value of Guaranteed Earnings [Are] on the Rise: Employees are increasingly more interested in guaranteed earnings and

2. High-Risk, High-Reward Work Environments [Are] Now Less Attractive: Instead, employees are more interested in high-quality management (Corporate Executive Board, 2004).

One of the requirements of being listed on one of the top employer lists is that the employer must have low turnover. Interestingly, there tends to be a correlation between financial performance and being a good place to work (low turnover). For example, a study conducted at DePaul University in Chicago found that the S&P 500 organizations that were ranked on the 100 Best Corporate Citizen's list for their employment and environmental policies outperformed their peers on the S&P 500 by an average of 10 percent on financial measures (Fulmer, Gerheart, & Scott, 2003). This study supports the relationship between positive financial performance and lower employee turnover. Top talent is more likely to remain with an organization that is performing well.

Types of Organizations

The way that market performance is measured varies by the structure of organization. Three types of organizations, public, privately held, and public-sector, differ in how they measure market performance. The solution needed to achieve stable or strong market performance varies for each of these organizational types.

PUBLICLY HELD ORGANIZATIONS. An organization that is traded on the stock exchange has very specific indicators that reflect its market performance, including stock price, profit, loss, annual reports, and public perception. When an organization's profits are high, the stronger that organization performs in the marketplace.

An example of an organization that shows a link between strong market performance and its ability to attract the top talent critical to the success and reputation of the organization is Google, based in Mountain View, California. The organization has over eight thousand employees and is known for hiring the best talent and making the best offers, and it continues to perform well in the marketplace, even during a down economy. Google receives more than 760,000 resumes each year—nearly a hundred times the number of employees currently employed (*Google take 2*, 2008).

PRIVATELY HELD ORGANIZATIONS. While publicly held organizations must disclose their market performance, privately held companies do not, which makes it more difficult for top talent to understand their market performance. There are, however, some key indicators that candidates can review to determine an organizations stability and growth opportunity:

- Announcements or press releases announcing growth, expansion, acquisitions, new product lines, or new service offerings;
- Positive press in the local trade and business journals; visibility of leadership in the community, speaking at functions such as local chambers of commerce meetings, and so forth;
- Announcements of increased budgets or greater investments into the company by private equity firms;
- Announcements of new accounts and large clients;
- Lack of announcements about layoffs; and
- Word-of-mouth or discussions from current employees who talk about future growth and opportunity.

These types of activities typically reflect an organization that is performing well in the marketplace and is likely to have a solid financial footing.

PUBLIC SECTOR ORGANIZATIONS. Market performance indicators for public sector organizations are unlike those of publicly traded companies, as there are usually no profits or revenues. Typically, the method of judging public sector organizations is by reviewing the "image" of the organization, the public's perception of the organization. The public's opinion can frequently influence budget allocations for these organizations.

Some public sector organizations rely on public awareness and positive public opinion to become attractive to top talent. For example, the popular televisions shows *CSI: Crime Scene Investigation*, the CBS television series, and its two spinoffs—*CSI: Miami* and *CSI: New York* have increased the public's awareness about this profession. These television shows routinely appear near the top of the Nielsen ratings, and the role of someone who is a crime scene investigator is fascinating to viewers. As a result, the Las Vegas Criminalistics Bureau, where the original version of the show is set, has seen a dramatic increase in the number of job applicants (Toobin, 2007). Moreover, the quality of candidates has improved in recent years (Edmondson, 2007).

EFFECTIVE RECRUITMENT STRATEGIES

Great organizations focus on searching for the best talent for their most critical roles. Recruiting budgets continue to grow, and keeping the talent pool infused with top talent for key roles is a critical organizational goal. Top talent, in turn, values being recruited by the right organization.

Need for Effective Recruiting

Top talent needs to be recruited and hired by an organization that is very attractive to them. Typically, top talent is generally employed, currently successful in their role, and not actively seeking new employment. Therefore, an organization must actively seek out these individuals. Top talent may become interested in a job change for a variety of reasons. They may have friends working for a company, they may be aware of marketplace success, they may desire a change in their work/life balance, or they may become interested because of the potential for professional growth and career advancement.

Even in times of high unemployment, there can be a lack of truly qualified top talent in any particular industry. Aggressive organizations that are determined to win the war for talent, primarily utilize a "poaching" strategy. Certainly, being recognized as a great place to work will increase the number and the quality of applicants (Sullivan, 2005).

Organizations use a variety of recruitment initiatives and take advantage of new technologies. Standard recruitment solutions include newspaper advertisements, internal employee referrals, open houses, college recruiting efforts, use of search firms, sponsorship of job fairs, use of internship programs, and working with business schools and technical schools as well job web sites. In years past, live networking events were a primary way to source candidates, but with the advent of sites like LinkedIn, Facebook, and blogs, social networking sites have emerged as a new way to source top talent. The following solutions identify some of the customary corporation responses for recruitment.

Social Networking

A new and emerging way to recruit top talent is through social networking sites. These sites can be a valuable and cost-effective way for organizations to connect with current employees, retired employees, and employees out on leave such as new parents out on maternity or paternity leave. In addition to providing a way for employees to collaborate, social sites can serve as an effective recruiting tool.

One organization that implemented a social networking site is Dow. The organization uses the site to as a way to keep its current workforce engaged and to cope with staff shortages. Like many organizations, Dow is faced with anticipated talent shortages, as 40 percent of its global workforce will be eligible for retirement by 2013. Dow also had many employees who were temporarily not working, for maternity leave or for other reasons. Dow recognized that they needed a creative way to use their retired and on-leave workforce more effectively—as mentors or part-time consultants or to reconnect them with current employees to transfer knowledge. The organization designed a social networking site where retirees, employees on leave, and current employees could connect. The end results were:

- Higher than expected participation—the targeted participation rate of 10 percent within a year was exceeded in two months;
- Users have applied for twenty-four FTE jobs and forty contracted jobs at Dow; and
- The job center receives the most visits from retirees.

Most importantly, the savings in rehiring alone offset the total cost of the project, demonstrating that social networking sites may be an effective tool for other organizations looking for ways to recruit top talent (Otter & Drakos, 2008).

Internal Referrals

The most highly effective means for attracting top talent is by leveraging the existing employee referral network. When current employees understand the organization's culture and long-term goals, referrals from those employees can yield excellent results. In fact, current employees are the most trusted source of information for candidates, yet ironically they are the most under-utilized. More than 80 percent of candidates believe that current employees are credible sources of information about organizations, yet fewer than 24 percent of employees proactively advocate for their organizations (Corporate Executive Board, 2006).

Various employee referral programs can be developed. Some employee referral programs include bonuses for existing employees of up to $3,000 per individual referred and subsequently hired, while other organizations offer gifts in exchange for referrals. These gifts can range in value and price and might include a vacation package at a location of the employee's choice. At Health Group of Alabama, a company in the laundry industry, employees are encouraged to refer potential employees with offers of an $80 bonus. Upon completion of the new employee's 90-day probationary period, employees who referred the new employee receive another $80. To encourage longevity, if the employee stays for a full year, the referring employee receives a $155 bonus (Frederick, 2002).

Organizations should also examine ways to leverage employee networks. At Pfizer, for example, employee networks are leveraged to gain access to "hard to attract" candidates. The organization provides organizational support and enables high-visibility sponsorship of events targeted to women, the Asian population, and gay and lesbian groups in an effort to attract candidates from these networks (Corporate Executive Board, 2006).

Open House Recruiting

Employers often use open house recruiting, any employer-sponsored public event that is intended to attract new candidates to the organization. An open house allows prospective employees the opportunity to learn about the organization and become familiar with other employees in a low-pressure atmosphere. The event also allows the employer a chance to informally assess a prospective employee.

Job Fairs

Job fairs are another great way to attract top candidates who may not be aware of an organization. A job fair may be held in the community where the organization exists or take place at an industry event or university.

A great example of an effective job fair is a professional development conference designed and hosted by Chicago-based Hyatt International Hotel. The conference is a free, one-day road show that teaches students how to interview and advance in the workplace. Additionally, the conference informs students about career opportunities within Hyatt. The conference has been known to attract between forty and one hundred potential employees at each site, even during a tight labor market (Hensdill, 2000).

Use of Recruiters

Using recruiters can be an effective way to surface passive top talent, candidates who are not actively seeking employment because they are somewhat satisfied with their current jobs, but they would consider a better opportunity if it arose. Passive candidates are generally viewed favorably by internal recruiting teams. External recruiting agencies, or headhunters, leverage their internal networks and actively pursue currently employed top talent.

Advertising

Advertisements in newspapers, trade magazines, and on the Internet have been a common method of recruitment, yet they are not always the most effective methods. Internet-based advertisements provide organizations with numerous employee applications, yet great, well-known organizations receive so many responses to Internet ads that it is difficult to keep up with the deluge of applications. Some organizations such as Google and Capital One use technology or pen-and-paper testing as a way to narrow the selection (Nicholson, 2000).

In spite of the number of applications received, even great organizations should apply the same standards of courtesy to the online applicant as is customary for traditional mail-in applications by responding with a letter. If there is a lack of communication, the applicant may be hesitant to apply to the organization in the future and it may damage the image of the organization in the eyes of the applicant.

EFFECTIVE SELECTION AND ATTRACTIVE OFFER

The interviewing process includes discussions held between prospective employees and the recruiting team and the hiring manager. These discussions can be formal or informal, but must be organized with clear objectives for the recruiting team before the interviewing process begins.

Interviewing is typically viewed as essential to becoming an employee of the organization, and candidates must experience the interviewing process as fair and impartial. Organizations must be on their best behavior and conduct fair and thorough interviews in an effort to create goodwill among all applicants, even applicants who are not hired or considered to be top talent.

Fairness and Timeliness

A fair and timely interviewing and selection process ensures that candidates have a positive experience and perception of the organization. A fair process means standardized selection criteria, a written hiring process, making decisions based on factual data, and considering all qualifications as well as work history. In addition, the organization must take into consideration the talents, education, and verifiable skill sets of the candidates. An unfair or lengthy process may result in candidates losing their motivation or interest in the job or the organization as a whole.

The Realistic Job Preview

Sometimes the cause for turnover is that the job or the workplace is not as expected. In their effort to win over candidates, managers could misrepresent the opportunity or the work, or could simply over- or under-state some elements of the job or work culture. An additional cause for turnover might be a mismatch between the job and the individual. This may be the result of interviewees who do not have clarity about their skills or strengths or misrepresent their abilities. Managers could be under pressure to fill a position and may make a poor assessment of an individual's ability to succeed in the role (Branham, 2005). Using a realistic job preview (RJP) is one way to clarify expectations of the organization and employee.

One organization that has successfully implemented the RJP is the Humane Society for Seattle. This organization has found that people sometimes have a romantic idea about what it's really like to work with cats and dogs all day. The organization was faced with high turnover of its adoption advisors, kennel technicians, and veterinary assistants during the first two weeks of employment. To reduce turnover and give job applications a more realistic preview of what it was like to work in their roles all day, they created a working interview, a chance for job applicants to job shadow for a day and be paid $10 per hour for their time. "It's a look/see on both sides," says Lisa Haneberg, HR consultant to the organization. "The organization has found that, by the end of the day, both the job applicant and the employer come to same conclusion. In fact, there is only a 50/50 chance that they will think it's a good match." The result has been that the organization has reduced turnover of new hires (Haneberg, 2008).

The RJP gives the candidate as well as the organization a chance to better understand the expectations and requirements needed in the role. Candidates who recognize that they are not the best fit for the role will be able to withdraw from consideration. The RJP process has been used successfully to increase retention.

A RJP can be conducted with a group of several candidates or in one-on-one interviews. Throughout the process, the applicant learns about what the organization is able to offer to assess how the opportunity matches up with his or her expectations. A RJP should cover the following topics, which are typical areas of misunderstanding between new hires and organizations:

1. How quickly the candidate can progress;
2. The level of responsibility the candidate will have;
3. The opportunity to grow personally through training;
4. How secure the job is;

5. The degree to which the candidate can operate independently;

6. The amount of coaching and mentoring the candidate would receive;

7. The degree to which the candidate can be creative;

8. The frequency at which long hours will be requested;

9. The amount of collaboration and teamwork required;

10. The frequency and duration of travel;

11. The pace at which work is demanded; and

12. The amount and frequency of organizational change.

(Branham, 2000)

Discussions like those during an RJP should not be limited to the time of hire, but held throughout the employee's first year of employment. Jobs and roles change and candid, frequent follow-up discussions are necessary to clarify and update obligations and expectations.

JOB FIT AND CAREER ADVANCEMENT OPPORTUNITIES

Job fit, alignment between what employees want to experience on the job and what the organization offers, results in more satisfied employees who will be more likely to remain in the organization for a longer period of time. Job fit also refers to the employee's ability to work effectively with the work team and within the organizational culture. Employees leave the organization sooner when they do not perceive proper job fit.

Criteria for Job Fit

During the interview, the following criteria should be discussed to help the applicant assess whether the job is a good fit.

- *Job role* describes the job in terms of the service provided or product being sold.

- *Job clarity* refers to the amount of certainty or risk required to be successful in the new position.

- *Job autonomy* describes how much independence the individual will have in accomplishing his or her goals.
- *Task importance* defines the priorities of the performance tasks that must be completed in order to meet job standards.
- *Task repetitiveness* describes the similar tasks or functions that must be completed over and over.
- *Task variety* defines the number of various tasks or functions in the job.

A detailed job description can provide all of these in detail and allow the applicant to determine his or her job fit. The three components of job fit applicants will be looking at include: person/organization, person/culture, and person/person.

PERSON AND ORGANIZATIONAL FIT (P/O FIT). When a new employee's work history and future job goals align with the job tasks required to deliver organizational products and services, then a perfect person/organization fit occurs. To determine person/organization fit, personal work characteristics may be assessed:

- Flexibility
- Autonomy
- Attention to detail
- Innovation
- Being a quick study
- Resourcefulness
- Dependability

In addition, an employee's personal values, career goals, and aspirations for the future need to fit within the organization's culture and the requirements of the job. All candidates should be assessed by the same objective criteria through behavioral interviewing techniques. In addition, selection tests have been shown to be successful in narrowing the number of candidates to the likely few who will be most successful (Phillips, 2002). Studies have shown that the better the fit, the greater the likelihood that an employee will feel professionally and personally tied to an organization and will stay in the job (Mitchell, Holton, Lee, Sablynski, & Erez, 2001).

PERSON-CULTURE FIT (P/C FIT). Organizations may seek out employees who demonstrate loyalty to their mission and the way that work is accomplished. The organization should seek out individuals who are aligned with its culture, but first, the organization must clarify how its culture is evidenced through employee behaviors.

For example, news media organizations understand that they are deadline-driven and should seek candidates who thrive on meeting deadlines and working extended hours when necessary to meet them. Similarly, technology organizations are known for working long but flexible hours, and individuals in these organizations often thrive on creativity. Recruiting efforts must align the culture and candidates who will thrive within that culture.

A study conducted by DBM, a career transition, career management, and outplacement organization headquartered in Boston, showed that more than 70 percent of executives who were terminated from their organizations were not terminated for performance, but because they did not fit the culture (Smith, 2001).

Finally, the hiring manager has to consider how the new employee's personal work characteristics will align with the culture of the work group. This can best be accomplished through a group interview by the work team.

PERSON AND PERSON FIT (P/P FIT). The final element of fit is person/person fit and refers to the experience of peer cohesion. Ask the simple questions: "Will this individual fit in with the people he/she will be working with? Will the individual create tension in the workplace?" While the questions may seem subjective, peer cohesion is critical. Employees are more likely to leave an organization if they do not feel accepted by their colleagues, so organizations must create an atmosphere of acceptance and offer team-building activities on a regular basis.

The Offer

After the right candidate for the job has been selected, an attractive offer must be extended. While it's impractical to extend the perfect offer, there are some elements of a more efficient and compelling offer. Some of the elements of an effective employment value proposition, or offer, include the rewards (compensation, benefits), the opportunity (organizational stability and growth, development opportunities), the organization (reputation, work environment), the work (work/life balance, job interest alignment) and the people (camaraderie, manager quality) (Corporate Executive Board, 2006).

It's a common perception that higher pay is the biggest motivator for accepting a new job; however, organizations that offer a well-known employment brand are able to offer less than market salaries and still hire top talent. When the total value of the offer (rewards, opportunity, the work, and the people) is attractive, only an 11 percent increase is needed to attract candidates Conversely, when the total value of the offer is not attractive, a 21 percent premium is needed to hire candidates, according to the Corporate Leadership Council.

Recognizing the importance of hiring top talent, FirstMerit's very aggressive recruitment strategy includes a most-wanted "interview-less" hire offer letter. The organization has developed a "most wanted" list of the five top performers at their competitors, as well as competitive intelligence about each of them. Additionally, the recruiting team has had a conversation with these "most wanted" candidates to verify that they were indeed highly desirable. Once the team has validated that the individual is a desirable candidate, the recruiting team then sends the individual, without warning or an interview, an offer letter (Sullivan, 2005).

ORIENTATION AND ON-BOARDING

The purpose of orientation and on-boarding is to help new hires become familiar and acclimated to the organizational culture, their peers, and their new jobs and roles. The orientation and on-boarding process is an excellent time for organizations to make a lasting impression with a new hire. Facilitating a professional experience makes a positive impact on turnover. A study conducted at Corning Glass revealed that new employees who attended a positive orientation session were 69 percent more likely to remain with the company three years later than those who did not attend such a session (Klienman, 2000).

Need for a Positive Orientation and On-Boarding Experience

The first day of a new job is a memorable experience associated with excitement as well as stress. Orientation is a time when people become familiar with the duties of their new jobs, become acquainted with the people they will be working with, and begin to learn more about the culture in which they will be working. The stress associated with something new is often difficult, and orientation helps new employees positively manage the stress by helping them learn about the company.

Borgata, an Atlantic City luxury casino, hotel, and spa, understands that successful on-boarding translates into success with the customer and improved employee retention. Having hired nearly five thousand people over a seven-month period in 2003, Borgota's branding efforts continued during the new employee orientation process with senior managers talking with new hires about company values. Borgota's orientation program, "One Borgata Way," helps new hires understand Borgota's way of doing business and helps new hires understand the organization's values: trust, confidence, respect, and support. Employees, including housekeeping staff, are viewed as critical to the customer experience and receive new hire orientation that helps them understand the goals and the mission of the organization as well as customer service. This program has paid off. The average turnover is 20 percent, less than two-thirds of the industry average (Overman, 2006).

In another example, ASDA, the UK's second-largest grocery, which is owned by Wal-Mart, earned recognition as Europe's number one great place to work in 2004 as a result of some of its employee engagement practices and its new hire orientation and on-boarding. All new hires go through twenty-five hours of training when they join the organization; part of that training includes developing a job ladder with the manager (Corporate Executive Board, 2004).

Successful orientation and on-boarding impact the perceptions and attitudes of new hires. Mitre asks new hires to complete a survey about their experience at regular intervals. New hires are asked about their first week experience, their first month, and their experience at the end of three months to ensure accountability of the line manager and the new hire's "buddy" (Corporate Executive Board, 2006).

Orientation Programs

A wide variety of orientation programs exist, but whether the orientation is large or small, formal or informal, the orientation needs to benefit both the new employee and the organization and provide a framework from which the new hire can begin a successful career.

The length or the intensity of the program is determined by the learning that has to take place. What are the desired outcomes of the program? The orientation program should be designed and developed with those outcomes in mind. For example, the military's orientation program, known as basic training, can last from six weeks to three months or more depending on the role of the individual. The objectives of the military's orientation program include attempting to change most aspects of the recruits' life habits, such as sleeping, eating, physical conditioning, skills, and behaviors. For some jobs in the private sector, orientation programs might last from fifteen minutes to as long as one year. The length of the orientation program depends on several factors, including:

- Organizational size and complexity;
- Importance of the orientation program to the organization;
- Resources available to run the orientation; and
- Number of objectives of the orientation process.

Orientation Outcomes

Effective orientation programs begin with clear learning objectives. Key objectives for a strong orientation solution might be as follows:

- Welcome new hires and ensure that they feel they have an important role;
- Inspire a positive attitude about the organization;
- Share important information about the organization, such as its history, mission, vision, values, and structure;
- Introduce new hires to their work environment;
- Describe benefit packages, how to access them and the company's pay practices;

- Provide time to complete any forms or documents necessary for finalization of employment;
- Communicate the policies and procedures; and
- Describe general expectations of employee performance.

Piloting the program with existing employees ensures that the program will be effective in soliciting candid input from new hires who have gone through the program can identify what they learned and what they feel they needed to learn during the orientation program. This feedback allows the organization to make improvements in the program.

The orientation program should be monitored continually for effectiveness, as the needs of the organization may change.

Organizations, like people, have only one chance to make a first impression. An orientation program that makes a good first impression may improve productivity and retention. The program must take both the new hire's and the organization's perspectives into account. A well-designed program is enjoyable for individuals and succeeds at giving people a head start in their new jobs.

FINAL THOUGHTS

This chapter described the six basic employee needs that relate to the recruitment process. The first two concerned the employee's desire to be associated with an organization that has a positive public image and brand and a track record of solid market performance. Ways to meet these needs with an employment brand and successful financial performance were discussed. The next two employee needs were around the recruitment and selection process. Specific solutions such as open houses, job fairs, and use of recruiters were illustrated, while the use of a realistic job preview and an effective offer were discussed. The final section of the chapter dealt with job fit and orientation and on-boarding. It comes down to ensuring that employees are selected for jobs that are in alignment with their skills and talents and helping them adjust quickly to the job, team, and organization. The next three chapters will continue the focus on employee needs and organizational solutions.

References

Branham, L. (2000). *Keeping the people who keep you in business.* New York: AMACOM.

Branham, L. (2005). *The seven hidden reasons employees leave.* New York: AMACOM.

Corporate Executive Board. (2004, March). *Key findings: Trends in employer of choice.* Washington, DC: Author.

Corporate Executive Board. (2006). *Attracting and retaining critical talent segments: Identifying drivers of attraction and commitment in the global labor market.* Washington, DC: Author.

Earth day 2007: Are American workers going green? (2007, April 10). Melville, NY: Adecco. www.harrisinteractive.com/news/newsletters/clientnews/2007_Adecco.pdf

Edmondson, B. (2007, May 16, 2007). *Forensic fever spins off scientists.* http://expertvoices.nsdl.org/tvscience/

Frederick, E. (2002, April). Your best source for finding new employees may be right beside you. *American Laundry News, 29*(4), 4.

Fulmer, I.S., Gerheart, B., & Scott, K.S. (2003). Are the 100 best better? An empirical investigation of the relationship between being a 'great place to work' and firm performance. *Personnel Psychology, 56*(4), 965–993.

Google take 2. (2008). San Francisco, CA: Great Place to Work Institute. www.greatplacetowork.com/best/100-best-2008-Google.pdf

Haneberg, L. (2008). Humane Society for Seattle, Washington. [Interviewed by author.]

Hensdill, C. (2000, March). Employee recruitment and retention tactics. *Hotels, 34*(3), 28.

Huff, C. (2007, August). Green recruiting helps bring in top talent. *Workforce Management Online.* www.workforce.com/archive/feature/25/06/24/index.php?ht=

Klienman, M. (2000, March 6, 2000). First impressions are lasting: Employee retention programs at various companies. *Discount Store News.* http://findarticles.com/p/articles/mi_m3092/is_5_39/ai_60122332

Long, G. (2008). Seattle, WA: Starbucks. [Interviewed by author.]

Mitchell, T.R., Holton, B.C., Lee, T.W., Sablynski, C.J., & Erez, M.. (2001). Why people stay: Using job embeddedness to predict voluntary turnover. *Academy of Management Journal, 44*(6), 1102–1121.

Nicholson, G., (2000, December). Automated assessments for better hires: Save time and money while reducing high turnover. *Workforce, 79*(12), 102.

Otter, T., & Drakos, N. (2008, March 27). *Case study: Dow's formula for social software.* Stamford, CT: Gartner.

Overman, S. (2006, April/June). Show off your brand. *Staffing. 2*(2).

Phillips P.P., (2002). *Retaining your best employees.* Alexandria, VA: ASTD.

Smith G., (2001). *Here today, here tomorrow.* Chicago, IL: Dearborn.

Stein, N. (2000, May). Winning the war to keep top talent. *Fortune,* pp. 132–137.

Sullivan, J. (2005, July 18). The best practices of the most aggressive recruiting department. www.ere.net.

Sutton, J. (2008). Portland, OR: Nike. [Interviewed by author.]

Toobin, J. (2007, May 7). The CSI effect: The truth about forensic science. *The New Yorker.*

Weddle, P.D. (2003, November 10). Your employment brand must lure the right people. CareerJournal.com.

CHAPTER EIGHT

Establish an Appropriate Work Environment

All employees, especially critical talent, need a work environment that allows them to thrive and prosper, Several factors work to create a positive work environment where top talent can thrive, including job satisfaction, workplace design, job security, and work/life balance. Table 8.1 contains a complete list of these factors as well as critical talent needs and appropriate solutions linked with these needs.

JOB SATISFACTION

Job satisfaction is the degree to which an individual feels content with his or her job. Patrick Lencioni, author of *The Three Signs of a Miserable Job*, tells a story to illustrate his perspective that a truly miserable job is one in which workers are anonymous, have roles that are seemingly irrelevant, and have virtually no visible impact on the business (Lencioni, 2007.) Traditionally, factors related to job satisfaction include:

- Satisfaction with the work itself
- Compensation

Category	Talent Needs	Solutions
1. Job Satisfaction	Satisfaction with the job	Design a personally rewarding and challenging job
2. Workplace Design	An attractive, functional work setting	Create an appealing and functional work area that promotes efficiency and productivity
3. Health and Safety	Assured of safety at work	Sustain a healthy work environment
4. Job Security	Confidence about employment continuity	Ensure employability and provide a stable work environment
5. Culture	Feel supported for individual values, gain respect and dignity	Create a culture that supports individual values and gives respect
6. Life/Work Balance	A sense of balance among work, family, and personal interests	Implement work/life balance programs
7. Diversity	Accepted as individuals regardless of differences	Build and support a fair and equitable diversity program

Table 8.1.   Critical Talent's Work Environment Needs and Solutions

- Opportunity for career development
- Good supervision
- Positive relationships with peers

Low ratings on these factors ma~ ·lt in low job satisfaction, which is linked to employee t~

N   ion

Given   forty-five hours a week at work,   itself bring a certain level of satisfactio   .es even more important because job satisfaction   productivity. In a 2006 survey by Randstad, 77   mployees and 75 percent of employers agreed that a   satisfaction is a key driver of productivity. Interest-   nt as job satisfaction is to productivity and personal happiness, 88 percent of employees said that they stay in jobs that they don't like, just to have a job. Moreover, 35 percent of employees surveyed indicated they were planning to leave their company for a new job within a year of the survey (Randstad Work Solutions, 2006).

Each of the five factors of job satisfaction mentioned above is important, yet these factors vary in importance by employee. For example, one employee might have a higher need for compensation than for positive relationships with peers. Another employee may have a greater need for satisfaction from the work itself than for compensation. In this chapter we will address the factor of the work itself. The other four job satisfaction factors are addressed in more detail in Chapter 9, Create Equitable Pay and Performance Processes, and Chapter 10, Build Motivation and Commitment.

The Work Itself

One way to create work so that it is satisfying and motivational for employees is to design it as such. There are many models for designing work that is satisfying. Hackman and Oldham's job characteristics model has stood the test of time as an effective way to design a job that is motivating for employees. The idea behind the job characteristics model is that people respond differently to the same job and that it is possible to alter the characteristics of a job to improve employee motivation, satisfaction, and performance (Hackman & Oldham, 1976).

According to the job characteristics model, when employees are matched well with their jobs, it will not be necessary to urge them to perform well because they will be internally motivated to perform well. Of the five characteristics of a job, three of them (skill variety, task identity, and task significance) contribute to the overall sense of meaningfulness of a job. The more an employee feels challenged (skill variety) by the job, the more he or she is able to see the whole and identifiable piece of work (task identity) and the degree to which the job impacts the lives of others (task significance), the more meaningful the job feels to the employee. These characteristics, combined with feedback and an appropriate amount of autonomy, result in employees who feel internally motivated by their work (Hackman & Oldham, 1976).

Measuring Job Satisfaction

Just as there are many models of job satisfaction, there are many methods for measuring job satisfaction. Typical measures of job satisfaction are through employee surveys that ask questions such as:

- I would recommend this company as a good place to work.
- I am clear about the department's goals and how they relate to me.
- Remaining at this company would be good for me in the long run.
- I am satisfied with my job.

Organizations may develop their own questionnaires or develop a customized questionnaire with an external vendor specializing in test development and administration. It is important that the person who constructs the assessment have a good understanding of assessment development and be able to run the appropriate reliability and validity tests to ensure that the test is indeed measuring what it is believed to measure. It is also helpful to benchmark the results against other organizations to isolate key areas that need focus and improvement. One job satisfaction questionnaire is the Minnesota Satisfaction Questionnaire, which measures an employee's satisfaction with his or her job. There is a long version, which requires fifteen to twenty minutes to complete, and a short version, which takes five minutes to complete. Another assessment is the Job Descriptive Index (JDI) from JDI Research based at Bowling Green State University. The JDI measures five facets of job satisfaction: Work on Present Job, Present Pay, Opportunities for Promotion, Supervision, and Co-Workers.

Job Satisfaction Solutions

While it may be important to measure job satisfaction, some have argued that high-performing organizations lead to satisfied employees more than highly satisfied employees lead to high-performing organizations (Rosenzweig, 2007). This may explain why the literature on job satisfaction drivers for top performers is sparse, as top performers are generally already aligned with high-performing organizations and job satisfaction does not surface as a concern for this talent group. Instead of focusing on improving job satisfaction, employers should focus on engaging employees and enabling performance. When performance is enabled by proper tools such as training, mentoring, feedback, and recognition for a job well done, all employees, including critical talent groups, are more likely to perform well and as a result, feel better about their jobs. Below are three key criteria to enable performance (Davenport, 1999):

1. *Focus on performance more than on job satisfaction.* Create a work environment in which people believe they can do their jobs to the best of their abilities.

2. *Develop supervisors and managers so that they become more effective managers.* Studies have consistently demonstrated a relationship between an employee's job performance and the effectiveness of his or her manager.

3. *Avoid over-engineering HR programs to create job satisfaction.* Focus more effort on engaging employees and making their jobs easier to do than engineering job satisfaction through HR programs.

WORKPLACE DESIGN

Workplace design is important to key talent groups and describes the way a work area is organized and arranged. Effective work areas need to be aesthetically appealing and support employees' activities and workflows in a way that helps them be more efficient and productive. Workplace design may also be viewed as the various kinds of jobs that employees perform on a regular basis.

Employee Need for Adequate Workplace Design

Buildings and workspace can communicate a lot about an organization and what it values. Top talent will assess the workplace as well as the job offer when considering whether to join a new organization. For example, are workstations set up to encourage collaboration? Are employees supported by new equipment or is the equipment old and outdated? Are employees valued and provided with ergonomic furniture and do they have access to natural light? (Herman Miller, 2004).

Not only are these factors important in attracting top talent, but research has also demonstrated that a well-designed workplace can boost productivity. A 2005 study by the Commission for Architecture and the Built Environment and the British Council for Offices found that good lighting and adequate daylight can reduce absenteeism by 15 percent and increase productivity by between 2.8 percent to 20 percent. The study also identified that one UK-based call center experienced an 11 percent reduction in turnover after a move to a new, improved, and more appealing location (Commission for Architecture and the Built Environment, 2005).

Functional Work Settings

Ideally, a well-designed workplace supports productivity, allows employees to communicate effectively, and is attractive. While a workspace does not need to be the newest or most expensive, it does need to be functional, providing employees with the tools, equipment, and space to accomplish their tasks. Additionally, the workspace needs to accommodate open communication and collaboration. Workplaces that are cramped can limit productivity which hinders spaciousness, which is known for advancing creativity—important to both attracting and retaining critical talent.

In one example, the design of the workplace was set up to reflect the values and priorities of the organization. For example, SEI Investments of Oaks, Pennsylvania, values productivity and communication, reflected in a design that distributes its workspace among 140 self-managed teams and lets each team arrange its space as it sees fit. Additionally, furniture is on wheels so that employees can create their own work areas and build stronger team relationships and promote employee retention as a result (From the Editor's Desk, 2000).

In another example, Monical's Pizza, a family-owned restaurant based in Illinois, incorporated workplace design as one of their employee retention tactics. In 1994, Monical's had one of the highest retention rates in the industry with management turnover of only 7 percent and restaurant-wide turnover of less than 100 percent in an industry where turnover can be as high as 300 percent (Monical, 2003).

To address turnover in 1994, Monical's created a long-term strategic plan that included management training, organization restructure, improved technology, and an improved work environment. These included upgraded kitchens and dining rooms and improved ventilation, air conditioning, and heating. Retention improved and turnover of front-line staff dropped to its current level of less than 100 percent. Monical's understood that their front-line, customer-facing employees were critical to the success of the organization and satisfaction of its customers (Bond & Reents, 2002).

Functional work settings may also include telecommuting from home or working from a temporary office or mobility center. For example, the roads near Microsoft's headquarters in Redmond, Washington, were not designed to handle the 35,000 workers who come to work each day. As a result, critical talent faces long commutes and the stress associated with intense traffic delays. To accommodate for this problem, Microsoft has implemented a program to allow more employees to work from home or at other off-site locations. This practice results in increased productivity, reduced real estate costs, and improved employee retention (King, 2007). In another example, VIPdesk.com, an Alexandria, Virginia-based call center provider, boasts 15 percent turnover in an industry noted for 80 to 90 percent turnover, all by allowing its employees to work from home (King, 2007).

The trend toward allowing employees to commute, once viewed as a luxury, is now becoming more common. In fact, 14 percent of the workforce already telecommutes, and this number is expected to increase to 17 percent by 2009. Allowing workers to work from home reduces stress and gives valuable time back to workers who may already be spending one to two hours per workday simply commuting to and from work (Reisner, 2007).

More and more organizations are considering ways to tear down walls and open communication—both literally and figuratively. Open workspaces have become more common and some business leaders have shunned the corner office in favor of working in close proximity with their teams. In the same way, senior leaders of British Petroleum, the world's third largest energy company, prefer to work in offices with without walls or doors in exchange for creating a more open environment (Girion, 2001).

Attractiveness

Although the attractiveness of any workplace may be limited by the type of work that is conducted in that space, even the most functional workspaces can be designed to increase attractiveness. For example, manufacturing facilities can be organized and have attractive, soundproof lunchrooms. The cab of a truck or bus can be clean and designed for comfort. Office cubicles can be well-designed, attractive, and personalized.

One element of attractiveness that is often overlooked is lighting. Lighting has been shown to alleviate seasonal affective disorder, improve the quality of sleep, improve performance of night shift workers, and to have an impact on brain activity. Research has shown that worker productivity is also impacted by lighting. In a study of the link between daylight and productivity, researchers found that during the winter months, workers in windowed offices spent more time on computer tasks than workers in interior offices without windows (Figueiro, Rea, Stevens, & Rea, 2002).

Employees with adequate lighting also view their workspaces more positively. A study of worker productivity and lighting also shows that people who rate their lighting space as more attractive are also happier, more comfortable, and satisfied with their environment and their work (DiLouie, 2004).

HEALTH AND SAFETY

Knowledge-based talent such as banking, IT, and professional services employees are more concerned about working in environmentally healthy environments than they are concerned about the physical safety issues posed by other careers such as manufacturing jobs, for example. In fact, these knowledge workers choose to avoid jobs that put them at physical risk. A recent study by consulting firm, Hill & Knowlton found that nearly half of 500 MBA students surveyed would be unwilling to work in the alcohol or chemicals sectors (MBA Graduates Spurn Tainted Jobs, 2008).

Other critical talent groups such as law enforcement employees, security guards, nighttime fast food workers, nurses and highly-skilled manufacturing and construction workers are more concerned about physical safety.

Need for Healthy and Safe Work Environment

While the safety profession was primarily regulation-driven in the past, with the age of terrorism and heightened awareness of environmental concerns, issues of health and safety have resurfaced as an important issue for all employees, including critical talent groups and top performers. The way that organizations handle safety concerns reflects their values and impacts how employees feel about the organization.

Griffin Hospital, rated one of the one hundred best places to work by employees, credits its award-winning work environment to its communication practices. Their communication policy regarding worker safety was put to the test not long after the September 11 terrorist attacks. In November of 2001, Griffin hospital admitted a patient who died due to anthrax inhalation and, while the hospital had confirmed the cause of death, the FBI had not yet confirmed the results. The FBI was clear that they did not want to release the news of the death until they had come to their own conclusions about the cause of death. In spite of the pressure from both the FB I and the local government to postpone a staff meeting to communicate the news about the cause of death, the hospital leaders chose to follow their policy of open and honest communication and tell their staff members about the death and its cause. Had the leaders chosen to keep the news secret, they would have destroyed the trust they had built with their employees. In the end, Griffin Hospital leaders were celebrated for their courage (Callo, 2008).

Given the necessary compliance concerns about safety, workers' physical safety may seem nearly irrelevant for discussion; however, in 2006, the Bureau of Labor Statistics reported more than four million worker injuries and more than 5,700 deaths in the private sector (Marquez, 2007). Additionally, in 2006, nearly 540 people were reported to the Bureau of Labor Statistics' Census of Fatal Occupational Injuries to have been killed by violence in the workplace. Workers who face the greatest risk of violence on the job are those who have contact with the public; exchange money; deliver passengers, goods, or services; work with unstable or volatile persons; work alone or in small numbers, especially late at night or during early morning hours in high-crime areas; or guard valuable property or possessions are at risk for violence on the job. In addition to the moral and ethical interests that employers have in protecting employees, they can also be liable for the safety of their employees (*Occupational Violence*, 2008). Moreover, organizations that have a solid reputation for taking extra measures for protecting their employees will stand out from other employers and be attractive to employees with critical skills in high-risk occupations.

Illness and Injury Prevention

All organizations must follow the legal requirements for occupational health and safety (OSHA). Failure to do so exposes an organization to potentially extreme punitive damages—especially if a loss occurs. The best safety practices begin with prevention. When employees recognize that preventative safety measures have been implemented, they are likely to feel secure and satisfied, resulting in a greater likelihood they will stay. A viable safety program begins with assessing the organization's safety needs to understand what is most important to employees.

Safety can begin before new employees even arrive by ensuring that the building is free of toxins and by conducting background checks for all new employees and any current employees who have not had backgrounds checked. Moreover, employers with employees who work in environments with a high risk of physical danger, such as manufacturing or construction workers and fast-food workers who work late at night, must take precautions to ensure that their employees are protected from potential physical harm.

When an organization is very clear about its policy about background checks, substance abuse, sexual harassment, and so on, they communicate the importance of worker safety to them.

Effective Health and Safety Programs

Health and safety programs include everything from health and safety policies to training programs. Organizations that fail to provide safe work environments can be held liable for illnesses, injuries, or fatalities that occur in the work environment. In years past, safety concerns were focused primarily on safe work practices such as machine handling, manufacturing chemical exposure, and the like. Throughout the last decade, issues such as violence at work and "sick building syndrome" have emerged as new concerns to workers.

Symptoms of sick building syndrome may include headaches; eye, nose, or throat irritation; cough; itchy skin; dizziness and nausea; difficulty in concentrating; fatigue; and sensitivity to odors. The syndrome can be caused by poor ventilation, chemicals from carpet or upholstery, and mold or bacteria, among other causes (Sick Building Syndrome, 2008). While the syndrome is somewhat controversial, the impact to an organization can be significant from a talent management standpoint and as a liability concern. For example, in

1997, Martin County sued the architect and builders for construction defects in a $13 million courthouse that led to mold damage. The value of the verdict exceeded the cost of the construction of the courthouse (Deering, 2001), illustrating the negative importance of health and safety prevention.

To provide a safe work environment, employers must implement safe work standards. One method to prevent injuries or illnesses on the job is to provide training for employees specific to the needs of the organization. One organization that has been effective at improving worker safety is Butterball, LLC, a large turkey producer with a workforce of six thousand employees, including two thousand who process turkeys each day. In 2006, the organization implemented a new approach to safety that included goal setting and performance tracking, detailed safety planning, a health facility and ergonomics team at each plant, and twenty to thirty hours of safety training annually for every manufacturing employee. In addition, safe work practices were documented for every job. Finally, an annual safety audit is conducted by safety managers and becomes a basis for safety improvements. The result is that the company will cut its casualty insurance costs by $1 million, clearly illustrating that the workplace has become a safer place for employees to work (Hansen, 2008).

Executive Commitment to Health and Safety

In summary, an organization can demonstrate its commitment to its employees through its policies, practices, and responses to health and safety concerns. Not only does this ensure that all employees feel safe, but extra measures to go above and beyond basic requirements are likely to foster a sense of trust and commitment from all employee groups. Moreover, organizations protect themselves from costly lawsuits and workers' compensations claims by taking a proactive approach to ensure their employees' health and safety.

JOB SECURITY

Providing employees, especially key talent groups, with job security gives them a sense of stability and the opportunity to buy homes, care for their families, and plan for the future. A lack of security or sense that the organization is not loyal to employees puts the organization at risk for losing critical talent groups.

Need for Job Security

Every employee has a need to feel a sense that his or her job is secure and will provide for him or her in the future. The common practices of corporate downsizing, mergers, and acquisitions have elevated job stability to critical importance. In a recent survey, only 25 percent of employees believed that their company was loyal to employees, yet 41 percent of employers believed they were loyal to their employees. When it comes to job security, generational differences exist. For example, Gen X and Gen Y are more interested in a career path and gaining new skills that will make them employable. Conversely, Boomers are more interested in promotions and pay increases (Randstad Work Solutions, 2006).

The downsizings of the last twenty years have taken a toll on all employees. The result is that employee commitment, productivity, and loyalty have dropped, even among employees who survive layoffs. The many years of layoffs and job uncertainty has fostered job hopping and has made it difficult for organizations to re-establish organizational commitment from its employees. One organization that has successfully found a way to curb job hopping is GE. Instead of leaving the organization after completing initial training, employees are directed to other departments in either a lateral move or move up the organization, to keep them engaged, retained, and committed to the organization (Cappelli, 2008).

Various Levels of Job Security

Organizations may offer various levels of job security, with the highest level being full job security—which is possible with the federal government and very few other organizations. Most organizations must respond to marketplace demands and operate within a restricted expense structure requiring that, at times, in an effort to survive, payroll must be cut. As the marketplace becomes more competitive and as organizational restructuring becomes more common, employees most likely must rely more on of the concept of *employability*, or the ability to quickly find another job, rather than on job security.

Guaranteed Employment

Few organizations do provide full job security to employees. Most famous for its guaranteed employment practice is Southwest Airlines, which hasn't laid off one employee since its inception in 1971. Southwest Airlines believes that providing job security is one way to build trust with its valuable people. In 2005, when Hurricane Katrina devastated New Orleans, Southwest Airline's service to the city, its largest hub, dropped from fifty-seven flights per day to only two flights per day. Southwest responded by offering the option of relocation to all of its 250 employees based in New Orleans (McCann, 2005).

Deciding to provide guaranteed employment cannot be taken lightly. Executives who decide to embrace this practice must ensure that they are thoughtful about the types of individuals they want to employ and clear about how they set the employees and the organization up for success.

Changing Employment Pay Rates

During times of change and uncertainty, organizations are wise to retain top performers, high-potentials and critical talent groups. To be effective, employers need to have a robust performance management process in place that allows them to clearly define who those top performers and key talent groups are.

One way to respond to tough economic times and keep top talent is to offer key employees the opportunity to work at different jobs within the organization at the appropriate market rate for those jobs, which may be less than what the employee current earns. Nucor Steel-Girder Plant in St. Joe, Indiana, faced significant challenges when orders fell 30 percent, and only twelve of the total 390 employees were able to work at their usual welding jobs. Rather than being laid off, welding employees were given other jobs to do, sometimes being paid less than half of their normal hourly rate. However, the company believed that offering job security to employees would pay off in the long run by allowing the company to retain a significant potion of their valuable workforce. Additionally, when customer demand for product increased, Nucor asked its staff to put in significant overtime. The company believes this strategy pays off in the long run and acknowledges that they would have a layoff if the survival of the company were at stake (Benjamin, 2002).

Sabbaticals

Sabbaticals provide a way for organizations to retain key talent through economic downturns as well as through specific milestones.

Intel provides an eight-week sabbatical with full salary to employees after each seven years of full-time service. This creates an incentive for employees to remain at the organization in order to earn their paid sabbaticals.

During economic downturns, voluntary sabbaticals can be used to retaining key talent and top performers. When Accenture faced a downturn in business in 2001, the organization created a program called FlexLeave which permitted employees to take a six- to twelve-month voluntary sabbatical at 20 percent of their salaries. Employees also retained their health benefits as well as their laptops and email accounts. While on sabbatical, they could volunteer, take another job, or travel. Two thousand of Accenture's employees took advantage of the program, and the organization was able to save 80 percent of its payroll for those two thousand employees. More importantly, the program created goodwill with the employees (Zimmerman, 2004).

Employability

When organizations are unable to offer guaranteed employment, they can increase employee loyalty by supporting their employees' employability. The concept of employability is especially appealing to knowledge workers, such as those who work in the technology industry. Key talent groups in industries like technology that face frequent downsizings and restructures know that their tenure at an organization can be limited. These critical talent groups are better able to cope with the flexibility of their work contracts knowing that they can build on their skills and prepare themselves for the next job while working in the current job.

Organizations can support employees' employability by offering training in new skills and opportunities to earn certifications and licenses. For example, they can provide programs such as tuition reimbursement, internal workshops, training and paid time off to attend classes or professional conferences. Multiple career tracks are yet another way to give employees options to grow their careers internally or externally. Washington Mutual Bank allows associates to create personal development plans that take them into multiple career paths (Thorness, 2007).

In another example, First USA developed a program to help employees identify their career aspirations and then create plans to achieve them within the organization. The program includes career-development training as well as follow-up guidance, but more significantly, the organization has created special facilities in the workplace that employees are permitted to use during company-paid time. The program was created after employee satisfaction surveys showed that employees were pessimistic about their future with the organization. After implementing the program, First USA found that employee satisfaction increased more than 25 percent on the topics related to career development. More importantly, the turnover rate among employees who participated in the program was 65 percent lower than the turnover rate among employees who did not participate in the program, resulting in a $2.2 million savings to the organization (Kiger, 2001).

Severance Packages That Encourage Employee Return

At times, a layoff becomes inevitable and organizations that want to promote goodwill to preserve their reputations in the marketplace or encourage employees to return in the future can promote loyalty by easing the employees' burden. Severance packages can include retention of health benefits and e-mail accounts. Moreover, organizations can offer assistance in finding new jobs by offering outplacement services.

During times of uncertainty, some severance packages can provide reassurance to employees and improve an organization's ability to continue to attract top talent and retain existing talent. When Yahoo was faced with a merger bid from Microsoft, the future of the organization grew uncertain for existing employees and could have posed a recruiting challenge to the organization. Instead, Yahoo's turnover rate was unchanged due to a new severance policy developed for all employees in the event of an acquisition. The new severance policy allows for four to twenty-four months of severance pay and health coverage. The program is unique in that the change-in-control clause covers not only executives, but all full-time employees (Ruiz & Frauenheim, 2008).

CULTURE

Culture is the sum of the attitudes, experiences, beliefs, and values of an organization. It reflects the norms shared by people within the organization and controls the way that people interact with each other and outside the organization. Culture varies from organization to organization. While culture cannot be prescribed, productive work cultures are usually intentional. Leaders carefully think through the values they wish to adopt and deliberately reward and recognize those behaviors that best reflect the values they wish to cultivate.

Organizational Culture

An organization's success or failure can be attributed to many factors, one of which is the organization's culture. Culture is typically defined and created by senior executives, and is a result of deliberate consideration of the values the executives wish to enforce. If not carefully considered, culture is the result of unconscious behaviors that create a culture that may be undesirable. Because the behaviors of senior executives tend to reinforce themselves and become the culture of the organization, it's critical to the long-term success of an organization to create a positive culture that is both attractive to critical talent and keeps that talent longer than the industry average.

When the culture of an organization is positive, employees stay with the organization and stay engaged. Hypertherm, Inc., a manufacturing company based in Hanover, New Hampshire, is a competitive and successful organization and yet has never faced a layoff. The organization's management values its employees, whom they call associates. To demonstrate how much they value their associates, the company cross-trains them to do a variety of jobs within the organization to provide both organizational flexibility and job skill development. The net effect is that associates feel a sense of job security. In exchange for that, employees contribute their ideas to improve business and reduce costs. The organization implements most of their employees' ideas and, in 2002, those ideas saved the company more than $2 million (Barnes, 2003).

Need for Supportive Organizational Culture

Culture is so important that it can literally determine why one organization succeeds and another goes fails. The best illustration of the link between culture and financial performance comes from The Great Place to Work Institute. The Institute's primary criteria for a great place to work is one where employees trust the people they work for, have pride in what they do, and enjoy the people they work with, as measured through employees' responses to an annual survey (Great Place to Work Institute, 2008). Great Place to Work organizations focus on developing trust, pride, and camaraderie within their culture also outperform the Standard & Poor's 500 by more than eight percentage points (Marquez, 2007), demonstrating a link between a positive culture and financial performance.

What characteristics of culture are important to employees? To answer that question, a recent worldwide survey revealed work/ life balance and open communication, followed by integrity and customer-orientation, are the most important aspects of an organization's culture according to employees who participated in the survey (Randstad Work Solutions, 2006). While this study is important, it's also important to recognize that the vital characteristics of culture vary by organization.

Selecting Employees to Fit the Culture

After the leadership of the organization has clearly identified the values and behaviors they will reinforce and model, the organization can ensure they hire employees that match their culture. Specific tools, as well as behavioral interviewing, can be used to identify candidates most likely to fit into the organizational cultural. Southwest Airlines has spent over ten years analyzing employee behavior and has developed specific needs and requirements for each job as well as for shared attributes such as common sense, judgment, and decision-making skills. During one year, Southwest interviewed seventy thousand candidates out of an initial pool of 160,000 applicants to hire five thousand new employees. Southwest believes that their hiring process, with a specific emphasis on hiring for both job fit and cultural fit, has contributed to Southwest's low turnover rate. The organization's 9 percent turnover rate for entry-level positions and 6 percent turnover rate for higher-level management is the lowest in the industry (Stein, 2000).

Employee Involvement

One way to improve culture is to listen to employees concerns. Culture must evolve over time, but what is important to employees changes over the year as the marketplace, economy, and organization change.

One airline, that wished to remain anonymous, is known for valuing its employees. This airline knows that employees will treat customers the way they are treated by the employer, and they recognize that customer-facing employees such as call center employees can be critical to the success of the organization. Turnover of call center employees is notoriously high, but this airline is noted for low turnover of 3 percent in their call center and they wanted to better understand what characteristics of their culture separated them from the rest of the industry. By comparing existing research on call center employees to results of an employee survey, they discovered that 62.7 percent of employees at other call centers live within ten miles of their employer. Conversely, only 36.7 employees of the airline studying the data lived within ten miles of the employer. Additionally, the average wage for employees of other call centers was $11.85 per hour, compared to $10.44 per hour. In other words, their employees were traveling farther to work to earn less than their industry counterparts. The survey results showed that employees chose to work at other call centers for the pay or until they found another job in their field. Employees of the airline chose to work at the organization because of the people, the positive work culture, and the benefit of free flights for employees. The conclusion is that people are willing to travel farther and work for less money when the work environment provides a positive experience (Butler, 2002).

Positive Communication

Retention can be influenced by communication practices. Emphasis on positive, informative communication contributes to employee retention. A survey by SHRM designed to measure employees' perceptions about corporate credibility and employee communications revealed that sharing both good news and bad news as promptly and as fully as possible was as the top choice for improving corporate credibility. Increasing two-way communication between management and employees was the next best method to strengthen organizational credibility among employees (Collison, 2002). Communication includes town hall meetings, open-door policies, and mechanism and practices for giving everyone a voice. The purpose of communication is to ensure that people understand the direction of the organization and their roles in that direction, and that they are heard, ideas are shared, and differences tolerated. Omni-Com Group, a large New-York-City-based advertising and marketing group, is committed to employee communication. OmniCom's networks often compete for the same clients such as Budweiser, Pepsi, and VISA. Despite this fact, OmniCom Group creates a culture that supports cooperation *and* competition. For example, the company conducts "jazz" sessions that allow the CEOs from their networks to meet to exchange ideas. These sessions allow the CEOs to feed off each other's ideas and enable all the embedded knowledge in the room to cascade into different networks. Additionally, the organization's twelve-member management team ensures that the environment remains frictionless. Interestingly, OmniCom's turnover rate of 18 percent is nearly 50 percent below the industry average (Stein, 2000).

Annual Surveys on Culture

Annual employee surveys allow an organization to assess its culture. The very act of asking employees for their perspective demonstrates that an organization cares about employees' needs. Survey reports provide management with insight regarding what is working well and what needs to be improved. In fact, the most important part of the process is management's response to the survey results. Some of the common topics on employee surveys include pay, job satisfaction, safety, diversity, and work/life balance.

Anonymous surveys make it possible for organizations to receive uncensored, honest feedback. This helps the organization address employees' biggest concerns. When the same survey is administered year after year, organizations can determine whether improvement has taken place.

WORK/LIFE BALANCE

Organizations expect employees to achieve organizational goals, yet employees have lives away from their work. Work/life balance refers to the need of employees to balance the workplace demands with their personal lives. Organizations that support employees' non-work activities help them with work/life balance and, as a result, employees are more satisfied and loyal.

Need for Work/Life Balance

The constantly growing competitive landscape, combined with increasing customer demand and globalization, has turned up the pressure to work 24/7. As a result the distinction between home life and work life has become less clear. For many managers, especially for senior managers, an unwritten expectation is that they are constantly accessible. Additionally, employees with international responsibilities regularly work off-hours to accommodate for meetings held across time zones. In a survey conducted by IRC/ORC Worldwide, 55 percent of surveyed employees reported that they do not take all of their earned vacation. More concerning is that employees continue to check e-mail or participate in conference calls, even when they do take that vacation (Cummins, 2007). Further, thirty-four percent of workers in the United States say that the demands of their jobs "seriously interfered" with their private lives (Wiltjer, 2005). In spite of worker's behavior, a study by Spherion Corporation indicates that 86 percent of U. S. workers said that ensuring work fulfillment and balance is a top career priority (Spherion, 2003). And the problem isn't limited to U.S. workers. Nearly two-thirds of Canadians have indicated that it is "somewhat" difficult to balance their work and family lives, and 28 percent have said that it was difficult or very difficult (Todd, 2004). In the United Kingdom, almost half of workers find it difficult to balance their work at least sometimes, and more than 25 percent indicated that it was difficult to balance their work all the time (Hurst & Baker, 2005).

The impact of work/life balance on retention is significant. A study by Spherion revealed that workers who take advantage of the work/life balance benefits offered by their employers indicated that they are 20 percent more likely to stay with their employers for the next five years (Spherion, 2003). Additional research has demonstrated that employees who perceive their organizations and supervisors as supportive to their family needs are more committed to the organization and more likely to remain with their employer (Jahn, 1998). Finally, one organization realized a savings of $70 million per year in reduced turnover by being sensitive to employees' needs and providing on-site subsidized child-care centers, a health-care facility, a fitness center, and a swimming pool (Schu, 2001).

Organizations must seek new and innovative ways to help workers achieve work/life balance, and companies need to rethink their ideas about the 8 to 5, Monday through Friday face-time if they want to engage younger employees and re-engage older employees. The number of employees who are willing to put their jobs before their families continues to decrease.

While each organization needs to consider the work/life balance programs best-suited to their employees, typical programs include flextime, telecommuting, compressed workweeks, and work-life benefits, such as a concierge services, on-site banking, or dry cleaning services provided on or near work—all of which are designed to maximize the amount of personal time available.

Part-Time Work and Flextime Schedules

Top talent may find value in flexible work schedules or being able to choose their own work hours. Part-time work or flexible work hours benefit both the organization and the employee because these programs reduce absenteeism and turnover and allow people to set their own work hours. Fifty-four percent of employees in 2006 stated that flexible work hours were important to them, and 35 percent stated that the option to work from home or telecommute was important (Randstad Work Solutions, 2006). Research sponsored by Alfred P. Sloan Foundation found that worker flexibility had a positive effect on productivity and customer service. In fact, Watson Wyatt, a human resource consulting firm, found that a flexible workplace is associated with a 9 percent increase in market value. Additionally, Eli Lilly found that the more flexibility and control over their work hours that employees had been given, the greater their job satisfaction, and they indicated that they were less likely to leave the company (Corporate Voices for Working Families, 2005). Some workers may even prefer to change from full-time to part-time, which can also be beneficial to both the employee and the organization.

According to a study by Catalyst, 46 percent of respondents who had switched from full- to part-time work reported an increase in productivity, morale, commitment to the company, and retention (McShulskis, 1998, January).

As a result of a tough economy in early 2000, Sun Microsystems, a technology organization, found it was unable to offer raises and bonuses to its employees, including it critical talent groups. Because the organization wanted to retain its critical talent during this time, the organization developed a flexible work option called iWork. Under the iWork plan, employees can access Sun's server from anywhere using special technology. Employees can work from any of Sun's global offices, flex offices, drop-in centers, cafes, or at home. As of 2008, fourteen thousand of Sun's thirty-five thousand employees take advantage of the program and Sun saved $65 million in traditional offices that it didn't have to build (Ruiz & Frauenheim, 2008) making the program a win-win for employees and the employer.

Family Support Options

Research has demonstrated that organizations can increase pro-ductivity or revenue, or both, by as much as 20 percent simply by implementing work/life balance programs (Withers, 2001). In a two-year study by Work in America Institute, the ten organizations profiled were found to improve absenteeism, customer service, over-time, stress, flexibility, collaboration, innovation and creativity by implementing life balance programs that address employees' personal needs.

Work/life support programs include:

- Flexible work hours, job sharing, or the ability to change to part-time work hours;
- On-site day care for children or on-site child care for times when children are sick;
- Nursing mothers' rooms;
- Allowing employees to use personal sick leave to take care of ill children;
- Allowing employees to use personal sick leave to take care of aging parents or offering elder care insurance;

- Paid maternity or parental leave;
- Sabbaticals that may be taken for any personal concern or interest after working a specified number of years;
- Exercise areas, including weight rooms, swimming pools, or walking paths; and
- Setting up special services such as flu shots or mammograms.

Organizations must assess the specific needs of their employees before implementing many of these costly programs to ensure that the results will be what they want. For example, at CapitalOne in 1997, attrition rose to 35 percent, and while this was low by industry standards, the organization sought to become an Employer of Choice and could see through lower than normal bi-annual employee survey ratings that a culture problem was arising. The organization developed a solution of an Amenities Center. The center included a fitness center, an Internet café, and a learning center and was piloted in one location. The organization realized a savings of $213 per employee through reduced attrition, improved attendance, and increased productivity (Curtis, 2002).

Balanced Programs

Organization's needs are based on the organization's culture and employee demographics and needs. Cross Country Staffing, a medical staffing company in Boca Raton, Florida, needed to improve employee retention and employee job satisfaction. By listening to the specific needs of their mostly female corporate staff, most of whom were working mothers, Cross Country Staffing implemented a series of family support programs including job sharing, telecommuting, and flexible work schedules. These programs resulted in reducing employee turnover, allowed the organization to grow, and culminated in their becoming listed as one of the best one hundred companies for working mothers by *Working Women* magazine (Corzo, 2000).

In another example, SAS Institute's attractive program of family support programs, benefits, and life balance has allowed the organization to retain employees in a highly competitive IT industry. SAS's headquarters includes child-care facilities, a health-care facility, a 55,000-square-foot fitness center including a swimming pool, dry cleaning services, and a massage and hair salon. Other offices enjoy day-care and health-club memberships. Break rooms offer free pastries, crackers, fruit baskets, pop, coffee, tea, juice, and chocolate. Each benefit has been studied for cost-effectiveness before it is adopted and the result is that SAS has saved over $70 million a year as the result of low turnover—as estimated by researcher Jeffrey Pfeiffer (Schu, 2001).

DIVERSITY

Not only do employees need a diverse work environment, but organizations must rely on a diverse workforce. With job growth and the employee shortage, organizations must include all types of employees, including the elderly and those employees who are physically and mentally challenged. All employees want to experience a workplace that has tolerance for everyone, regardless of differences. Not only does a diverse workforce create a more welcoming environment for workers from diverse backgrounds, but a diverse workforce may actually be linked to improvements in the bottom line. Catalyst, a research and advisory organization, has found a link between the number of women board members and the financial performance of the organization and the relationship is significant. Fortune 500 organizations with a higher percentage of female board members had 42 to 66 percent higher returns on sales, equity, and invested capital (Allen, 2008).

Need for a Diverse Work Environment

As the labor pool continues to shrink in the years to come, being able to provide a work environment in which all kinds of employees can thrive, regardless of their age, gender, or ethnicity, will provide an organization with a competitive edge. Moreover, a lack of tolerance and acceptance of diverse groups negatively impacts the employees who are considered to be "different" as well as individuals who see the inequitable treatment. Employee retention suffers when employees feel preferential treatment is given to one group of employees. Additionally, tolerance, acceptance, and fairness help organizations avoid non-productive time addressing diversity complaints.

Benefits of Diversity Policies and Programs

Diversity used to be a compliance issue concerned with preventing discrimination against minority populations. Today, some organizations have shifted their diversity concerns from compliance to an active interest in diversity as a way to better connect with customer groups and/or to enhance creativity and innovation.

From a compliance perspective, organizations must write clear policies on diversity practices that reflect the overall corporate mission before developing diversity programs. For example, Allstate's employee booklet, *The Allstate Partnership*, identifies what employees and the organization can expect from one another. This handbook clarifies its diversity policies in three explicit statements related to diversity. Employees are expected to exhibit no bias in interactions, promote an environment that is inclusive and free from bias, and foster dignity and respect (Wah, 1999). Creating an environment in which people from diverse backgrounds feel included and welcomed attracts employees to an organization.

In addition to compliance, organizations are focused on creating diverse employee groups because they know it pays off in the attraction of customers. Borders Group, Inc., a Michigan-based bookseller, received a top rating from the Human Rights Campaign, an organization that champions gay, lesbian, bisexual, and transgender community issues. Borders received the award because of its diverse workforce, and while the organization has made no direct link to how this has paid off in store traffic, the organization does recognize that the gay, lesbian, bisexual, and transgender market spends $680 million a year on books and that this particular market looks at a company's policies when they shop (Whitesall, 2008).

Finally, a focus on building a diverse workforce can lead to the creation of innovative products that pay off for the organization. For example, PepsiCo has focused their diversity efforts on working closely with several affinity groups, groups of employees who are united by gender, race, ethnicity, or other traits. The employees from these groups have generated successful ideas for new products and market strategies for the organization. For example, at Frito-Lay, a division of PepsiCo, the Hispanic employee affinity group provided input for a line of guacamole-flavored potato chips, a product line that developed into a $100 million product line for the organization (Johansson, 2005 , October).

There are great benefits to an organization that creates a strategic approach to attracting and retaining diverse employee populations, especially for organizations focused on innovation.

Leadership Practices

An accepting work environment for diverse populations must be demonstrated through organizational practices and the actions of top executive leadership. Through role modeling, leaders establish practices that are visible to employees and set the tone for acceptance of diversity. Leaders and managers must be open to make changes based on feedback from employees. One way to learn what employees are thinking is to conduct a focus group or individual interviews. In focus group settings or in one-on-one discussions, employees can be asked specific questions about their own work experiences as they relate to an open, accepting work environment. These discussions must focus on both positive and negative experiences without concentrating on the poor treatment of diverse employees. Key to making this process successful is to ensure that the focus groups are reflective of the entire organization. Care must be taken in ensuring an adequate sample size is used to reflect the entire organization.

Targeting Specific Populations

In order to recruit specific diverse populations, first ensure that the organization serves the needs of those diverse populations. For example, if an organization wants to recruit more women, it must first ensure that the organization meets the needs of female employees. Ernst and Young, a professional services organization, has implemented a program to attract more women. The organization was able to double the number of minorities in its organization, with nearly half of its workforce being women (15,000 out of 33,000), due to implementing programs specific to the needs of this population, including mentoring, networking opportunities, and flexible work arrangements. The result is that the organization has successfully retained women (Tapping into Diversity, 2001).

In another example, Ford Motor Company recruits prospective employees at universities and gives special attention to disability groups within the local community. In order to reach the diverse communities such as women and minorities, the organization targets universities with a higher percentage of women and minority groups in addition to becoming involved with disability groups (Tapping into Diversity, 2001).

FINAL THOUGHTS

In this chapter we presented the topic of employee needs and solutions for an acceptable work environment. We reviewed issues such as leadership, job satisfaction, workplace design, safety, security, culture, work/life balance, and diversity and shared a variety of solutions that have been shown to ensure that employees have the supportive and safe surroundings they need to remain in the organization and productive on the job.

References

Allen, S. (2008, February). The death of groupthink. *BusinessWeek*.

Barnes, E. (2003, July). No layoff policy. *Workforce*, pp. 96–99.

Benjamin, M. (2002, February 15). Jobs built to last. *US News and World Report: Career guide 2002*.

Berta, D. (2001, June 18). Job satisfaction: The key to low turnover. *Nation's Restaurant News, 35* (25), 18.

Bond, H., & Reents, J. (2002). Reinvigorating a mature company. In J J Phillips & P.P. Phillips (Eds.), *Action: Retaining your best employees*. Alexandria, VA: ASTD.

Butler, D.L. (2002). Culture matters! Retaining employees and increasing profitability. In J.J. Phillips & P.P. Phillips (Eds.), *Action: Retaining your best employees*. Alexandria, VA: ASTD.

Callo, C. (2008, February). Creating a great place to work: Griffin Hospital created an award-winning work environment by honoring its commitment to open communication. *BusinessWeek*.

Cappelli, P. (2008). *Talent on demand: Managing talent in an age of uncertainty*. Boston, MA. Harvard Business School Press.

Centex-Rooney Construction Co. v. Martin County. (1997). (706 So.2d 20, Fla. 4th Dist. Ct. App. 1997).

Commission for Architecture and the Built Environment. (2005, May). *The impact of office design on business performance*. London:

Commission for Architecture and the Built Environment. www.cabe.org.uk/AssetLibrary/2191.pdf.

Corporate Voices for Working Families. (2005, November). Business impacts of flexibility: An imperative for expansion. *Corporate Voices for Working Families Report,* researched by WFD Consulting, sponsored by the Alfred P. Sloan Foundation, pp. 13–16.

Corzo, C. (2000, September 11). Boca Raton, Fla.-based medical staffing firm puts brakes on high turnover rate. *The Miami Herald.*

Collison, J. (2002, August). *Corporate credibility and employee communications survey.* Alexandria, VA: SHRM/Council of Public Relations Firms.

Cummins, S. (2007, October). Life, liberty, and the pursuit of balance. *BusinessWeek.* [www.businessweek.com/managing/content/oct2007/ca20071023_799034_page_2.htm].

Curtis, D. (2002). Measuring the impact of an amenities center on attrition, attendance, and performance. In J.J. Phillips & P.P. Phillips (Eds.), *Action: Retaining your best employees.* Alexandria, VA: ASTD.

Davenport, T. (1999) *Human capital: What it is and why people invest in it.* San Francisco, CA: Jossey-Bass.

Deering, A. (2001, November). Beyond sick building syndrome: Mold litigation enters the main stream. *Risk Management.* http://findarticles.com/p/articles/mi_qa5332/is_200111/ai_n21479749/pg_2?tag = artBody;col1

DiLouie, C. (2004, September/October). Lighting and productivity: Missing link found? [www.archlighting.com/industry-news.asp?articleID=453031&sectionID=0].

Figueiro, M.G., Rea, M., Stevens, R., & Rea, A. (2002). Daylight and productivity: A possible link to circadian regulation. *Proceedings of the Light and Human Health: EPRI/LRO 5th International Lighting Research Symposium.* Palo Alto, CA: The Lighting Research Office of the Electric Power Research Institute.

From the editor's desk. (2000, May). *Harvard Management Update,* 5(5), 11.

Girion, L. (2001, May 13). Office design. *Los Angeles Times.*

Great Place to Work Institute. (2008). *What makes a great place to work?* San Francisco, CA: Great Place to Work Institute. www.greatplacetowork.com/great/index.php

Hackman, J.R., & Oldham, G.R. (1976). Motivation through design of work. *Organizational Behavior and Human Performance, 16,* 250–279.

Hansen, F. (2008, February 18). Ensuring safety in a dangerous industry. *Workforce Management.* www.workforce.com/archive/ feature/25/38/85/253887.php?ht =

Herman Miller. (2004). *Mutual attraction: How to get the attention of the top performers who fit.* [www.hermanmiller.com/hm/content/research_ summaries/pdfs/wp_Mutual_Attraction.pdf].

Hurst, J., & Baker, S. (2005, February). *The 24/7 work life balance survey* (p. 4). Leicestershire, UK: Work Life Balance Centre.

Jahn, E.W. (1998, July). The impact of perceived organizational and supervisory family support on affective and continuance commitment: A longitudinal and multi-level analysis. *Dissertation Abstracts International Section A: Humanities and Social Sciences,* 59(1-A), 0237.

Johansson F., (2005 , October). Matters of the multicultural. *Harvard Business Review.*

Kiger, P. (2001, March). At First USA Bank, promotions and job satisfaction are up. *Workforce,* pp. 54–46. [www.workforce.com/archive/feature/22/27/40/index.php].

King, R. (2007, February). Working from home: It's in the details. *BusinessWeek.*

Lencioni, P. (2007). *The three signs of a miserable job.* San Francisco, CA: Jossey-Bass, 2007.

Marquez, J. (2007, June 25). Kindness pays . . . or does it? *Workforce Management,* pp. 40–49.

MBA graduates spurn tainted jobs. (2008, January 17). *Management Issues.* http://216.128.29.163/2008/1/17/research/mba-graduates-spurn-tainted-jobs.asp

McCann, K. (2005, October 11). *Gary Kelly: Southwest Airlines CEO on the business of building trust.* Austin, TX: McCombs School of Business. www.mccombs.utexas.edu/news/pressreleases/lyceum05_kelly_ wrap05.asp

McShulskis E., (1998, January). Part-time plans have a positive impact. *HRMagazine,* 43(1), 26.

Monical. (2003, May 12). Monical's turnover rate reduced dramatically with Harvard business program. www.monicals.com/navbar/index.shtml

Occupational violence. (2008, June 16). Washington, DC: National Institute for Occupational Safety and Health. www.cdc.gov/niosh/topics/violence/.

OSHA safety equipment standard done. (2007, November 20). *Workforce Management Online.* www.workforce.com/archive/ article/25/23/03.php.

Randstad Work Solutions. (2006). *2006 employee review.* Atlanta, GA: Randstad Work Solutions.

Reisner, R. (2007, March). Telecommuting now and forever. *BusinessWeek.*

Rosenzweig, P. (2007). *The halo effect.* New York: The Free Press.

Ruiz, G., & Frauenheim, E. (2008, April, 10). Yahoo tackles talent needs amid upheaval caused by merger bid, takeover talk. *Workforce News in Brief.* www.workforce.com/archive/article/25/47/02.php?ht =

Schu, J. (2001, October). Even in hard times, SAS keeps its culture intact. *Workforce, 80* (10), 21.

Sick building syndrome. (2008, February 20). *Indoor air facts no. 4* (rev.). Washington, DC: U.S. Environmental Protection Agency. www.epa.gov/iaq/pubs/sbs.html#Causes%20of%20Sick% 20Building%20Syndrome

Spherion. (2003). *2003 Spherion emerging workforce study* (p. 1). Ft. Lauderdale, FL: Spherion Pacific Enterprises. www.spherion.com/ downloads/pov/POV_Work_Balance_ (LR-BW). pdf.

Stein, N. (2000, May). Winning the war to keep top talent. *Fortune,* pp. 132–137.

Tapping into diversity. (2001, May). *globalhr,* pp. 21–25.

Thorness, B. (2007, June). Best places to work 2007. *Seattle Business Monthly.*

Todd, S. (2004). Improving work-life balance—What are other countries doing? Ottawa, Ontario, Canada: Human Resources and Skills Development, Canada. www.hrsdc.gc.ca/en/lp/spila/wlb/pdf/ improving-work-life-balance.pdf.

Wah, L. (1999, July/August). Diversity at Allstate. *Management Review, 88*(7), 24.

Whitesall, A. (2008, May). The future of diversity: Changing focus, practices can create new business. *Workforce Management Online.*

Wiltjer, P. (2005, August 29). Numbers suggest job security improving for U.S. workers, but work-life balance is more difficult to achieve. *ISRInsights.*

Withers, P. (2001, October). Finders keepers. *CMA Management, 75*(7), 24.

Zimmerman, E. (2004). Despite painful cutbacks, these companies still have recruiting power. *Workforce Management Online.* www.workforce.com/archive/article/23/65/30.php?ht =

CHAPTER NINE

Create Equitable Pay and Performance Processes

I n this chapter we review the critical issue of pay and recognition for top talent. We explore what top talent needs in terms of pay and benefits, as well as their need for recognition and rewards. The essentials necessary to effectively manage job performance are also covered.

Table 9.1 presents the four categories associated with pay and performance for top talent as well as the needs in for category and the related possible solutions.

PAY

Almost no one feels paid adequately, yet most employers think that they do indeed pay their employees fairly. Compensation is most crucial for critical talent pools who can be easily lured away with attractive compensation packages. Unwanted turnover can occur when compensation for top talent is not handled properly. More importantly, effective compensation programs are great levers for improved performance —especially among highly motivated, top performing talent groups.

Category	Need	Solution
1. Pay	To be paid fairly and equitably	Use a pay system that is fair, equitable, and competitive.
2. Benefits	To have competitive benefits to meet individual needs	Offer economically feasible employee benefit programs tailored to individual needs.
3. Rewards and Recognition	To be rewarded and recognized for contribution	Implement a rewards and recognition program tailored to individual needs
4. Job Performance	To know performance expectations for success and growth	Implement a performance management process.

Table 9.1.   Top Talent Needs and Solutions for Equitable Pay and Performance Processes

Need for Adequate Pay

Pay is more than total value of the compensation package. Pay also acknowledges the worth and value of the employee's contribution to the organization. A review of nineteen thousand exit interviews from employees uncovered that feeling devalued was a key driver of turnover and the study concluded that unfair pay practices were at the root of feeling devalued (Branham, 2005). The solution is not as simple as paying everyone at the highest level possible, nor is that practical for organizations, yet getting pay right is critical to an organization. In a recent job satisfaction survey conducted by the Society for Human Resource Management, 70 percent of surveyed individuals indicated that compensation was the most important factor in job satisfaction, illustrating the importance of developing an effective pay solution (Thorness, 2007.)

Fair Pay

Employees have a real need to feel that they are paid fairly. One of the biggest challenges facing employers today is that employees are able to research salary information online and frequently there is a wide gap between the salary information that employees find online and the data provided by salary surveys that HR departments conduct. This poses a dilemma for employers with respect to how they pay all employees, including critical talent groups in a way that feels fair to employees, yet accurately reflects the market data. Pay equity consists of both *distributive justice* and *procedural justice*. Distributive justice means that employees feel that the organization distributes pay fairly across all employee groups. When employees feel that the organization has fair practices around the distribution of pay, the employee's intent to leave is lower than those who feel pay is unfairly distributed (Liang, 2000). The second type of pay equity is *procedural justice* which is defined by the process by which pay is administered and how employees can address any pay concerns.

Equity or fairness is determined by both company communication about pay and employees' perceptions about pay. This can pose a problem for organizations that reward their key talent groups or top performers differently than the rest of the employee base, yet a blanket approach for all employees runs the risk of driving away key talent. In fact, two common errors with compensation programs exist. The first is a program that is focused on minimizing expenses and scrutinizing every cost—including compensation. The result is that motivation, creativity, and productivity are lost among top talent. The second type of compensation error is sprinkling the same raises or bonuses to everyone, regardless of performance. While managers believe this is fair, the result is that companies run the risk that their top performers will head for the door (Welch & Welch, 2008).

To retain critical talent or top performers, organizations must reward critical talent groups and top performers differently. The perception that pay practices are unfair can be mitigated by utilizing an outside resource to conduct an audit to eliminate any suspicion about unfairness of pay practices and by following and communicating some basic guidelines for selecting pay strategies.

Guidelines for Selecting Pay Strategies

Many organizations are seeking the secret to the perfect pay solution. Pay can be compared to industry standards and local market data. Sometimes organizations will engage a consulting firm specializing in comparative pay data to analyze the competitiveness of the organization's pay strategy. An effective pay program considers the following:

1. Job expectations must be clear and employees must know what is expected of them.

2. Employees must be classified correctly in their jobs.

3. Job grade assignments need to be equitable compared to others in similar job grades throughout the organization.

4. Pay ranges must be competitive based on salary surveys and desired market competitiveness.

5. Performance ratings must be fair and accurately reflect performance.

6. Performance evaluations must reflect contribution of the individual.

7. The guidelines for pay increases need to reflect the corporate philosophy around compensation practices.

8. Pay should be linked to performance of the individual.

9. Increases should stay within the established budget.

10. A clear policy on appeals by employees regarding their pay should be in place and adhered to.

11. The base pay program should be aligned with or integrated with other programs.

(Greene, 2003)

Typical Pay Solutions

Base pay is a significant portion of the package for most employees, although, among executives and sales people, variable pay (such as stock options, commission, and bonuses) can be the largest portion. Getting base pay right requires that both the organization and the employee view base pay as:

- Equitable in comparison to other roles within the organization;
- Competitive in the employment marketplace;
- Providing a livable wage and affordable by the organization;
- Legal and defensible; and
- Easy to understand.

(Greene, 2003)

Two basic approaches to paying top performers and key talent are merit pay and person-based pay.

MERIT PAY. The purpose of merit pay is to pay employees based on the market value of the job, together with how well they have mastered the job and their performance in that job. Merit pay programs are limited when budgets are limited and when a system for rewarding top performers is not in place. To impact performance, the largest increases must go to the individuals who are low in their pay range, yet performing well. The smallest increases, or no increase during years when merit budgets are low, go to those who are high in their range and performing in low levels. The risk of paying the same amounts to all employees is that the highest performing individuals will leave the organization (Greene, 2003).

To ensure that a merit pay program work well, the following factors must be taken into consideration:

- The jobs must be valued both internally and for market competitiveness;
- The performance evaluation techniques and standards must be clearly communicated to employees;
- Managers must be competent at providing feedback, setting direction, providing support and evaluating performance; and
- The guidelines for merit must be clearly communicated and adhered to.

(Greene, 2003)

PERSON-BASED PAY. Another way is to pay people based on the value they bring to the organization rather than the role they are fulfilling at a certain point in time. This can be a potentially risky way to pay employees due to perceived issues around fairness and lack of clarity around common practices of this type of pay. There are three basic approaches to person-based pay including: skill-based pay, knowledge-based pay and credential-based pay (Greene, 2003). Table 9.2 illustrates these types of pay and provides an excellent framework to developing criteria for paying individuals based upon the value that they bring to your organization.

Pay Increases

It is important to achieve a balance between what employees need (in order to remain with the organization) and what the organization can

Skill-Based Pay	Knowledge-Based Pay	Credential-Based Pay
Based on the job-related skills the employee has learned or mastered. Some type of test must determine skill mastery.	Based on what an individual is capable of doing based on his or her expertise within a particular occupation or discipline. Typically defined as career ladders.	Based on formal credentials earned by an employees who serve to clearly designate who is able to serve in certain roles.

Table 9.2.   Types of Pay
From Greene, 2003

afford to pay. In an increasingly competitive world marketplace, it is more challenging for organizations to remain competitive both from an operations side and from an employee attraction and retention side. Merit increases have gone up slightly but continue to hover around 3 or 4 percent. In addition, organizations are faced with the cost pressure of increasing benefits, the costs of which outpace inflation (Dovey, 2006).

In spite of these pressures, organizations must find solutions around pay increases for top performers. Organizations must remember that top performers think and behave differently than other employees. Years of research on motivation since 1933 provide insight into motivation of individuals and the differences between top performers and less motivated individuals. McClelland's concept of achievement motivation and Herzberg's motivation-hygiene theory show that those individuals who have high achievement motivation are more interested in the job itself and look at pay as a scorecard. In other words, high-achievement motivation individuals—those individuals who are likely to be top performers—want feedback and compensation is a measure of how well they are doing in their job. Conversely, people with low achievement motivation are more interested in their work environment and how others feel about them. One way to ensure that pay increases are clearly understood and motivational to high-achievement individuals is to communicate specific, high-impact goals (Reilly, 2005).

One example illustrates how setting and communicating clear goals can impact performance as well as retention. Southeast Corridor Bank, a regional bank operating in four states with sixty branches, experienced a turnover rate of 71 percent among the tellers, compared to an industry average of 26 percent. The bank discovered that the cause of turnover was lack of opportunity for employees to advance or learn new skills, in addition to lack of pay. The organization developed a solution around skill-based pay that allowed employees to advance and earn a greater income upon learning new skills. The result was that the turnover dropped to 35 percent, saving the company nearly $2 million in one year (Phillips, 2002). In addition the organization gained increased individual performance from employees who improved their skills and as a result, likely improved their performance effectiveness.

Retention Bonuses

Historically, retention bonuses have been used to retain talent during times of turbulence and workforce reductions. As the demand for employees with critical skills increases, retention bonuses are beginning to be considered for key talent groups to keep them from leaving the organization, even during times when the organization is not facing difficult changes. For example, private-sector organizations are eager to recruit key talent from the U.S. Army Special Forces. The military is unable to compete with the compensation packages offered by private-sector firms. As a result, the military has developed a retention strategy that, among other tactics, includes a retention bonus. The military's Critical Skills Retention Bonus program offers twenty-year special operations employees in the Army, Navy, and Air Force bonus payments that range from $8,000 for a one-year service extension to $150,000 for six years. This payment is tax-free if a service member is deployed in a combat zone when the bonus is paid. Additionally, employees who are in the middle of the their careers receive and additional $375 a month in pay, and those employees with twenty-five years or more of experience receive $750 a month more. These types of programs are likely to grow in popularity as more organizations recognize that retaining critical talent even during non-difficult times is necessary (Kiger, 2005).

Pay for Performance

Pay for performance has become a way for organizations to legitimately reward top performers differently than average performers.

One way to recognize top performers is by distributing merit pay according to performance. More often than not, organizations are faced with very limited merit budgets. Merit increases of 3.5 percent and 4 percent are most common for most industries in the United States (Dovey, 2006). This poses a challenge for organizations looking for ways to reward top performers, however, experts recommend rewarding top performers double the average increase of average performers. Organizations can also use their short-term bonus plans to reward top performers differently than their lower performers. Again, a rule of thumb is that the top performers, likely 10 percent of the employee population, would receive double the average bonus pay out (Hansen, 2007).

A final consideration is that employees may be less likely to set stretch goals so that they are assured of meeting them and thus receiving a pay increase at the end of the year. Moreover, employees are less likely to indicate that they need improvement in certain areas when that could impacts their ability to earn a pay increase. But research has shown that pay-for-performance practices can be effective provided employees:

- Value the financial award for performance;
- Understand what they have to do to earn the reward;
- Believe that it is possible to reach the performance measure; and
- Believe that the company will honor its commitment to the program.

(Petrimoulix, 2007)

Employee Ownership

Employee ownership is another effective way to add to employee's total compensation package and retain all talent pools, including critical talent. USA 800 Inc., a four-hundred-employee contact and fulfillment center with offices across the United States, was experienced turnover of 70 percent until they transitioned to 100 percent employee ownership. Since this transition, the organization's revenues have increased almost 30 percent and turnover has dropped to 23 percent. In addition, the organization has been able to develop management talent from within, as opposed to recruiting from outside. Since this program began, the organization has promoted 80 percent of its managers from within (Branham, 2005).

BENEFITS

The cost of benefits continues to outpace inflation. Typically, the benefit package has many elements to it, including medical insurance, dental insurance, and paid time off such as vacation time and sick time. Other benefits may include flextime, part-time work, daytime care for sick children (taking place in a medical facility), job sharing (in which one job is shared by two employees), elder-care insurance (nursing-care coverage for elderly relatives with deteriorating health), and use of physical fitness facilities.

Need for Adequate Benefits

A 2007 study by MetLife found that employee retention is the top benefits objective among employers. Moreover, the study found that, for the first time since the study's inception, utilizing benefits as an employee retention strategy was a higher priority than controlling costs. According to the study, 72 percent of respondents said workplace benefits were the reason employees joined their current employer, and 83 percent said it is a factor for remaining there (MetLife, 2007).

As the cost of health care continues to rise, employers have been shifting more of the costs onto employees. Employees have been required to pay more for medical care through deductibles and coinsurance (Shea, 2008). In 2008, a Towers Perrin survey estimated that the average cost per employee for health-care benefits was just above $9,300 per year, up 7 percent from 2007. A study released by the Kaiser Family Foundation and the Health Research and Educational Trust found that the employers' premium costs increased an average 6.1 percent in 2007, with the average premium for family coverage reached $12,106. An average of $8,825 of that amount was reported to be paid by the employer and the balance paid by the employee (Shea, 2008).

In spite of the rising costs, employers must find a way to meet the needs of employees, especially top performers who help set the organization apart from their competitors. But providing a benefit package addresses only half of this need—the other half is communicating what the benefits do for employees and their families.

Communicating Benefits

Great benefits without good communication fall short of expressing appreciation to the employee. Although benefits such as health care and 401(k) plans can be difficult to communicate about, it's important that employees understand these benefits. To ensure that benefits are communicated effectively to all employees, the messaging must clearly describe what the benefits are, what they are worth, and how to use them. Communications should be straightforward, and all supporting documentation must support all employees so that everyone receives the same information. For effective communications following these guidelines:

- Clearly define the main message and repeat this same key message throughout the communication materials and meetings;
- Use straightforward language, yet use a conversational tone;
- Use an active voice so that employees are clear about what they need to do;
- Explain why a change occurs or why a particular program exists; and
- Describe how employees may take advantage of the benefits.

Collateral for the communication efforts include paper documents, brochures, online media, email, and PowerPoint presentations. Communicate benefits in small group meetings when possible, and utilize technology to meet live with virtual or remote employees when an in-person meeting is not possible. Ensure that materials include FAQs, forms, and tools (for example, calculators) where possible. And finally, when communicating bad news about a benefit such as terminating a current benefit or passing greater health care costs on to the employees, conduct a face-to-face meeting to allow for questions and answers and minimize the risk of resentment or anger toward the organization (Tyson, 2007).

Flexible Benefit Packages

Due to the high cost of standard benefit programs such as health care, organizations are looking for unique benefits they can offer that set them apart from their competition and allow them to attract top talent. For example, many trucking companies faced with a shortage of long-distance drivers are luring new employees by making the on-the-road workplace more like home. Features like better suspension seats, satellite radio, and cellular phones are attractive to new recruits. Moreover, the industry is recruiting more married couples as team drivers and providing larger sleeper berths, microwave ovens, and more storage space (Taylor, 2007).

In another example of offering flexible benefits, UCG, a business information publisher in Rockville, Maryland, has no set number of vacation or sick days. Instead, the company leaves it up to the employee and the manager to come up with a plan to keep customers served but provide the employees with the time off they need (Taylor, 2007).

The consulting industry faces high turnover as a result of job burnout. Consultants who travel frequently and spend time away from home are less likely to remain at the organization for a long period of time, and yet this talent is the key to the organization's success. Triage Consulting Group, based in San Francisco, sends hospital consultants on four- to eight-week projects in client cities. To make the experience easier on the employees, the company provides them with work apartments instead of hotel rooms and flies them home every weekend. If an employee chooses to stay on the job site for the weekend, the company flies a guest out to stay with them (Taylor, 2007).

Finally, as the price of gas continues to increase, employers in large metropolitan areas will be forced to address this very important economic concern. A survey conducted by WorldatWork found that 84 percent of the U.S. workforce said that they expected their employer to take measures to help offset the rising cost of gasoline. The survey revealed that employees' expectations about how their employer will provide assistance include: (1) instituting or expanding car-pooling programs (61 percent); (2) providing incentives for the use of mass transit (51 percent); (3) permitting working from home (51 percent), and (4) providing a gasoline allowance to cover additional commuting costs (42 percent) (WorldatWork, 2008a).

More interestingly, in July of 2008, Utah Governor Jon Huntsman announced the Working 4 Utah program, a condensed four-day work week program designed to alleviate the burden of soaring gas prices on many government workers. Other states are soon to follow (WorldatWork, 2008b). As the worldwide demand for gas continues to outpace the supply, the issue will continue to be important for the workforce in general, as well as for critical talent groups.

Benefit Surveys

Employees' specific benefit needs can change over time. The best way to ensure that the benefit program addresses employees' changing needs is through an employee satisfaction survey. In addition to conducting an annual employee satisfaction survey, organizations may consider conducting an annual benefits survey that is more specific to the organization's benefits. This is particularly useful for global organizations that have various benefit plans by region, as they can customize the survey items by region.

To be truly effective, benefits need to match employee needs. For some employees a great retirement plan is most important, while adult-care benefits for aging parents or on-site day care may be more important to others. Flexible organizations address the need for benefits tailored specifically to employees' needs by allowing employees to choose from a variety of benefits. For example, organizations might allow employees to buy and sell a limited number of vacation days, providing employees with different abilities to trade cash for time off and vice versa.

REWARDS AND RECOGNITION

All employees want to feel important and be recognized for a job well done. Effective rewards and recognition acknowledge great performance and motivate employees toward continuous improvement. Not only do rewards and recognition impact the individuals being recognized, but the entire organization can experience the commitment to excellence.

To be effective, rewards and recognition programs need to be credible and meaningful. If employees believe that their performance goes unnoticed or is not valued or that others in the organization are rewarded for the wrong behaviors, the programs will be demotivating to employees and result in turnover.

Need for Rewards and Recognition

Recognition contributes to both employee satisfaction and retention. A study conducted in partnership with the Saratoga Institute revealed that feeling devalued and unrecognized was one of seven primary reasons why an employee leaves an organization (Branham, 2005). While a pay increase or bonus is important to employees, less tangible benefits such as praise and a pat on the back go a long way toward making employees feel valued. In addition, providing employees with stretch assignments that are stimulating makes employees feel that they are valuable contributors.

Rewards can be one of the keys to avoiding turnover. Rewards often are more effective if they are immediate and appropriate. Most important, they should be personal or relevant to the employee. Key talent or top performers may be motivated by different rewards or recognition programs than those of the general employee base. For example, top performers may be more interested in and feel more rewarded by significantly challenging projects or speaking at a conference, whereas the general employee base may be more motivated by serving on a special committee or attending a conference.

Designing a Rewards and Recognition Solution

To be truly effective, rewards and recognition programs must align with what is most motivating to employees and align with the organization's interest. In a ground-breaking study of 845 workers on the state of the work ethic, researchers found that "being recognized for individual contributions" was one of the top four motivators for encouraging employees to invest extra effort into their work (Yankelovich & Immerwahr, 1984). Specifically, rewards or recognition programs that communicate respect from peers and included employees in important business strategy formulation are especially motivational. In addition, recognition can also come from outside the organization, such as friends and the local or professional community (Davenport, 1999).

Use the following guidelines to create an effective rewards and recognition solution for your organization:

1. Make rewards and recognition available immediately by having a clearly developed program unencumbered by red tape. Managers

giving rewards must have the authority to make decisions without having to go through a lengthy approval process.

2. Ensure that rewards and recognition are appropriate to the behavior being recognized.

3. Create relevant rewards and recognition programs that fit the needs and interests of the target audience. While the general population may be motivated by a $200 spot bonus, top performers may be more motivated by the opportunity to attend or be supported to speak at a prestigious conference.

Ideas for rewards and recognition solutions that may appeal to key talent groups are

- Any opportunity to enhance special skills such as speaking at or attending a prestigious conference, support for authoring an article in an important journal or blog, or to participate in a unique development program, either internally or externally;
- Presenting work in front of peers;
- Teaching or training at a college or university;
- Participating in a unique or special project that is highly visible or important to the overall strategy of the business;
- Interaction with senior executives; or
- Participating in a mentoring program, either as a mentor or mentee of a highly regarded individual.

In addition, small acts of recognition can be important to all employees. Sometimes, a personal note from the CEO or a senior manager may mean more than a generic company award.

Meaningful and Motivational Rewards

Finally, to design effective rewards and recognition programs, it is important to understand what is motivating for individuals. A manager who gains a sense of accomplishment from reaching year-end business goals and also works to receive a bonus associated with that accomplishment is both intrinsically and extrinsically motivated. Three primary factors influence whether employees are intrinsically motivated (1) the individual's personal characteristics; (2) the nature of the role; and (3) the nature of the organization. Contrary to popular belief, non-cash rewards can be more effective than cash rewards. In a study by WorldatWork, non-cash reward programs were found to achieve three times the return on investment, compared with cash-based programs. In a recent Incentive Federation survey, it was discovered that, on average, 79 percent of respondents said that non-cash reward programs were effective in motivating employees to achieve sales and marketing goals (Daniel & Metcalf, 2005). These findings are further supported by a study by the International Society of Performance Improvement that revealed that when incentive programs were implemented and tracked correctly, individual performance increased by an average of 22 percent. In addition, team incentives increased performance by as much as 44 percent (Daniel & Metcalf, 2005).

In summary, it is important to first discover which types of rewards and recognition programs are most valuable to your key talent groups before designing and implementing solutions.

Retaining Top Performers

As stated, any organization may benefit by rewarding top performers, rather than average performers. In a study by Hudson, IT workers are more likely to believe that their organization will give a greater pay to stronger performers (Rasmussen Reports, 2005). Part of the secret to GE's success in attracting and retaining top performers is that the organization is focused on identifying its top performers and then generously compensating them. GE's compensation program rewards top performers as much as possible and employees understand the "payback" that comes with superior results (Welch & Welch, 2008).

Employees who are viewed as the most talented seem to want the assurance that, if they perform better, they can increase their earnings (Branham, 2000) This approach of focusing rewards and recognition on top performers as a retention strategy is validated by the research. Research has demonstrated that compensation packages were the third and fourth most important factors in retaining top performers (Harpur, 2002) and in a study of a critical talent group of knowledge workers, linking pay to performance was a primary factor in determining the commitment of these employees to the organization (Kinnear & Sutherland, 2000).

Performance Management

Performance management is the ongoing dialogue between an employee and his or her manager to ensure that the employee is working on the right goals and meeting or exceeding expectations. Regular feedback is essential. In fact, job satisfaction may be linked to a work environment that enables performance. When all employees have the coaching, feedback, and development they need to be successful, they perform better and also report feeling better about their jobs (Caudron, 2001). Without feedback, employees are working in a vacuum and, as stated earlier in this chapter, high-achievement individuals are even more interested in receiving feedback. Interestingly, in a pay and performance report by Hudson, 34 percent of those surveyed said that they rarely or never receive a formal performance review and another 34 percent were unsure about the review criteria (Rasmussen Reports, 2005).

Need for Performance Management

The impact of individual job performance on turnover has been researched for years. A study by Randstad showed the 86 percent of employees said that feeling valued by their employer was necessary to stay happy in their jobs, yet only 37 percent of those same employees said they received the feedback they needed to feel happy (Randstad Work Solutions, 2006). The impact of this on turnover can be significant. In a study conducted by an Australian international banking organization of nearly four thousand employees in 611 branches and business outlets, it was shown that job performance impacts voluntary turnover (Iverson & Deery, 2001).

Performance problems can play out and result in turnover in several ways. First, employees who do not perform well move to another organization to avoid the consequences of their poor performance. Other employees who are performing poorly but are not aware of their poor performance might be "shocked" by a poor performance review and seek employment elsewhere. And employees who feel that their performance is at least average but under-valued might decide to leave an organization. Recent studies of top performers and key talent has shown that the positive feedback afforded by such processes as performance management is essential to the retention of key talent. Studies in the financial services industry have found that a sense of self-esteem and knowing that one's opinions were listened to were in the top ten issues for key talent groups (Harpur, 2002).

Communicating the Performance Review

A key component of performance management is communication between the manager and the employee. In addition to providing for an exchange of important information, communication allows managers and their employees to develop trust. One study found that a perceived sense of honesty of management by key talent groups was the most important determiner of retention of these talent groups (Harpur, 2002).

The importance of open, honest feedback was illustrated in a recent survey of managers who received ratings from their employees about whether or not their organization had a good performance management process. The group of managers who received high, positive ratings from their employees was compared with those managers who received low, negative ratings about their company's performance management process. The primary factor in whether or not employees believed the company had a good performance review process was communication that the employees had with their managers. Managers with high, positive ratings had direct reports who said that their managers provided frequent feedback and partnered with them to create goals. Managers who received low, negative ratings from their employees about the performance review said that their managers focused on the review form and the process of the review rather than on the content of the review (Lounsberry, 2007).

Setting goals that are clearly linked to the organization's overall performance helps the organization achieve those goals. In addition, employees feel connected to the business and feel that their role contributes to a greater purpose. Ideally, goals are communicated to all employees. A well-designed performance review process serves to answer the following questions for employees:

- How am I doing?
- Am I on track?

- What am I doing well?
- What can I do better?
- How will the organization help me improve?

Aligning Performance Goals with Strategic Objectives

Before designing a performance management system, an organization must identify its strategic goals. To better understand why organizations fail to execute on strategy, Franklin Covey surveyed over 250,000 global leaders in more than two thousand organizations across eighteen industries and discovered four main reasons why execution breaks down. The research revealed that only 15 percent of employees know the goal that they are to be working toward; only 15 percent of employees know what to do to achieve the goal; only 12 percent keep track of how they are doing; and only 26 percent are held accountable to reaching their goals. In effect, although the goal-setting process is key to organizations hitting their numbers, they do not necessarily ensure that each employee understands his or her role (Simpson, 2007).

Goals need to be aligned from the top of the organization to the individual level. For example, an organization might have a goal to increase market share by 20 percent. At the individual level, an employee might align his or her individual goal to the corporate goal by helping to design and develop new marketing materials to improve market share. Alignment helps individuals feel engaged by helping them to understand how what they do on a day-to-day basis contributes to organizational success.

Key Components of Successful Performance Management

Managing performance with all employees, including critical talent, is key to maximizing organizational performance. Nucor Steel, one of the very few remaining steel companies in the United States, has a unique pay program linked to its performance management program. Employees receive up to 25 percent of their salary based on return on assets (ROA) and can also earn money based on their individual performance. While their base pay is lower than industry average, they can receive a bonus for exceptional performance if they exceed hourly quotas. Employees see a direct relationship between their performance and their pay, and the organization has high productivity and low absenteeism (Smith, 2001).

To ensure a successful performance management program, consider the following:

1. *Align performance with top-line organizational objectives.* Give employees a clear line of sight to the overall organizational goals and ensure that goals are in alignment with them.

2. *Create goals in partnership with employees.* When setting individual goals, create goals in partnership with employees by discussing organizational goals and best ways that employees can align their individual goals to the overall business strategy.

3. *Ensure that goals are specific, measurable, attainable, realistic, and time-oriented.* In particular, create real stretch goals that will create a sense of meaning and purpose for high-achievers and top performers.

4. *Create opportunities for ongoing dialogue.* Engage in real conversations with employees about performance. Performance management should be a positive experience that helps employees gain a sense of energy and commitment toward learning and contributing.

5. *Keep employees on track.* Pay attention to when employees begin to slip on performance goals and help them get back on track by recognizing their barriers to success and helping them to overcome these roadblocks.

6. *Conduct positive quarterly, mid-year, and end-of-year reviews.* Conduct regular reviews to check in on progress toward end-of-year reviews. Focus on development of the employee.

7. *Provide rewards for performance.* All employees need to understand how their individual performance pays off at the end of the year. Reward employees according to the level of their contributions.

In summary, performance management is an excellent way for organizations to align individual and organizational goals so that everyone is working toward a common purpose. The performance management solution also helps employees understand how their roles link to the overall organizational objectives. When poor performance management is the cause of turnover, the nine key components of the performance management solution listed above can help to improve retention.

FINAL THOUGHTS

Adequate and equitable pay is one of the critical reasons employees, including top talent choose to remain in an organization, and pay is more than "dollars and cents." Pay is significant in that it also acknowledges an employee's worth and the value of his or her contribution. In this chapter we presented guidelines for selecting the best pay solutions and some typical pay strategies, such as pay for skill and knowledge and retention bonuses.

In some instances, employees have a greater need for benefits than for pay. Some typical benefit solutions, such as medical insurance, day care for children, and elder-care insurance were discussed. Providing a benefit program that addresses of the specific needs of employees will help to promote employee satisfaction and improve retention.

In addition to pay and benefits, employees need to be recognized for a job well done. We offered guidelines for designing a rewards and recognition program that will contribute to both employee satisfaction and retention.

Finally, we addressed the often-difficult topic of performance management, explaining how a performance review can be used to align individual goals with organizational objectives. We presented nine key components for an effective performance management solution.

References

Adams, B.; Mahaffey, G., & Norm, R. (2002). Omaha, NE: First Data Resources. [Interviewed by author.]

Branham, L. (2000). *Keeping the people who keep you in business.* New York: AMACOM.

Branham, L. (2005). *The seven hidden reasons employees leave.* New York: AMACOM.

Caudron, S. (2001, February). Job satisfaction may not be everything. *Workforce*. www.workforce.com.

Daniel, T.A., & Metcalf, G.S. (2005, May). The science of motivation. SHRM white paper. www.shrm.org/hrresources/whitepapers_published/CMS_012666.asp#P-4_0

Davenport, T. (1999). *Human capital: What it is and why people invest in it.* San Francisco, CA: Jossey-Bass.

Dovey, C. (2006, January). Compensation trends. SHRM white paper. www .shrm.org/hrresources/whitepapers_published/CMS_011730.asp.

Greene, R.J. (2003, September). Effectively managing base pay: Strategies and programs for success. SHRM white paper. www.shrm.org/ hrresources/whitepapers_published/misc/CMS_005590.asp.

Hansen, F. (2007, November 5). Pushing money toward the top. *Workforce Management*, p. 44.

Harpur, A. (2002). *Retention factors affecting knowledge workers in the financial services sector.* Unpublished MBA project report. Johannesburg: University of the Witwatersrand.

Herzberg, F., Mausner, B., & Snyderman, B.B. (1959). *The motivation to work.* New York: John Wiley & Sons.

Hutchins, J. (2002, March). How to make the right voluntary benefit choices. *Workforce, 81*(3), 42.

Iverson, R.D., & Deery, S.J. (2001). Job performance and voluntary turnover: An examination of linearity, curvilinearity, and the moderators of time, unemployment rate, and perceived ease of movement using event history analysis. *Academy of Management Proceedings*, 1.

Kiger, P. (2005). Keeping your best troops. *Workforce.* www.workforce.com/archive/feature/24/15/59/index.php?ht=

Kinnear, L., & Sutherland, M. (2000). Determinants of organisational commitment among knowledge workers. *South African Journal of Business Management, 31*(3), 106–112.

Liang, K-G. (2000, June). *Dissertation Abstracts International: Section B: The Sciences and Engineering, 60*(11-B), 5818.

Lounsberry, C. (2007). *Compensation and performance management comparison.* Seattle, WA. Corbis. [Interviewed by author.]

McClelland, D.C. (1958). *Talent and society: New perspectives in the identification of talent.* Princeton, NJ: Van Nostrand.

MetLife. (2007). As talent wars escalate, U.S. employers rate "retention" as the top benefits objective, ahead of controlling costs, according to annual MetLife study. *General News: 2007 Press Releases.*

Moss, B. (2000, December). Chain of loyalty. *SDM: Security Distributing and Marketing, 30*(15), 79.

Pay for performance report. (2002). Newark, NJ: Institute of Management and Administration, Inc.

Phillips, P.P. (2002). *Retaining your best employees.* Alexandria, VA: ASTD.

Petrimoulix, S. (2007, January). *The problems with pay-for-performance plans (and what to do about them).* Alexandria, VA: SHRM. www.shrm.org/rewards/library_published/compensation/nonIC/CMS_019977.asp.

Randstad Work Solutions. (2006). *2006 employee review.* Atlanta, GA: Randstad Work Solutions.

Rasmussen Reports. (2005, June). *Survey: Tenure trumps performance for determining pay.* Alexandria, VA: SHRM Compensation and Benefits Forum. www.shrm.org/rewards/library_published/compensation/nonIC/CMS_012971.asp

Recruit and retain. (2000, November). *National Petroleum News, 92*(12), 48.

Reilly, M. (2005). Pay for performance or pay for the masses? WorldatWork. www.3ccomp.com/TrendsIssues/Pay_for_Performance_or_Pay_for_the_Masses_.pdf

Reimers, B.D. (2001, August 6). Keep talent from taking flight. *Network Computing, 12*(16), 42.

Shea, T.F. (2008, January). No turning back. *HR Magazine.* www.shrm.org/hrmagazine/articles/0108/0108Shea.asp, Jan. 2008.

Simpson, M. (2007, February 23). [recording of Franklin Covey's monthly web-cast]. *The four disciplines of execution.* Salt Lake City, UT: Franklin Covey.

Smith, G. (2001). *Here today, here tomorrow.* Chicago, IL. Dearborn Trade Publishing.

Taylor, S. (2007, October/December). Red-carpet treatment. *Staffing Management Magazine.* www.Shrm.org/ema/sm/articles/2007/1107taylor.asp Oct-Dec, 2007

Thorness, B. (2007, June). Best places to work 2007. *Seattle Business Monthly.*

Tyson, R. (2007, August 24). Dear workforce: How do I effectively present our benefits program to employees? *Workforce Management.*

Welch, J., & Welch, S. (2008, January). Give till it doesn't hurt. The Welch way. *BusinessWeek.* www.businessweek.com/magazine/content/08_06/b4070092840947.htm?chan=careers_the+welch+way_the+welch+way.

Wheatley, C. (2001, October 23). British software services firm Logica plots course for good year. *Sunday Business.*

WorldatWork. (2008a, June 19). *Employees expect help with soaring gas costs.* www.worldatwork.org.

WorldatWork. (2008b, July 1). *Energy costs push Utah to move to four-day workweek.* www.worldatwork.org/waw/adimComment?id=27058#.

Yankelovich, D. & Immerwahr J., (1984). Putting the work ethic to work. *Society, 21*(2), 58–76

CHAPTER TEN

Build Motivation
and Commitment

In the previous three chapters we discussed the typical needs that all employees, in particular top performers and critical talent has in the workplace as well as the ways to address those needs. In this chapter we present some final solutions and explore the issues of building commitment and growth. Table 10.1 shows the six employee needs for all employees including critical talent groups around motivation and commitment and the organization's solutions for meeting these needs.

QUALITY OF LEADERSHIP

Great leaders inspire confidence in employees and motivate them to stay in an organization. In addition to setting strategy and making the right decisions about the direction of the organization, effective leaders are able to guide, coach, and mentor employees. Each organization has its own unique culture and performance needs. The challenge for any organization is to develop the right individuals into leadership roles, resulting in retaining key employees. Typical leadership solutions include developing leadership competencies, creating leadership development plans, training, hiring consultants,

Category	Need	Solution
Quality of Leadership	To have a leader who is respectful and one who inspires employees	Provide leadership mentoring and coaching, development training, and development
Empowerment	To be involved in job decisions and allowed to take actions on job issues	Implement an empowerment program
Teamwork	To be part of a supportive, productive team	Create team-building programs; build effective, productive teams
Trust and Integrity	To work in a trusting and ethical environment	Implement an ethics program; treat people fairly, openly, and honestly
Organizational Commitment	To be attached to the company, the team, and other employees	Create team-building programs that improve employee commitment at all organizational levels
Professional Growth and Career Advancement	To have a variety of skills and competencies. To have the opportunity to grow and prosper with the organization	Offer a variety of training and development programs to improve skills. Implement a career management system

Table 10.1. Needs and Solutions for Building Motivation and Commitment

role modeling, coaching, and participating in on-going development such as reading discussion groups.

Need for Effective Leadership

Some experts argue that the most important measure of leadership is the leader's ability to retain employees. In a review of 19,000 exit interviews from employees, a leading cause of turnover was attributed to employees' loss of trust and confidence in senior leaders (Branham, 2001). Good managers and leaders are pivotal to employee retention and even more so for critical talent as they have a greater choice about where to work. In a landmark study of more than 80,000 interviews conducted by The Gallup Organization, the front-line managers was identified as key to attracting and retaining talented employees. By focusing on great leadership, organizations can impact employee retention (Buckingham & Coffman, 1999).

Developing Leadership Competencies

In order to select and develop the most appropriate leaders for an organization, leadership competencies must be developed. These competencies need to align with current and future business requirements. To be effective, these competencies must be lined-owned. In other words, the senior business leaders must be able to articulate the behaviors required of leaders throughout the company that are necessary for business success. If the competencies are developed solely by HR, they are only important to HR, and the behaviors will not be reinforced and role-modeled by senior leaders. Once competencies have been developed, leadership training and development must focus on these key competencies. With clearly defined competencies, plans for and training to improve specific skill levels can be developed.

One way to identify competencies is by expressing them as a distinct set of talents, skills, and knowledge that are unique to fulfilling customer's and investor's expectations. This concept is known as Leadership Brand, a term coined by David Ulrich and Norm Smallwood. Leadership Brand is described by organizations that organize their people to serve customers, motivate their employees to be customer-focused, and measure their success through customer behavior. Organizations that have implemented this approach include GE and Johnson & Johnson, among others. For example, GE's tagline is "imagination at work," and the organization is known for developing leaders who are both conceptual and decisive. They can take imaginative concepts and put them to work by creating products for the company.

Johnson & Johnson has effectively aligned its leadership competencies with its brand in the marketplace. Johnson & Johnson's credo statement, which reflects its values, begins with, "We believe our first responsibility is to the doctors, nurses, and patients, to mothers and fathers, and all others who use our products and services." The organization is known for its leaders who develop high-quality, scientifically sound products and services. Leadership competencies include social responsibility and product development in a disciplined way. What these two organizations have in common is that their leadership competencies reflect their marketplace brand, ensuring alignment in what their employees do and what the market expects from the company. Not only is this level of focus and alignment attributed to the organization's ability to retain talented employees, but it also plays out positively for these organizations as measured by price/earnings ratio. When price/earnings ratios of organizations with a strong leadership brand were compared to their competitors, they had consistently higher p/e ratios (Ulrich & Smallwood, 2007).

Creating Leadership Development Plans

The purpose of leadership development plans is to identify the competencies for which an individual excels and those that need improvement. By understanding their weaker areas, managers can develop those specific competencies. Generally, a manager conducts a self-assessment of his or her competencies by referencing a competency model. The supervisor also conducts an assessment of the manager, by utilizing the same competency model. Upon completion of the assessments, both the supervisor and the direct report meet to discuss the competency assessment and identify successful demonstration as well as areas to improve. Sometimes, a 360-degree assessment can be used. A 360 assessment asks the manager's peers, subordinates, and superiors to assess the manager's behavior. The results are compiled and provided to the manager being evaluated. This feedback can be used to develop or refine the manager's development plan. In this way, a leadership development plan can be implemented to track, measure, and assess leadership improvement.

Training

Leadership training must be aligned with the organization's desired leadership competencies. It may be conducted in a classroom setting, via e-learning, or through a combination of both.

Top companies recognize the link between developing great leaders to run the business and employee retention. A 2007 study of top companies for leaders conducted by Hewitt revealed that nearly all of the top companies measured the overall effectiveness of leadership in their organizations, compared to only 59 percent of all other companies. In addition, 94 percent of these top companies also tracked retention of key employees as a measure of leadership success (Hewitt, 2007).

Training for new managers is usually focused on the basic skills that managers need to master to be successful in their new roles. Macy's new manager training, "Lights, Camera, Action: A New Store Executive's Guide to Stardom," trains new managers on the basic skills managers need to be successful. This program includes training on how to run meetings, complete performance evaluations, and interview job candidates. The senior leadership at Macy's recognizes the importance of leadership training to the success of its business. "Sales and profit are our number one objective, but retention is our number one priority," states Macy's CEO. "We couldn't afford for our turnover to get any higher at the same time we were enjoying good business," said the human resource group vice president (Breuer, 2000).

One organization that has utilized leadership training to reduce turnover is Bubba Gump Shrimp Company, a chain of twenty-five restaurants based in San Clemente, California. The restaurant industry has long been recognized as one plagued by high turnover, however, Bubba Gump Shrimp was intent on developing the most competent, motivated, and loyal talent group possible. The restaurant chain estimated that they were spending 10 percent of its estimated annual sales per year in recruiting costs alone due to turnover. One element of the of the restaurant's solution to reduce turnover included training and development. Since establishing their training programs, turnover in the managerial ranks has reduced from 16 percent down to an industry low of 8 percent (Kranz, 2007).

Mentoring and Coaching

Today's organizations are leaner and faster moving than in generations past. More importantly, employee loyalty to the organization is no longer a given and, to gain trust and respect from employees as well as to energize them, leaders must excel at interpersonal skills such as communication and relationship skills. In addition, to create a culture that values these behaviors, leaders must effectively model strong interpersonal skills. It's no longer enough to only expect strong personal skills from senior leaders; today's front-line supervisors as well as mid-level managers must demonstrate competence in the soft skills. Unfortunately, organizations find these skills increasingly in short supply, which creates a demand for leaders who have mastered both the functional skills of a leader and the soft skills. Despite all of the progress made in leadership training, structured, classroom or online leadership training alone is still unable to develop employee soft skills (Sherman & Freas, 2004).

Mentoring and/or coaching are two appropriate solutions for developing the interpersonal skills of leaders. Both mentoring and coaching work with the objective to increase the leader's work-related effectiveness within the work/organizational culture; however, there are distinct differences in the way that the mentoring and coaching works. For example, mentoring is done by an individual who has a track record of success in the topic that the mentee wants to improve or learn about. The mentor is an advise-giver and, at times, a door-opener. The mentor does not need to have any specific training or certification to be a mentor; but must have or build credibility with the mentee.

A coach, on the other hand, must have participated in training specific to coaching and be certified as a coach to call him- or herself a coach. In addition to a coaching certification, a coach may also have an education in psychology or organization development. A coach and his or her client work together toward very specific, identifiable goals and are held accountable to the organization to meet those goals. Unlike a mentor, a coach does not provide advice and does not "tell" the client what to do, but rather uses provocative questions to expand the individual's awareness and desire to change (Nielson, 2006). Coaching is not the right solution for every leader, and careful thought should be given to using it as a solution, especially as it is an expensive solution. For example, when a leader does not know "how to" do something, training, mentoring, or advising is an appropriate solution and usually the least costly.

In an example of the impact of coaching on retention, in 2006, a global media company faced 12 percent turnover of first-year employees. New hires were voluntarily departing the company prior to their one-year anniversary due to stated chaos, disorganization, and confusion within the organization, which were likely caused by the number of new employees. Through a coaching program, new hires learned how to navigate the organization and get the direction and support they needed to be successful. The program positively impacted retention and produced a 251 percent ROI (Edwards & Lounsberry, 2008).

Reading and Discussion Programs

In addition to more formal approaches to learning such as classroom-based training or formal mentoring and coaching programs, leaders can develop their leadership awareness and knowledge through reading and discussion programs. In these types of programs, participants read books relevant to leadership, such as business strategy, qualities of successful leadership, and operational excellence. Typically these books align with the necessary leadership competencies of the organization. The reading group may have a written assignment based on the reading that they report out and generally a discussion is held about the book and practical applications are reviewed.

Many leadership books and materials exist. Exhibit 10.1 lists the ten most popular books on leadership from Amazon.com.

1. *Good to Great: Why Some Companies Make the Leap . . . and Others Don't* by Jim Collins
2. *Predictably Irrational: The Hidden Forces That Shape Our Decisions* by Dan Ariely
3. *The Four-Hour Workweek: Escape 9–5, Live Anywhere, and Join the New Rich* by Timothy Ferriss
4. *Nudge: Improving Decisions About Health, Wealth, and Happiness* by Richard H. Thaler and Cass R. Sunstein
5. *StrengthsFinder 2.0: A New and Upgraded Edition of the Online Test from Gallup's Now, Discover Your Strengths* by Tom Rath
6. *The Black Swan: The Impact of the Highly Improbable* by Nassim Nicholas Taleb
7. *Stop the 401(k) Rip-Off!: Eliminate Costly Hidden Fees to Improve Your Life* by David B. Loeper
8. *Getting Things Done: The Art of Stress-Free Productivity* by David Allen
9. *The Five Dysfunctions of a Team: A Leadership Fable* by Patrick M. Lencioni
10. *The Tipping Point: How Little Things Can Make a Big Difference* by Malcolm Gladwell

Exhibit 10.1.   Top Ten Best-Selling Leadership Books on Amazon.com

EMPOWERMENT

Employees are empowered when they have clear lines of authority, have the responsibility of making decisions about their work, and are supported in their decisions. Being empowered allows employees a way to exercise authority and control within the span of their job. Top performers and critical talent groups who are fully capable of doing exemplary work will feel stifled if they are not empowered to make decisions about their work. Leaders and managers throughout the organization are wise to empower all to make their own decisions; however, a culture is not open to the concept becomes uninspiring for everyone and is difficult for managers and leaders to overcome.

Need for Empowerment

Empowerment has been shown to have a positive impact on organizations. When employees are empowered in their jobs, they take more responsibility for what they produce, which results in higher-quality products and services, less absenteeism, better decision making, timely problem solving, and lower turnover (Dennison, 1984). For example, technicians at General Electric (GE) plant in Durham, North Carolina, who represent a critical talent group for GE, work on some of the world's most powerful jet engines and are empowered to make changes when necessary. When technicians install any of the ten thousand parts in engines that weigh up to 8.5 tons, they sign off on each step of the process by inputting their initials into the computer terminal. That signoff step is not just for accountability. When employees find something isn't working as planned, they have the authority to make a decision to make it work correctly. The result is that employees take ownership and responsibility of the decisions that they make (Fishman, 1999).

Empowering employees not only makes employees feel positive about their work, but also pays off for the organization. A study of managers who were empowered to make decisions about how they wanted to improve the results of a company-wide survey within their own teams or departments found that their survey results in the following year significantly improved (Lounsberry, 2008). The managers benefited from the positive associations they had by making their own decisions about how to approach the problems revealed in the survey, and the company benefited by having improved survey results in the following year.

Empowerment Solutions

Level of empowerment varies based on the size of the company, the nature of the work, and the situation. For example, in smaller organizations, it is relatively easy, and in fact, necessary, to expand an individual's authority and responsibility. However, larger, more complex organizations generally have a difficult time empowering employees due the multiple layers, standard processes, and decision-making procedures.

A smaller organization that has seen how empowerment impacts retention is Allyis, a technology firm based in Bellevue, Washington. Allyis fosters a culture of trust, empowerment, and accountability that has resulted in 95 percent retention of its critical technology employees. Key to making empowerment work in this organization is understanding that mistakes do happen, but what is most important is to learn what to do differently next time (Hewitt, 2007). The added benefit of empowerment to the organization is the knowledge it retains from its mistakes. Because retention is high, the learning that occurs as a result of any mistakes remains in the organization, rather than the organization going thru the pain of making the mistake again with a new employee.

A larger organization that has effectively used an empowerment solution to retain critical talent is Children's Hospital in Omaha, Nebraska. The shortage of nursing talent is dramatically impacting the healthcare industry. This poses a real challenge for hospitals, both as it relates to scheduling and to critical talent retention. Nurses who consistently work long hours are more prone to making errors and more likely to be dissatisfied with their organization, making them more likely to leave if they don't get the work hours they want. Children's Hospital implemented a solution that empowered nurses to schedule their own work hours. While it's too soon to evaluate the impact that this solution has on retention of nurses, management of Children's Hospital is hopeful that the freedom to schedule one's own work hours will result in improved retention (Rafter, 2008).

Clearly, organizations that empower their employees experience less turnover. When employees can see that they have a choice and can control the quality of their work, they are happier in their jobs. Key elements of empowerment include levels of empowerment, structure, timeframe, and review process.

Potential Problems

While empowerment can positively impact an organization, if not managed properly, it can have a negative effect. For example, when an organization is not clear about which decisions employees have the authority to make, or when employees are not equipped with guidelines about how to make decisions, the potential for error and mistakes greatly increases. Finally, for empowerment to build trust within the organization, the leaders and managers must be willing to accept that employees will make mistakes and that employees must have the opportunity to learn from their mistakes. If employees are not given this opportunity to learn from their errors and are instead punished, all trust between the employee and employer will be lost.

Factors of Empowerment

Effective employee empowerment has significant benefits to the organization when the following factors are considered:

Level of empowerment defines the situations and freedom that employees have to make decisions and take action without seeking additional approval. If the level is not clarified, employees may assume more authority than has been granted. Additionally, if the organization does not communicate the reasoning behind these levels of empowerment, employees may feel a lack of satisfaction or feel a sense of frustration.

Structure of empowerment identifies who can give authority for empowerment within the organization. One way to ensure that the proper structure has been set up is to establish an office that monitors performance and advocates for empowerment changes. This ensures that empowerment levels that are hurting the organization are modified or changed.

Timeframe of empowerment defines the expected length of time for the empowerment structure. In order to assume the responsibility they desire, employees may need weeks or months to be trained in key areas.

Finally, *the review process* evaluates the successes of and areas for improvement of empowerment. Without a review process, there is no opportunity to maintain what is working well and change what needs to be improved.

TEAMWORK

A team is a group of employees working together toward a common goal. Typically, teams are set up with the idea that productivity and effectiveness improve as a result of processing work within organized groups. In addition to coordinating actions and improving communication, employees also typically experience bonding and develop trust and respect for one another.

Need for Teamwork

All employees want to be part of a supportive, productive team. A 2001 Australian study of teams in seventeen private- and public-sector industries found that organizations with team structures had higher labor productivity, a flatter management structure, and reduced employee turnover (Glassop, 2002).

Teamwork can be a part of the retention solution when other means of retention fail. A survey of mid-level administrators of a large public doctoral research university found that the administrators had high satisfaction levels, but turnover rates were also high. The survey revealed that teamwork had a positive impact on morale and a substantial indirect effect on intent to leave (Edwards, 2001). Organizations can increase the likelihood that teams will remain intact by creating closely knit teams to carry out projects (Cappelli, 2000).

Building Teams

Teams are often created to serve a specific purpose or to accomplish a specific goal such as developing a new product, improving a process, or improving a work culture. The goal of such a team must be clearly identified so that employees know when the goal is achieved. When employees are a part of a group it helps them to have a sense of belonging and purpose.

Whole Foods, an Austin, Texas-based organic and health food store with 270 locations in the United States and the United Kingdom, is well-known for its democratic operating style and innovative teamwork. Each of the stores is composed of an average of ten self-managed teams with identified team leaders and clear performance targets. In addition, all of the team leaders of a store are a team; the store leaders of all of the regions are a team; and the regional presidents of all of the regions are a team. Teams are involved in decisions that would normally be left to managers in other companies. For example, teams make hiring decisions and are supported with an open-book approach to the finances—everyone can see the financial performance of the business. While team collaboration works throughout the organization, teams also compete against each other for bonuses, recognition, and promotions on specific performance measures such as store quality, service, and profitability. In addition to low turnover, this 100 Great Places to Work organization's efforts to make empowerment, autonomy, and teamwork the foundation of its business has paid off. The grocery retail industry is notorious for low profit margins, but because of its teams, net profits at Whole Foods are double industry average (Fishman, 2006).

Team Chartering

A team charter is a written document that clarifies the purpose of the team, the specific goals of the team, and roles and responsibilities of team members. A charter must have leadership support to be effective. A team charter includes:

- Purpose—identifying the end product of the team
- Goals—stating clear and achievable goals
- Authority—defining levels of power and responsibility
- Roles—establishing the power of the team leader and team members
- Division—creating the division of work
- Process—defining how problems may be raised, addressed, and solved; identifying how the team will respond to requests for information, products, and services

The team charter concept comes from quality management principles such as Deming management philosophy and Six Sigma. In addition to utilizing the team charter to communicate and clarify roles and responsibilities, it is an effective way to clearly define the purpose and desired outcome of the team as well as decision-making authority. Some organizations utilize a "coach" to facilitate the team chartering process. The coach is trained in quality management or Six Sigma principles and partners closely with the team leader. Initially, the coach plays a significant role at the start of the team project and, gradually, over time diminishes his or her level of involvement by transferring greater responsibility for managing the team to the team leader.

Virtual Teams

As the economy continues to become more global, many critical talent groups such as technology employees are working in virtual teams. A virtual team is a group of people located around the country or the world to accomplish a specific task or goal. Just like other teams, virtual teams are used to develop new products, improve processes, or resolve other critical organizational concerns. Many challenges exist with running effective virtual teams, including cultural differences, time zone constraints, greater likelihood for communication problems, and lack of group bonding due to distance. In a study by SHRM, several best practices in creating effective virtual teams include:

- Find creative ways to build team trust such as finding a way to work face-to-face at regular intervals, implementing specific ways to recognize individuals regularly through e-mail and voice mail;

- Overcome time zone constraints by setting regular conference calls and clearly identifying due dates and times;

- Adapt technology to the team's needs by setting up a separate site for team members only where individuals can post and share work;

- Establish agreed-on rules such as how meetings are run and ensure that everyone participants in conversations;

- Build an easy-to-reference knowledge database that reminds members who has expertise or knowledge about specific areas; and

- Overcome cultural barriers by educating the team at the beginning about possible cultural differences.

While virtual teams pose some specific barriers to creating loyalty among team members, with careful planning, virtual teams can be as productive as non-virtual teams (Rosen, Blackburn, & Furst, 2006).

Fostering Interpersonal Relationships

Effective teamwork is dependent upon good working relationships among team members. When teams are able to develop interpersonal relationships that help them to rely on each other, they can be more effective. People can establish connections with others in many ways. Some examples include luncheons, dinners, outdoor recreational activities, contests, motivational meetings, brainstorming sessions, and personal development activities. Members can learn more about each other's personal communication style or personality types through assessments such as DiSC or MBTI. In addition, team members might select symbols or mementos that help team members affiliate themselves with the team, such as tee-shirts, mugs, or caps. The purpose of all of these is to foster a sense of belonging and to improve teamwork.

One organization that has used teams to reduce turnover is River-Point Group, an information technology consulting organization that once experienced turnover of 60 percent. The turnover was attributed to the fact that most of the company's employees worked offsite, in isolation from each other. To create a stronger common culture and unite their critical talent groups to each other, the company now schedules quarterly staff meetings and social outings so that employees can become better acquainted. In addition, to ensure "face time" and bonding, account managers are required to go onsite with the associates. Finally, when employees start new projects they receive bagels at the new worksite and birthday cake on their birthdays. The result has been dramatic. Turnover dropped 25 percent (Branham, 2005).

Building Teams Through Recognition

As noted in the previous chapter, recognition is a driver of employee retention. This also applies to teams. When awards to the team are meaningful and motivational, dedication to the team is fostered. One example of rewarding teams is illustrated by Harrah's Hotel and Casino. Harrah's has more than eight hundred employees and strives to retain them through team rewards, recognition, feedback tools, and compensation. A special chairman's award goes to teams that go above and beyond normal job expectations.

TRUST AND INTEGRITY

Surveys of exit interviews have shown that a loss of trust and confidence in senior leaders and/or one's immediate supervisor is one of the key drivers of turnover. Specifically, this study found that one reason employees leave an organization is that they believe that senior leaders are out of touch with reality, greedy, lack concern and appreciation for employees, are isolated from employees, and mismanage change (Branham, 2005). All is not lost, however. In his book *Speed of Trust*, Stephen M.R. Covey defines thirteen leadership behaviors that provide the foundation for trust:

1. Talk straight
2. Demonstrate respect
3. Create transparency
4. Right wrongs
5. Show loyalty
6. Deliver results
7. Get better
8. Confront reality
9. Clarify expectations
10. Practice accountability
11. Listen first
12. Keep commitments
13. Extend trust
    (Covey, 2006).

Organizational integrity is the degree to which behaviors of organizational leaders match what they say. Communication must be timely, accurate, and honest. When there is bad news to share, leaders need to release information to employees as soon as it's available. If leaders wait to share information, employees may perceive that they are being kept in the dark and that either leaders don't care or do not trust employees with information. Even when the news is bad and involves potential layoffs, employees trust leaders who tell the truth and are careful not to gloss over details or place too much positive spin on the message.

Not only must the organization communicate honestly, but it should also follow through on what is says it will do. For example, if the organization states that it is going to implement a new bonus plan within a certain timeframe, it should do so. If it is unable to implement the plan when promised, the organization should be forthcoming as to why it cannot meet its promise. Keeping promises is a central criteria for integrity.

Need for Trust and Integrity

Although it may seem too "soft" to measure, trust has been linked to organizational financial performance. Consulting firm Watson Wyatt has found that organizations with high employee trust levels outperform organizations with low trust levels by as much as 186 percent (King, 2003). A recent survey of the American workforce has shown that the level of distrust in the workplace and in senior leaders is significant. Eight-two percent of respondents said that they believe executives work to serve themselves at the expense of the organization. Moreover, only 39 percent of workers said that they trusted leaders, and only 50 percent of respondents said that they believed the managers in the organization are concerned for the well-being of the employees (Branham, 2005).

Additionally, an organization's ethical climate directly influences employee job satisfaction and employees' commitment to the organization (Schwepker, 2001). In fact, the Ethics Resource Center (ERC), a Washington, D.C.–based nonprofit educational organization, found a direct correlation between employee satisfaction and employers' ethical practices. High ethical standards and satisfied employees mean lower turnover (Ethics Resource Center, 2001).

Developing Supervisory Trust and Integrity

The basic foundation of a functional team is trust between the team and supervisor (Lencioni, 2005). All employees, including critical talent and top performers, expect and want supervisors who are competent, trustworthy and ethical. When organizations hire and promote people who are both competent and capable of forming positive and trusting relationships with subordinates, the result is positive for everyone—the organization, leaders, and employees.

When behaviors do not match words, trust deteriorates. To develop trust and integrity, organizations must require that supervisors act with integrity and keep their commitments. In addition, organizations can reward leaders and employees who tell the truth, even when it might be easier to exaggerate accomplishments. Finally, leaders who treat employees fairly, openly, and honestly build trust. Trust can be sustained through team-building activities (Heathfield, 2002). Whether trust is built by the leader or through the expectations and actions of the organization, it is an important part of employee retention.

Developing Organizational Trust and Integrity

Organizational integrity is key to developing and sustaining employee trust. At the basic level, organizations must have clear policies and practices that are fair and provide a mechanism for employees to seek equity if they are not perceived as fair or equitable.

Examples of betrayed trust have been plentiful in recent years. The most well-known example of betrayed trust can be seen in the Enron scandal. When Enron misused the funds of employee 401(k) retirement accounts, employees' entire life savings vanished. Employees were devastated both emotionally and financially because of the unethical behavior of Enron's corporate officials. When senior executives demonstrate truthfulness and ethical behavior, employees are able to trust the organization.

The publicity following the Enron scandal surfaced additional corporate scandals. In fact, the Sarbanes-Oxley Act of 2002 was enacted to deal with the increasing number of corporate scandals. Ethics are based not only on organizational values, but on organizational behaviors. For example, Enron's stated corporate values were communication, respect, and . . . integrity. Clearly, a statement of values is not enough. Leaders must *live the values* in order for the values to mean something.

Employees develop trust for the organization when they can answer "yes" to the question, "Does the organization treat all employees equally?" While this does not mean that everyone receives the same pay, benefits, the same work hours, or the same work responsibilities, it does mean that employees believe that the treatment of employees is fair. For example, is the timing of pay increases are consistently distributed to all employees throughout the organization and is the review process the same for everyone. In addition, employees are more likely to trust an organization when pay and perks of the executives are not dramatically different from those of the rest of the employees. In fact, when profit sharing, which is often targeted only for the most senior leaders, is available for the entire employee population, employees are more likely to develop a sense of trust and fairness for the organization.

Finally, employees must feel that there is a fair mechanism in place for them to resolve issues. Employees need to know that there is a process to follow to resolve complaints. This can be as simple as an open-door policy for employees to express their concerns to their supervisors or to the next-higher level of management.

One excellent example of how to create and sustain trust among all employees, including key talent, is demonstrated by Yarde Metals. While organizations can attempt to train employees to be more trusting or kinder to others and can even expect ethical compliance, a better way to gain employees' trust is to be transparent and share their profits with employees. Yarde Metals has many employee perks such as a company nap room, an on-site kennel for employees' dogs, and a work-out facility, but it's their management practices that develop employee trust. Yarde was a privately held organization until 2006, but has been transparent about the finances of the organization since the company began in 1996. Each month, employees learn about the company's financial status and, since its inception, the company shares one-third of its profits with employees. The company credits its open-book management style to its ability to pull through a particularly tough year in 2001. The leaders of the organization communicated with employees that if the company did not make a gross profit of 1.85 percent, they would default on the bank loan. Employees committed themselves to helping the company reach that target goal and as a result the organization was able to hit its financial goals (Marquez, 2007). Establishing trust with employees not only serves employees but serves the organization.

Ethics Programs

The Sarbanes-Oxley Act of 2002, along with the public shame felt by leaders of organizations who demonstrated unethical behavior, have done much to ensure that organizations communicate, support, and reinforce ethical behavior. Still, organizations feel the weight of ensuring that their employees comply with the law or may be held liable for unethical practices within their organization.

The director of organizational programs for the Society for Human Resource Management (SHRM) and an ethics specialist lists six key aspects to an effective ethics program:

- Make ethical behavior a priority and communicate the ethical position;
- Obtain buy-in for an ethics program and solicit help for maintaining the program;
- Appoint an HR manager (or executive management leader) to assume the role of chief ethics officer;
- Create an ethics task force that creates a statement of ethics pledging the organization's commitment to ethical behavior;
- Require that management models high ethical standards; and
- Require ethics training sessions using real-world scenarios and provide support programs and an ethics hotline for employees who find themselves conflicted about appropriate conduct on the job.

(Ethics Resource Center, 2001)

Professional Codes of Ethics

Many professional groups have established codes of ethics that govern their behavior and professional conduct. For example, the International Coaching Federation (ICF) has a code of ethics and also operates as a certifying organization of individuals who wish to be coaches. Their code contains general moral imperatives as well as specific professional responsibilities. There are numerous examples of industries and professions adopting codes of ethics, including home inspectors, realtors, electrical engineers, computer programmers, journalists, ecologists, sociologists, civil engineers, reporters, fundraisers, archivists, Internet professionals, photographers, auditors, travel agents, lawyers, and health care professionals (Google.com).

Leadership and Ethical Behavior

Integrity, trust, and ethical behavior cannot exist in an organization if the leaders do not demonstrate these behaviors and hold their subordinates accountable for the same behaviors. Only the leaders of an organization can build the foundation of trust. They must model trustworthiness, honesty, and ethical behavior. When leaders are found to "fudge" or exaggerate numbers in order to achieve goals, it sends a mixed message to employees. Leaders should demonstrate only the highest standards, which does have an impact on talent retention.

ORGANIZATIONAL COMMITMENT

Commitment to the organization has become known as "employee engagement" and describes the degree to which an employee is so committed to an organization that he or she will invest extra effort in the work. Organizations can benefit greatly from such highly engaged employees. High levels of organizational commitment promotes retention of talent, improved customer loyalty, better organizational performance, and stakeholder value (Lockwood, 2007). Consider that employee turnover is not a single event, but rather a process of disengagement (Branham, 2001), and that employees who are not committed are more likely to eventually leave the organization as they become less and less engaged.

Need for Commitment

Employee commitment has consistently been shown to be related to turnover. One study has shown that employees with the highest level of commitment are 87 percent less likely to leave the organization (Lockwood, 2007). In addition, commitment is also associated with productivity. Employees with the highest level of commitment perform 20 percent better (Lockwood, 2007).

Employees who are involved in their work processes, such as conceiving, designing, and implementing workplace and process changes, are more likely to be committed to the their jobs and to the organization. In a recent study of 132 manufacturing firms, employees who had this level of involvement in their work processes also had higher productivity (Lockwood, 2007).

Forms of Commitment

There are two main forms of commitment:

- *Rational Commitment*—the degree to which a job serves an employee's financial, developmental or professional self-interest
- *Emotional Commitment*—the degree to which a job serves an employee's values, enjoyment and belief in what they do

(Buchanan, 2004).

Each of these forms of commitment is distinct. Employees may be committed to the organization because it fulfills a logical and rational need to provide an income or source of financial stability. An employee may also be committed to a job because it serves a long-term purpose related to career goals and professional needs. However, emotional commitment, gaining a sense of meaning and joy, is where discretionary effort kicks in. Emotional commitment has four times the power to impact performance; yet only 11 percent of the workforce is committed that level. Thirteen percent of the workforce has very little commitment at either the rational or emotional level, and the remaining 76 percent of the workforce is somewhere in the middle, with strong commitment to one aspect of the job, such as income, and can take or leave the rest. More importantly, the lesser the degree of commitment, the greater the likelihood that the employee will leave the organization (Buchanan, 2004).

To increase and maintain commitment from employees, an organization must address both forms of commitment listed above.

Building Employee Commitment

Think of the employee who chooses to stay late to help a co-worker with a client project that is due in the morning; or the employee who talks proudly of his or her organization to friends and encourages them to apply for an open position at the organization. When employees are both rationally and emotionally committed to an organization, they willingly go above and beyond the call of duty. Committed employees are more likely to:

1. Put more into their job then required by their job descriptions;
2. Invest this extra effort when needed; and
3. Focus extra effort on the most important priorities.
   (Johnson, 2006)

Commitment can be measured in business impact and positive commitment can result in significant cost savings to an organization. For example, Molson Coors, a Denver, Colorado–based company, found that employees who were committed and engaged were five times less likely to have a safety incident and seven times less likely to have a lost-time safety incident than their non-committed counterparts. The cost of a safety incident for the committed or engaged employee was only $63, compared to an average of $392 for the non-committed employee. As a result of improving employee engagement, the organization was able to save $1.7 million in safety costs in 2002 (Lockwood, 2007).

Good management practices are central to building employee commitment. Specifically, managers must be clear about business goals and how employees' individual roles contribute to that goal and provide positive feedback or re-direct behaviors when necessary. Celebrate successes. Finally, managers need to recognize that everyone is unique and that they must find ways to maximize people's performance and feelings of success by plugging them into roles that leverage their natural abilities.

Organizing Work Around a Project

One way to effectively build commitment is to organize employees around a specific project. When the project goes well, employees receive the credit, which increases their prestige and helps to establish commitment because the team members don't want to let other team members down. The higher the standards are for performance, the greater the commitment is to quality and to the other team members. The auto industry is one example where organizing employees around a project has improved employee commitment and made improvements in quality and overall employee performance (Cappelli, 2000).

IDENTIFYING EXPECTATIONS AND BENEFITS. Identifying expectations and the benefits of meeting those expectations also helps to build commitment, even in temporary or short-term employment. In a temporary job, employees understand that they will eventually have to leave. However, when organizations explain expectations and help them achieve the benefits of completing their temporary work assignments, commitment can be created. Employees with positive experiences may remain committed long after they leave the organization. For example, McKinsey and Company is famous for the level of commitment it enjoys from its former consultants, even after layoffs. Another example was at the Wharton School, where members of the first-year class were asked to explain how they were managed in their previous jobs. Nearly without exception, those employees who worked in temporary jobs, such as for an investment bank as a junior analyst, were positive about their former employers. The reason was due to receiving a clear idea of organizational expectations, what was gained through their efforts, and knowledge of their fixed departure date (Cappelli, 2000).

Measuring Commitment

Many organizations measure employee commitment to improve productivity and gain insight about potential turnover concerns. The Gallup Organization has identified twelve indicators that link employee commitment to productivity, profitability, retention, and customer satisfaction. These indicators, now known as Q12, are measured by the following questions in its assessment:

1. Do you know what is expected of you at work?
2. Do you have the materials and equipment you need to do your work right?

3. At work, do you have the opportunity to do what you do best every day?

4. In the last seven days, have you received recognition or praise for doing good work?

5. Does your supervisor, or someone at work, seem to care about you as a person?

6. Is there someone at work who encourages your development?

7. At work, do your opinions seem to count?

8. Does the mission/purpose of your company make you feel your job is important?

9. Are your associates (fellow employees) committed to doing quality work?

10. Do you have a best friend at work?

11. In the last six months, has someone at work talked to you about your progress?

12. In the past year, have you had opportunities at work to learn and grow?

(Buckingham & Coffman, 1999).

PROFESSIONAL AND CAREER ADVANCEMENT

Professional growth is about continued development, including learning additional skills, acquiring new knowledge, or personal development that allows for improved interpersonal relationships or opportunities for advancement. Professional growth may consist of taking educational courses, receiving internal training programs, experiencing a new assignment that requires use of new skills, becoming certified or licensed in a new function or participating in professional associations. Professional growth benefits both the employee and the organization.

Need for Professional Growth

As job uncertainty becomes more common, all employees, and in particular top performers and critical talent groups, must be able to grow in their careers by improving skill sets and gaining experience in desired positions so that they can advance in the organization, remain valuable to the organization, or be easily employable elsewhere. Professional growth may mean that employees work in areas that lead to new challenges, such as special projects or being a part of special teams, but professional growth goes beyond leadership development or training programs described earlier in the chapter. Unless leaders address individual career development, employees are always likely to move to another organization (Story, 2002).

Higher Education Programs

Another way for employees to experience professional growth is by receiving additional education through high schools, colleges, and universities. Such programs are a means through which employees can improve knowledge and skills. One federal agency faced 38 percent turnover of its technical specialists. This placed a strain on the agency to recruit and train new employees. While exit interviews revealed that employees were leaving for higher competitive salaries, the agency was unable to compete with private-sector salaries. Adding to the problem, the agency found that they needed to continuously update the technical skills of the employees. However, the annual employee survey revealed that employees had an interest in an internal master's degree program in information science. The agency implemented a solution to offer such a program in-house and saw a decrease in turnover and resulted in a 153 percent return on investment (Phillips & Phillips, 2002).

Licenses and Certificates

Another way to offer professional growth is through a license or cer- tificate. One organization that has created such a program in which its management team can achieve improved professional growth is JD Wetherspoon, a chain of English pubs. This organization has introduced a professional qualification program for its managers to improve the career path of its staff and improve retention. Wether- spoon has thirteen thousand employees and had been working on retention for five years because of its high turnover problem. The chain, which will be adding another ninety pubs to its present 570, is now establishing formal education that will be required for all management. According to Wetherspoon's personnel and training director, "It's part of an ongoing drive to help staff build a career path in the pub industry. We want to send out the message that you can join the trade, get good training, a professional qualification, and move up the career ladder." The course is being developed in cooperation with Leeds Metropolitan University and is called the "Professional Diploma in Licensed Retail." It will last two years and consist of workplace training and a series of exams. Wetherspoon has reduced front-line staff turnover through improved pay and training from 180 percent in 1997 to around 48 percent. The turnover among management has dropped from 25 percent to 12 percent (Pub Group Sets Course. . ., 2002).

Developmental Assignments and Projects

In addition to structured training or education, employees can develop their careers through interesting work assignments and development stretch assignments. This type of on-the-job training can offer new challenges, such as special projects or working on a process-improvement team. A developmental assignment should be suited to the abilities of the employee, but also allow for the individual to stretch and learn something new. For example, let's assume that a relatively new employee might be assigned to compile and organize a technical training manual for shift supervisors. Teamed with a boss who outlines specifics, the employee can gain experience in the organization and meet presenters from different departments. The employee would be able to research different aspects of the company and demonstrate initiative in bringing the project together. The result would be personal growth and hands-on orientation with others in the organization.

When designed well, developmental assignments can prepare employees for more responsibilities. These assignments require employees to use skills that are not required on the job. New projects and assignments provide a way through which employees can increase skills on the job through doing new tasks. Critical to employee success in these situations is the guidance and assistance of leadership. With mentoring, employees can undertake new assignments that both increase their own knowledge and skill level and meet the organization's goals. Employees who experience professional growth are more inclined to remain with the organization.

FINAL THOUGHTS

In this chapter and the previous three, we described the needs of employees in the workplace, along with possible solutions to these needs. In this chapter we specifically addressed motivation and commitment. Solutions offered include empowerment and team-building programs, building trust, displaying ethical behavior, offering opportunities through training, and employee development for job growth and career advancement. By satisfying key needs, organizations can strengthen employee commitment and loyalty and reduce turnover.

References

Branham, L. (2001). *Keeping the people who keep you in business: 24 ways to hang onto your most valuable talent*. New York: American Management Association.

Breuer, N. (2000, August). Shelf life: Retaining employees in the retail trade. *Workforce Management*.

Buchanan, L. (2004). *The things they do for love*. Boston, MA. Harvard Business School Press.

Buckingham, M., & Coffman, C. (1999). *First break all the rules*. New York: Simon and Schuster.

Cappelli, P. (2000, January/February). A market-driven approach to retaining talent. *Harvard Business Review*, *79*(1), 103.

Covey, S. M.R. (2006). *The speed of trust*. New York: The Free Press.

Denison, D.R. (1984). Bringing corporate culture to the bottom line. *Organizational Dynamics*, *13*(2), 5–22.

Edwards, L., & Lounsberry, C. (2008). *Measuring ROI in coaching for new-hire employee retention: A global media company*. San Francisco, CA: Pfeiffer.

Edwards, R.L.R. (2001, August). The morale and satisfaction of midlevel administrators: Differentiating the constructs and their impact on intent to leave. *Dissertation Abstracts International Section A: Humanities and Social Sciences*, *62*(2-A), 482.

Ethics Resource Center. (2001, June 15). Ethics plans pay off in staff retention and profits. *HR Briefing, 7*.

Fishman, C. (1999, October). Engines of democracy. *Fast Company*, pp. 270–280.

Fishman, C. (2006, April). Whole Foods is all teams. *Fast Company*.

Glassop, L.I. (2002, February). The organizational benefits of teams. *Human Relations, 55*(2), 225–249.

Google.com. (2002, October). (Search: Code of Ethics).

Heathfield, S. (2002). *Trust rules! The most important secret.* Available: http://humanresources.about.com/library/weekly/aa041401a.htm

Hewitt, M. (2007, January). Finding and keeping the best: Three ways to ensure that employees stay. *Workforce Management.* www.workforce .com/archive/article/24/62/99.php?ht =

Hewitt Associates. (2007). *Top companies for leaders.* www.hewitt associates.com/_MetaBasicCMAssetCache_/Assets/Articles/2007_ Top_Companies_NorthAmerica_Highlights_100507.pdf.

Johnson, L. (2006, August). *Motivating employees to go above and beyond.* Boston, MA: Harvard Business School Press.

King, R. (2003, November). Great things are starting at yum. *Workforce Management.* www.workforce.com/archive/feature/23/54/58/index.php?ht =

Kranz, G. (2007, June). A menu for management. *Workforce Management.* www.workforce.com/archive/feature/24/97/14/index.php?ht =

Lencioni, P. (2005). *The five dysfunctions of a team.* San Francisco, CA: Jossey-Bass.

Lockwood, N. (2007). *Leveraging employee engagement for competitive advantage: HR's strategic role.* Alexandria, VA: Society for Human Resource Development.

Lounsberry, C. (2008). Seattle, WA: Corbis. [Interviewed by author.]

Marquez, J. (2007, June 25). Opening up the books to win workers' trust. *Workforce Management,* p. 45.

Nielson, C. (2006, April 24). Dear workforce: What is the distinction between coaching and mentoring? *Workforce Management.* www.workforce.com/archive/article/24/77/33.php?ht =

Phillips, J.J., & Phillips, P.P. (2002). Using an internal degree program to reduce the turnover of technical specialists: An ROI approach. In J.J. Phillips & P.P. Phillips (Eds.), *Action: Retaining your best employees.* Alexandria, VA: ASTD.

Pub group sets course to push staff retention. (2002, April 16). *Personnel Today,* 3.

Rafter, M. (2008, May). Right on schedule. *Workforce Management.* www.workforce.com/archive/feature/25/53/55/index.php?ht =

Rosen, B., Blackburn, R., & Furst, S. (2006, May 23). *Technology and training.* SHRM Foundation Research Grant. Alexandria, VA: Society for Human Resource Management.

Schettler, J. (2002, March). Federated Department Stores, Inc. *Training,* *30*(3), 65.

Schulte, L.E. (2001, December). Undergraduate faculty and student perceptions of the ethical climate and its importance in retention. *College Student Journal, 35*(4), 565.

Schwepker, C.H., Jr. (2001, October). Ethical climate relationship to job satisfaction, organizational commitment, and turnover intention in the sales force. *Journal of Business Research, 54*(1), 39–52.

Sherman, S., & Freas, A. (2004, November). The wild west of executive coaching. *Harvard Business Review.*

Story, M. (2002, March). Winning the battle for talent. *New Zealand Management, 49*(2), 39.

Ulrich, D., & Smallwood, N. (2007). *Leadership brand: Developing customer-focused leaders to drive performance and build lasting value.* Boston, MA: Harvard Business School Press.

CHAPTER ELEVEN

Match Solutions to Needs

A s discussed in the previous four chapters, a wide range of solutions are available to organizations that want to reduce turnover. The challenge is to match the solution to the cause of turnover. In some cases, the cause of turnover is clear and the best solution to address the cause is very clear. More often than not, pinpointing the right solution to the cause of turnover is neither easy nor obvious. Too often, organizations apply solutions that are not related to the cause of turnover, or apply too many solutions, rather than focusing on the priority of the various causes of turnover. Ways to determine the biggest drivers or causes of turnover and present your conclusions to various groups so that a proper solution can be found are covered in this chapter. Only the solutions with maximum payoffs should be attempted. In addition, we will explore ways to avoid mismatches, along with techniques to ensure the match you choose is appropriate and effective.

COMBINING DATA FROM DIFFERENT SOURCES

In Chapter 5 we explored the various approaches to determine the causes of turnover. Frequently, multiple methods are used so it is necessary to combine the data in a meaningful way in order to identify and address the primary causes of turnover. For example, some organizations review their annual feedback survey results to determine causes of turnover. Or they may review exit interview data or conduct focus groups to explore specific reasons why employees are leaving. The challenge is to combine and organize the data in a meaningful way that allows the organization to decide on appropriate solutions. The approach to use depends on the consistency of the data from various sources.

Ideally, all of the data sources point to the same causes of turnover and the task is to combine the data so that it illustrates their priority. In some situations, considering the most important causes of turnover may be as simple as reviewing the strength of the data. For example, if the input measure is on the same scale (for example, a 5-point scale), it is much easier to identify the most important causes of turnover. However, this situation is less likely because some data sources are more credible than others, some input is more reliable than others, and some input scales are different. The challenge lies in addressing the inconsistencies.

There are four basic considerations when managing inconsistent and conflicting data from different sources. The first consideration is to let the relative strengths and weaknesses support or cancel each other. This is a mathematical approach. For example, if one report shows the need for flexible working hours as the number 1 reason for turnover, but another source has this problem listed as number 5, then a convenient average of the data is used. The downside is that the main cause of turnover may be located somewhere between numbers 1 and 5.

A second consideration is to examine the relative strength of the data. For example, if the nominal group technique was used and the number 1 cause of turnover was unfair treatment by supervisors, by a wide margin, this information should not be ignored, even if this information did not come up from another data collection technique. Strength of the ranking always must be a consideration.

The third consideration is the credibility of the data-collection method. Was the data collected anonymously? Did respondents have an opportunity or a reason to be biased? Was there a motive for respondents to provide data that is either inaccurate or purposely distorted? The most critical consideration here is the objectivity of the data and the credibility of the source. For example, anonymous data will be more credible if the respondents clearly perceive that the data-collection process *is* anonymous. Other methods, such as the nominal group technique, can be used to refine the input, digging deeper into the issue, and using the synergy of the group to help understand why people make decisions to leave an organization. The nominal group technique is more credible when the groups represent a cross-section of the target population. The point here is that you must rank the data sources in terms of their credibility.

The final consideration is to use expert input from individuals who understand the retention issues in the organization the best. These may include human resource specialists or team leaders from the areas where the turnover is occurring. Individuals need not have ownership of the solution; but must have knowledge about the retention issue. The group can use consensus to decide the actual causes of turnover, given the conflicting data sources. More information about consensus decision making is provided later in the chapter.

DETERMINING THE SIGNIFICANCE OF THE CAUSE

After all of the data has been combined, the next step is to judge the relative strength of the cause. The main task here is to determine how much turnover is being impacted by a particular issue or could be prevented by addressing that particular issue. The starting point is to determine the relative strength of the cause to develop the potential payoff for addressing a particular cause. Four methods are appropriate to tackle this issue.

First determine the most impactful cause of turnover by examining relative rankings of the data. For example, on the annual feedback survey, the highest-rated issue is likely to be driving the highest percentage of turnover. After examining the data, allocate the percent

Turnover Cause	Points	% of Total	% of Turnover
#1. Inadequate Pay	252	21.8	7.6
#2. Feedback and Recognition	193	16.7	5.8
#3. Ability and Opportunity	102	8.8	3.1

Sample Calculation:

Total points from the Nominal Group Process –all causes	1155
Total points for number 1 cause	252
Percent of total (252 ÷1155)	21.8%
Total turnover rate	35%
Turnover rate allocated to number 1 cause (22% × 35%)	7.6%

Exhibit 11.1. Allocation of Turnover

of turnover to various causes. For example, it might be seen that the top ten issues account for 80 percent of the turnover. If the turnover rate is 30 percent, 24 percent (80 percent × 30 percent) is caused by the top ten reasons. That 24 percent should then be allocated according to the relative strength of the rankings. In another example, each ranking determined from using the nominal group technique could be translated into turnover, assuming that the points assigned represent all causes of turnover. Exhibit 11.1 shows a sample calculation for the first three causes of turnover, taken directly from a nominal group progress data.

In this example, a 35 percent turnover in an 820-employee group results in 287 turnovers in a given year. The number one cause of this turnover, inadequate pay, accounts for 21.8 percent of that figure, or 63 turnovers. In other words, if the perception of inadequate pay was removed, there would be 63 fewer turnover statistics in the group during the year.

A second way to isolate the most important cause of turnover is to ask participants to provide input. As the data are collected (either by survey, focus group, or interviews), the participants should be asked to indicate the percentage of turnover that is caused by a particular issue. Although this is an estimate, it can be adjusted for error by applying techniques described later in this book. One way to gather this information from participants is to ask participants to allocate the turnover causes in a pie chart with the end result representing 100 percent (that is, all turnovers during a specified time period, such as a month or year, are considered a complete pie). Participants

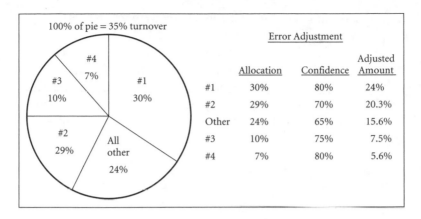

Figure 11.1.   Allocation of Turnover

then indicate their level of comfort with each of their allocations. As participants consider each piece of the pie, they indicate the level of confidence they have with the allocation to a particular cause. Figure 11.1 shows a sample pie chart from a group using this method.

Participants may report the same level of confidence for each of the allocations, or they may be more comfortable with some allocations than others. After allowing participants to reflect on the certainty of their estimations, multiply the two percentages, discounting by the level of confidence to allow for error. For example, if participants indicated that 30 percent of turnover is caused by unfair treatment from supervisors and they are 80 percent confident, then at least 24 percent (30% × 80%) of the actual turnover can be attributed to this particular issue.

A third method to determine the most significant causes of turnover is to use the experiences of others. For example, if other organizations have found that problems with the direct supervisor account for the majority of turnover, this may mean that finding solutions to this problem should be given a higher priority. Experience gained through previous projects should also be used to reach a conclusion about the relative strength of any cause.

The fourth method of determining the most significant cause of turnover is to use the input of an expert, that is, those who may understand the causes of turnover and have an understanding of the relative strength of those issues. Examples of internal experts include the HR staff and the line managers directly involved in the areas where turnover is excessive.

It is important to bring all of those who are familiar with and affected by the turnover problem together to decide on the best solutions. The group must understand the underlying assumptions and clarify any issues in an entirely open manner before coming to a agreement about which solutions should be used to address the turnover problem.

PRESENTING DATA FOR DECISION MAKING

After organizing the data gathered from various sources, the next step in the process is to present the data to the primary stakeholders of the project, showing the relative priority of the causes. It is important to present the data in a way that is clear and simplified. Three very simple methods can be used, although others could be appropriate.

Pie Charts

One of the most common ways to present any type of data is to utilize a pie chart. Three to five "slices" work well. The largest piece of the pie would reflect the most significant cause of turnover; the second largest cause would be the second, and so on. Figure 11.2 is an example of a pie chart on the causes of turnover.

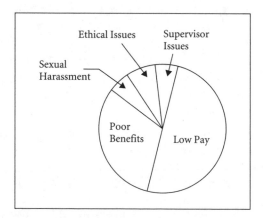

Figure 11.2.   Causes of Turnover

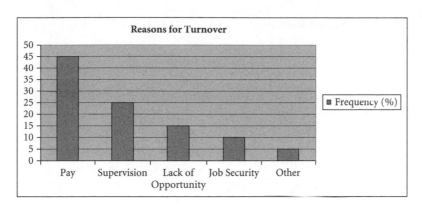

Figure 11.3.   Pareto Chart on Turnover

Pareto Charts

The Pareto chart is a way to display information so that the most critical issues are easily recognized. Once the priorities are determined, the percent of their impact is revealed. The example in Figure 11.3 shows a Pareto chart on the causes of turnover in a particular situation.

In this figure, four primary causes of turnover are identified and the remaining causes are combined into one category. Pay is identified as the most critical cause and accounts for 45 percent of the total turnover. The quality of supervision is next and accounts for 25 percent of the turnover problem. Lack of opportunity is the next cause, accounting for 15 percent of turnover. The chart quickly illustrates the key problem areas and the causes that must be addressed. Pareto charts can be used in three potential scenarios.

1. The original turnover problem can be presented in terms of regions, job categories, race, and ethnic backgrounds, or any combination totaling 100 percent. The chart will reflect where the turnover has occurred most often.

2. The chart can also be used to display the actual causes of turnover, as was illustrated in Figure 11.3. Detailing the causes in chart form quickly reveals the areas where attention is needed.

3. Finally, Pareto charts can be used to reflect the actual costs of turnover and illustrate which categories represent the most critical turnover costs. This can give impact to a presentation when showing a fully loaded cost profile.

Trend Lines

Another basic method for presenting turnover data is the use of trend lines or line charts. Trend lines show changes over a designated period of time. The most likely use of these charts would be to track turnover to show the effect of other events that have occurred during the time frame that might influence turnover (seasonal or otherwise). Another way to use a trend chart is to plot turnover by regions or job groups to show how the turnover varies in different categories. Finally, the causes of turnover could be displayed over time. For example, a certain category of responses from exit interview questions could be plotted to show the monthly reasons for leaving. The most common measure could be charted to show how turnover causes are changing and to measure reaction to a particular solution designed to decrease it.

MATCHING SOLUTIONS TO NEEDS

The most difficult part of the process is to match the best solution or solutions to the needs or causes of turnover. This is as much an art as it is a science. Several principles should be followed during this process to ensure that the solution addresses all the needs or causes.

A cause can't automatically be translated into a solution. Not every cause has an obvious solution. For example, if managers are not providing positive feedback or creating a supportive work environment, it does not necessarily mean that they need training. Too often a training solution is identified when, in fact, other solutions may be more appropriate. Ensure that you know enough about the cause to identify the right solution. In other words, if managers are not providing positive feedback or creating a supportive environment, is it because they don't know how to do it (a training issue), is it because there's been no requirement (a policy issue), or is it because there has been no role modeling for that type of behavior (a coaching issue)?

Some solutions are obvious. Some causes point directly to a solution. If the employees need more flexibility in scheduling their work hours, flexible scheduling is the obvious solution. If employees need the flexibility to work at home, telecommuting is an appropriate solution. Although there are important design issues, the solutions become obvious in these situations.

Solutions can come in different sizes. Solutions come with a full range of possibilities and represent a broad scope of investment needs and levels of complexity. For example, if employees have expressed a need for better child care, the solution could range from identifying recommended child-care facilities to operating an on-site center completely funded by the organization. It is helpful to understand what would be considered an acceptable solution to prevent turnover, versus not addressing the issue at all.

The design of the solution is critical. Because there may be a wide variety of solutions, the actual design of the solution is often just as important as finding the solution. For example, if employees indicate that they want their salary connected directly to their performance, there are dozens of ways to fulfill this need; however, some designs may be counterproductive and perhaps create more problems, whereas others can be very motivating and uplifting. The design should be considered in relationship to the cause of turnover to ensure that any concerns are addressed. This may mean that more analysis is required to find what would actually correct a problem.

Some solutions take a long time. While some issues may respond to a short-term fix, such as flexible working schedules, others will take a long time to rectify. For example, if employees are leaving because of the public image of the organization (bad press, recent negative events, tarnished image, etc.), it could take a long time to repair the situation. It has to start from the top of the organization. This must be recognized early and it may take a long time to build trust and credibility with all of the employees.

Solutions should be tackled for the highest priority items first. While this is an obvious principle, it requires further discussion. Those issues causing the most turnover are also those demanding the most attention, perhaps even the most investment. The next section describes this issue in more detail.

Designing a solution under these guiding principles will serve to identify the appropriate mix of solutions so that an effective solution to resolve major issues can be designed. The results of these steps are easily presented as a matrix diagram.

Using a Matrix Diagram

A matrix diagram is a way to organize a large group of information. It can be used to arrange the information so that elements are logically connected and presented in a graphic form. A matrix also shows the importance of each connecting point in a relationship and presents the relationships that exist among these variables. The matrix diagram can be "L" shaped, where there is one column across the top and one down the side of the page, or it can be "T" shaped, in which two columns containing two types of data are compared with a third.

In Figure 11.4 a "T" shaped matrix diagram presents a plan to reduce turnover in four job groups. The job groups with the most turnover in this large banking organization are listed at the top of the matrix. Six causes of turnover are identified along the middle of the diagram, with each matched to a job group. Listed at the bottom are the solutions that are matched to the particular causes. For example, Install Pay for Skills is aimed primarily at the branch teller group and

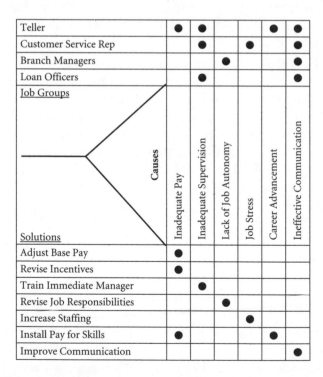

Figure 11.4.   Matrix Diagram of a Plan to Reduce Turnover

focuses on both the concern about inadequate pay and the lack of career advancement. As an alternative, words can be used in place of a dot to indicate the relative priority, strength, or importance of a particular cause, solution, or job group. Matrix diagrams provide an excellent way of summarizing information about turnover causes and relating them to job groups, regions, or other breakdowns. In addition, as shown in Figure 11.4, it can also be used to relate to solutions.

SELECTING SOLUTIONS FOR MAXIMUM PAYOFF

The next step is to make sure that the focus is only on those solutions that will have the maximum payoff. Two major issues can affect that payoff: the cost of the solution and the monetary benefit from the implementation. To achieve the maximum payoff, costs should be considered—the smaller the cost, the greater the potential payoff. (ROI will be covered in detail in the next two chapters.) From the benefits side, the greater the benefits, the greater the potential payoff. Several issues must be considered.

Short-term versus long-term costs. Some solutions, such as building a day-care center, will be very expensive to implement on a short-term basis. This solution will have high initial cost for the organization and may not be feasible. Other solutions, such as implementing an incentive plan, may have very little up-front cost, but a tremendous long-term expense   one that may exceed the actual payoff. Compensation plans are usually perceived as long-term and to be carefully considered before implementing. The short-term versus long-term cost implication always must be considered.

Consider forecasting ROI. Chapter 12 illustrates a method for forecasting the ROI forecast for a solution. Such a forecast can be developed showing the expected monetary benefits compared to the projected cost of the solution. The solutions with the highest forecasted ROI value become the best prospects for implementation.

The time needed for implementation. Some solutions can be implemented quickly, while others will take a long time. This may mean that long-term solutions should be implemented in conjunction with short-term fixes. In other words, the organization should recognize that both quick fixes and long-term changes are in store. This shows employees that the organization is taking steps now and also building for the future, which results in enhancing commitment and loyalty.

Avoid Mismatches

As possible solutions are considered, the impact of a mismatch must be taken into consideration. If a solution proves to be inappropriate, what will be the consequences? Some mismatches can result in tremendous morale issues. For example, having to discontinue an employee incentive plan can affect job satisfaction. Mismatches can cause three major problems:

1. The funds are wasted because money is spent on a solution that didn't correct the problem and drained the organization's resources.

2. Some solutions have a negative impact if they're inappropriate. For example, if training is implemented as a solution when there's no deficiency in knowledge and skills, the impact can be adverse. The participants being trained (for example, supervisors or managers) may resent the training because they've been coerced into participating in a program that has no value for them or develop skills that they already possess.

3. When time, effort, and money are spent on a solution that is mismatched, an opportunity to implement the correct solution has been missed. This may be more important because an unmet need still exists—the cause is still there, still causing damage to the organization while resources have been wasted on other solutions.

The message: Avoid mismatches at all costs!

Tackling Multiple Solutions

There is no clear answer to whether an organization should tackle a turnover problem with more than one solution at a time. To a certain extent, the answer depends on the relative priority of the causes. Clearly, too many solutions undertaken at the same time can reduce the potential effectiveness of each of the solutions and result in confusion and waste.

It is essential to examine the top priorities to determine which are feasible, given the current resources, the time it takes for implementation, and the level of involvement needed from others. This may translate into taking on three or four (five, at the most) solutions. Beyond that, it may be too much of a problem. Avoid the quick fix, especially if it is not a quick-fix issue. Most turnover problems are not solved through quick-fixes and are usually issues that have evolved over time (either internally or externally). As a result, they will take time to correct.

Consider the level of involvement and support needed for the solution. Most employees must be involved in the solution in some way, requiring time away from routine duties or time to keep track of what's being developed. The level of support from managers is also important. They need to be supportive of solutions and their implementation. How much they can (or are willing to) support is an important issue.

Finally, the available resources are a very important issue. For most organizations, the costs of the solutions can be substantial and taking on too many solutions may drain available resources. The result may even have an impact on the earnings of the organization, potentially creating another serious problem.

Verifying the Match

After identifying the possible solutions, it's necessary to verify that a match exists between the need and the solution. It is often helpful to return to the source of input (focus groups, employees, etc.) to affirm that the solution meets the needs. This approach is not applicable for every solution, as employees may be biased. However, their input may provide insight into progress made or indicate whether a solution is on target or off base. When input was obtained from interviews or focus groups, it may be easier to return to these groups to check whether a solution is addressing the cause of turnover. The important point is to find a way to discover whether a mismatch exists.

Upon initial implementation of the solution, obtain feedback to ensure that the solution is a fit and is working. Early feedback can bring out adjustments that need to be made, or in worst-case scenarios, suggest abandonment of the solution altogether. This represents another opportunity to involve a group of experts.

In addition, communicate the early results quickly. Letting the target group know that a solution has been implemented and that the results are positive (or developing, or need improvement) provides an opportunity to collect feedback from them. Employees need to see that action is being taken, progress is developing, and, more important, that the organization is responsive.

FINAL THOUGHTS

In this brief chapter we have tackled the critical issue of matching the solution to the actual cause of turnover. Although some may consider this an obvious step, it can be one of the most critical steps because mismatches can be disastrous! If the cause is not fully understood, the solution will not be appropriate. If the solution addresses the cause in an ineffective way, the results will be less than optimum. In addition, taking on too many solutions can create significant problems in the organization, diminishing the overall effort of retention management. It is important to ensure that the real causes are understood, the relative priority of the various causes is known, solutions are matched to those causes, and that the high-priority, high-payoff solutions are addressed quickly to manage retention effectively.

CHAPTER TWELVE

Forecast ROI
of Retention Solutions

ometimes, there is confusion regarding when it is appropriate to develop the ROI for a retention solution. The traditional approach is to base ROI calculations strictly on business results obtained from the retention solution. This chapter will illustrate that ROI calculations are possible at several different stages—even before the retention solution is implemented.

WHY FORECAST ROI?

Although ROI calculation based on post-implementation data is the most accurate way to calculate ROI for a retention solution, it is often important to know the ROI forecast before the solution is implemented or the final results are tabulated. Forecasting the impact of a solution, even before the project is pursued, is an important issue when the reasons for the need for a forecasted ROI are examined. Here are the five reasons that usually surface:

1. To Minimize Risk and Uncertainty

It is helpful to reduce uncertainty in a new retention solution whenever possible. In a perfect world, the sponsor (client, senior management) would like to know the expected payoff before any action is taken. Realistically, knowing the exact payoff may not be possible and, from a practical standpoint, may not be feasible. However, the desire still exists to take the uncertainty out of the situation and act on the best data available. This can push the project to a forecasted ROI before any resources are expended. Some senior managers will simply not budge without a pre-project forecast for a retention solution. They need some measure of expected success before allocating any resources to the solution. They want to "see the money."

2. To Make Go/No-Go Decisions

In some cases, even a pilot retention solution is not practical until some analysis has been conducted to examine the potential ROI. For example, if the solution involves a significant amount of work or costs, a senior manager may not want to expend the resources, even for a pilot, unless there is some assurance of a positive ROI. This is particularly true for solutions involving changes in compensation. The pre-project ROI becomes an important issue in these situations, prompting some clients to stand firm until an ROI forecast is produced. Then an appropriate decision can be made to go with the project—or not.

3. To Make a Follow-Up Comparison

Whenever there is a plan to collect data on the success of the application and implementation, impact, and ROI of the retention solution, it is helpful to compare actual results to pre-project expectations. In an ideal world, a forecasted ROI should have a defined relationship with the actual ROI—or at least one should lead to the other with some adjustments. One important reason for forecasting ROI is to see how well the forecast holds up under the scrutiny of post-project analysis.

4. For the Sake of Efficiency

Several cost-saving issues may prompt the ROI forecast. First, the forecast itself is often a very inexpensive process because it involves estimations and several assumptions. Second, if the forecast itself becomes a reliable predictor of the post-project results, then the forecasted ROI might substitute for the actual ROI, at least with some adjustments. This could save the costs of the post-project analysis. Finally, the forecasted ROI data might be used for comparisons in other areas, at least as a beginning point for other types of solutions. Thus, the forecasted ROI might have some transfer potential to other retention solutions.

5. For Compliance

More organizations are developing policy statements—and in the case of government agencies, enacting legislation—even passing laws to require a forecasted ROI before major projects are undertaken. For example, in one organization, any project exceeding $300,000 must have a forecasted ROI before it can be approved. In one foreign government, a company can receive partial refunds on the cost of a project if the ROI forecast is positive and likely to enhance the performance of the organization. This formal policy and legal structure is a growing reason for developing the ROI forecast.

Collectively, these five reasons are causing more organizations to examine ROI forecasts (or at least during a project) so that the retention solution coordinator will have some estimate of the expected payoff.

THE TRADEOFFS OF FORECASTING

The ROI can be developed at different times and at different levels. Unfortunately, the ease, convenience, and low cost involved in capturing a forecasted ROI create tradeoffs in accuracy and credibility. As shown in Figure 12.1, there are five distinct time intervals during the implementation of a retention solution at which the ROI can actually be developed. The relationship with credibility, accuracy, cost, and difficulty is also shown in this figure.

The time intervals are

1. A **pre-project forecast** can be developed using estimates of the impact of the retention solution. This approach lacks credibility and accuracy, but it is also the least expensive and least difficult ROI to calculate. The value in developing the ROI on a pre-project basis—observed earlier—will be discussed in more detail in the next section.

ROI with:	Data Collection Timing (Relative to Retention Solution)	Credibility	Accuracy	Cost to Develop	Difficulty
1. Pre-Project Forecast	Before solution is started	Not Very Credible	Not Very Accurate	Inexpensive	Not Difficult
2. Reaction and Satisfaction Data	At the beginning of project, after team members have been exposed to solution				
3. Learning Data	At the beginning of project, after team members learn how to implement the solution				
4. Application Data	During project implementation, after team members have applied the solution				
5. Business Impact Data	After project is complete	Very Credible	Very Accurate	Expensive	Very Difficult

Figure 12.1. ROI Possibilities

2. **Reaction data** can be extended to develop an anticipated impact, including the ROI. Team members collect data after they have been exposed to the solution through briefings, explanations, or training sessions. In this case, team members actually anticipate the chain of impact as a retention solution is applied, implemented, and turnover measures are influenced. While the accuracy and credibility increase from the pre-project basis, this approach still lacks the credibility and accuracy desired in most situations.

3. **Learning data** in some retention solutions can be used to forecast the actual ROI. Data are collected after team members learn how to use the solution, usually following a training program. This approach is applicable only when learning data shows a relationship between acquiring certain skills or knowledge and subsequent business performance. When this correlation is available (usually developed to validate a test), test data can be used to forecast subsequent performance. The performance can then be converted to monetary impact and the ROI can be developed. This has less potential as an evaluation tool due to the lack of situations in which a predictive validation can be developed. Because of the limited use of this forecasting situation, additional detail is not offered in this chapter.

4. In some limited situations, when frequency of skills and actual use of skills and knowledge are critical, the **application and implementation** of those skills or knowledge can be converted to a monetary value using estimations. This is particularly helpful when competencies are being developed as a major part of the solution and values are placed on improving competencies. Because of the limited use of this application and the preference to use business data (i.e., turnover), this approach is not explored further in this chapter.

5. Finally, the ROI can be developed from **business impact data,** usually turnover, converted directly to monetary values and compared to the cost of the solution. This post-project evaluation is the basis for the ROI calculations used in the next chapter. It is the preferred approach because of the pressures outlined above; it is important to examine ROI calculations at other times and at levels other than using business data.

In this chapter we will discuss, in detail, pre-project evaluation and the ROI calculations based on reaction data. The ROI calculations developed from learning and application data will not be discussed, but are examined in other publications (see Phillips & Phillips, 2007).

PRE-PROJECT ROI FORECASTING

Perhaps one of the most useful steps in convincing a client that a retention solution expense is beneficial is to forecast the ROI for the solution. The process is similar to the post-project analysis, except that the extent of the impact must be estimated along with the forecasted cost of the solution.

Basic Model

Figure 12.2 shows the basic model for capturing the necessary data for a pre-project forecast. This model is a modification of the post-project consulting ROI process model presented in the next chapter, except that data are projected instead of being collected during the various time frames. In place of the data collection is an estimation of the change in impact data expected to be influenced by the solution. Isolating the effects of the retention solution becomes a non-issue, as the estimate of output takes the isolation factor into consideration.

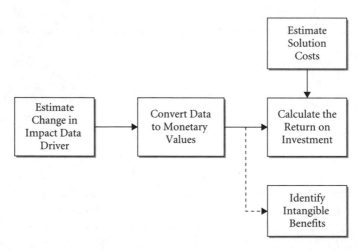

Figure 12.2.   Basic Model for Capturing Data for Pre-Project Forecast

For example, when an individual is asked to indicate how much of the particular improvement can be driven by the solution, the influence of other factors is already taken into consideration. Only the solution factor is an issue because the other factors have been isolated in the estimation process.

The method to convert data to monetary values is exactly the same because the data items examined in a pre- and post-analysis should be the same. Estimating the project's cost should be an easy step because costs can easily be anticipated based on previous solutions using reasonable assumptions about the current solution. The anticipated intangibles are merely speculation in forecasting but can be reliable indicators of which measures may be influenced in addition to those included in the ROI calculation. The formula used to calculate the ROI is the same as in the post-analysis. The amount of monetary value from the data conversion is included as the numerator while the estimated cost of the solution is inserted as the denominator. The projected cost-benefit ratio can be developed along with the ROI value (%). The steps to develop the process are detailed next.

Steps to Develop the ROI

The detailed steps to develop the pre-project ROI forecast are presented in simplified form below:

1. Develop the implementation and impact objectives with as many specifics as possible. Developed from the initial needs analysis and assessment, these objectives detail what would actually change as the retention solution is implemented and identify which business measures (usually turnover) would actually be influenced.

2. Estimate or forecast the monthly improvement in the turnover data. This is considered to be the amount of change directly related to the solution and is denoted by $\Delta \sim P$.

3. Convert the turnover data to monetary values using the methods described in Chapter 5. This value is denoted by V.

4. Develop the estimated annual impact for the improvement in turnover. In essence, this is the first-year improvement from the retention solution, showing the value for the change in turnover

directly related to the solution. In formula form, this is $\Delta I = \Delta P \times V \times 12$.

5. For long-term retention solutions, improvement may be forecast for a period greater than one year. In this case, additional years should be factored into the analysis if a solution will have a significant useful life beyond the first year. These values may be discounted to reflect a diminished benefit in subsequent years. The client or owner of the retention solution should provide some indication as to the amount of improvement expected (turnover reduction) in years two, three, etc.; however, it is helpful to obtain input from as many team members as possible.

6. Estimate the fully loaded costs of the retention solution. Using the direct cost and indirect cost categories, the fully loaded cost would be estimated and projected for the retention solution. This is denoted as C. Again, all direct and indirect costs should be included in the calculation.

7. Calculate the forecasted ROI using the total projected benefits and the estimated cost in the standard ROI formula:
$$\text{ROI}(\%) = \frac{\Delta I - C}{C} \times 100$$

8. Use sensitivity analysis to develop several potential ROI values with different levels of improvement ($\sim\Delta P$). When more than one measure is changing, that analysis should be developed using a spreadsheet showing different possible scenarios for output and subsequent ROI values.

9. Identify potential intangible benefits by securing input from the individuals most knowledgeable of the project and retention solution. These are only anticipated and are based on assumptions from previous experience with this type of solution.

10. Communicate the ROI projection and anticipated intangibles with much care and caution. The target audience must clearly understand that the forecast is based on several assumptions (clearly defined), and that the values are the best possible estimates. However, there is still much room for error.

These ten steps make the ROI forecast feasible. The most difficult part of the process is the initial estimate of performance improvement. Several sources of data are available for this purpose, and are described next.

Forecasting/Estimating Performance Improvement

A variety of input is available when attempting to estimate the performance improvement that will be influenced by a retention solution. In most retention solutions, the performance improvement will involve turnover reductions only. The following sources should be explored when estimating performance improvement:

1. Those individuals in the organization with experience in a similar, previous retention solution or similar solutions may help form the basis of the estimate. Utilizing a breadth of experience can be an important factor as comparisons are rarely, if ever, exact.

2. The retention solution team may have experience with similar solutions in other organizations or in other situations. Here, the experience of the designers, developers, and implementers involved in the solution will be helpful as they reflect on their experiences with other organizations.

3. The input of external experts (usually retention consultants) who have worked in the field or tackled similar retention solution in other organizations can be extremely valuable. Consultants, suppliers, designers, or others who have earned a reputation as knowledgeable about this type of solution in this type of situation may be helpful.

4. Estimates can be obtained directly from a subject matter expert (SME) in the organization. This is an individual who is very familiar with the internal processes being altered, modified, or improved by the retention solution. Internal SMEs are very knowledgeable and sometimes the most favored source for obtaining conservative estimates.

5. Estimates can be obtained directly from the senior manager or the sponsor of the project. This individual, who is ultimately making the implementation decision, may be capable of providing data or input on the anticipated change in a measure linked to the retention solution. The influential position of this individual makes it a credible source.

6. Individuals who are directly involved in the retention solution, often labeled participants or target audience, may know how much of a measure can be changed or improved with a specific

retention solution. These individuals understand the processes, procedures, and performance measurements being influenced. Their close proximity to the situation makes them credible and often the most accurate sources for estimating the amount of change in turnover.

Collectively, these sources provide an appropriate array of possibilities to help estimate the value of an improvement. Pre-program forecasting is the weakest scenario in the ROI forecast and deserves the most attention. The stakeholders in a forecasted ROI project should understand the source of the estimates. More importantly, the sponsor must view the source as credible. Otherwise, the forecasted ROI has little utility.

CASE EXAMPLE

It may be helpful to illustrate how a forecasted ROI can be developed using the processes explained here. A manufacturing plant of a large multinational corporation was experiencing serious turnover problem—a 60 percent annual rate in an industry with an average of 25 percent. An assessment and initial analysis identified several needs. The solution was comprehensive team leader training program. However, before pursuing the project and contracting for the training, a forecasted ROI was needed. Following the steps outlined earlier in this chapter, it was determined that several business impact measures would be influenced by the implementation of this training.

With comprehensive supervisor training in place, team leaders and supervisors should improve work unit performance (productivity and quality) and increase job satisfaction, as well as team manager retention. However, the forecasted ROI would be developed on turnover alone.

To determine the extent to which turnover would be reduced, input was collected from four sources:

1. Analysts (who identified the causes of turnover and recommended solutions) provided input on expected reduction in turnover.

2. Department managers (responsible for the supervisors and team leaders) provided input on expected reduction in turnover.

3. Project sponsors (plant manager who initiated the project) provided input on the anticipated reduction in turnover.

4. Finally, the training supplier and facilitators (who designed and delivered the training) provided input on expected turnover reduction based on previous experience.

When input is based on estimates, the actual results may differ significantly; however, the project sponsor was interested in a forecast based on very limited analysis but was strengthened with the best expert opinions available. After some discussion of the benchmarking data and examining turnover cost studies for similar types of jobs, it was decided to use a standard value of 75 percent of annual wages as the cost of a turnover statistic.

The forecasted ROI calculation was developed for this plan only. After reviewing the possible scenarios, it was decided that there could be a range of possibilities for reducing turnover. The value should be in the range of 10 to 25 percentage points, bringing turnover down from 60 percent to 35 to 50 percent. Four scenarios were developed using a 10, 15, 20, and 25 percentage point decrease.

The turnover reduction was easily converted to monetary values using standard values. The cost for the proposed training was easily estimated based on input from the training contractor. The total cost of training was developed to include facilities for training session, lost time for learning activities, and coordination. This fully loaded project cost, when compared to the benefits, yielded a range of expected ROI values. Table 12.1 shows a list of the four possible scenarios.

The ROI values range from a low of 30 percent to a high of 400 percent. With these values in hand, the decision to move forward was a relatively easy one, as even the worst-case scenarios were very positive, and the best case was over ten times that amount. Thus, the decision was made to move forward with the project. As this example illustrates, the process needs to be kept simple, using the

Potential Turnover Reduction (Annualized Values)	New Annual Turnover Values	Expected ROI (%)
10%	50%	30%
15%	45%	100%
20%	40%	250%
25%	35%	400%

Table 12.1.   Expected ROI Values for Various Scenarios

most credible resources available to quickly arrive at estimates for the process. Although this is an estimate, its advantage is simplicity and low cost, and these factors should be considered when developing the processes.

Forecasting with a Pilot Program

Although the steps listed above provide a process for estimating the ROI when a pilot or trial implementation is not conducted, a more favorable approach is to develop a small-scale pilot of the retention solution and develop the ROI based on post-implementation data from the pilot. This scenario involves the following steps:

1. As in the previous process, develop implementation and impact objectives.

2. Initiate the retention solution on a very small-scale sample as a pilot project, without all the bells and whistles. This keeps the cost extremely low without sacrificing the fundamentals of the solution.

3. Conduct the pilot solution and fully implement it with one or more groups of target audiences who can benefit from the retention solution.

4. Develop the ROI using the ROI methodology for post-project analysis. This is the same ROI methodology used in the previous chapters.

5. Finally, decide whether or not to implement the retention solution throughout the organization based on the results of the pilot implementation.

This approach provides a much more accurate analysis, withholding full implementation until results can be developed from the pilot study. In this scenario, data can be developed using all six types of measures outlined in the next chapter.

FORECASTING ROI WITH REACTION DATA

After participants in the retention solution become involved in the solution, usually through training or briefings, a reaction questionnaire is often administered. When a reaction evaluation includes

Planned Improvements

1. As a result of this retention solution, what specific actions will you attempt as you apply what you have learned?

   a.

   b.

   c.

2. Please indicate the amount of change in turnover, as a result of your actions.

3. Estimate the cost of one turnover statistic.

4. What is the basis of this estimate, if it is not provided to you?

5. As a result of anticipated changes above please estimate (in monetary terms) the benefits over a period of one year. $_____

6. What confidence, expressed as a percentage, can you place in your estimate of improvement? (0% = no confidence; 100% = total certainty) _____%

Exhibit 12.1.   Important Questions for a Forecast Based on Retention

planned application, this important data can be used in ROI forecast calculations. With questions focusing on how participants plan to use what they learned, higher-level evaluation information can be developed. The questions presented in Exhibit 12.1 illustrate how these types of data are collected with a reaction questionnaire. Participants are asked to state specifically how they plan to use the retention solution and the results they expect to achieve with it. They are asked to convert their planned accomplishments in turnover into annual monetary values and show the basis for developing the values (if not provided). Participants can adjust their responses with a confidence factor to make the data more credible and allow them to reflect their uneasiness with the process. With advanced notice, discussion of the questions, explanation of the use of the data, encouragement to provide data, a simple typical example, and ample time to complete the form, a high participation rate can be achieved. Eighty to 90 percent is normal.

When tabulating data, the confidence levels are multiplied by the annual monetary values, which produces a more conservative estimate for use in the data analysis. For example, if a participant estimated that the monetary impact of the retention solution would be $50,000 but was only 50 percent confident in his or her estimation, a $25,000 value would be used in the ROI calculations ($50,000 × 50%).

To develop a summary of the expected benefits, several steps are taken. First, incomplete, unusable, extreme, or unrealistic data are discarded. Next, an adjustment is given for the confidence estimate as previously described. Individual data items are then totaled. Finally, as an optional exercise, the total value is adjusted again by a factor that reflects the subjectivity of the process and the possibility that participants will not achieve the results they anticipate. The implementation team can estimate this adjustment factor. In one organization, the benefits are divided by two to develop a number to use in the equation. Finally, the ROI forecast is calculated using the anticipated net benefits from the retention solution divided by the solution costs. In essence, this value becomes the expected return on investment once the confidence adjustment for accuracy and the adjustment for subjectivity have been made.

This process can best be described using an actual case. Integrated Systems, Inc. (ISI), designs and builds large commercial systems for banks and financial service companies. Retention is always a critical issue at ISI and usually commands much management attention. To improve the current level of performance, a retention solution was initiated for software designers, project engineers, and system integrators. The retention solution focused on culture change. After implementing the solution, managers were expected to improve the retention in their departments. At the end of the implementation sessions, mangers completed a comprehensive reaction feedback questionnaire, which probed specific action items planned as a result of the retention solution and provided estimated monetary values of the planned actions. In addition, managers explained the basis for estimates and placed a confidence level on their estimates. Table 12.2 presents data provided by the first group of participants. Only fifteen of the twenty managers supplied data. Approximately 50 to 80 percent of participants will usually provide data on this series of questions. The total cost of the retention solution, including managers' time, was estimated to be $105,000. Prorated development costs were included in this figure.

The monetary value of the planned improvements was extremely high and reflected the managers' optimism and enthusiasm at the end of a very effective retention solution from which specific actions were planned. As a first step in the analysis, extreme data items were omitted. Data such as "millions," "unlimited," and "significant" were discarded, and each remaining value was multiplied by the confidence value and totaled. This adjustment is one way of reducing high subjective estimates. The resulting tabulations yielded a total

Participating Managers	Estimated Annual Reduction in Turnover (Number)	Monetary Value of Turnover (100% of Annual Salary)	Confidence Level of Estimate	Adjusted Value
1	2	$96,000	60%	$ 57,600
2	3	$152,000	70%	$ 106,400
3	0	0	0	0
4	4	$183,000	80%	$ 146,400
5	5	$212,000	30%	$ 63,600
6	0	0	0	0
7	3	$139,000	60%	$ 83,400
8	1	$45,000	50%	$ 42,500
9	8	$420,000	40%	$ 168,000
10	10	$525,000	20%	$ 105,000
11	0	0	0	0
12	6	$275,000	60%	$ 165,000
13	3	$140,000	70%	$ 98,000
14	2	$100,000	60%	$ 60,000
15	0	0	0	0
			TOTAL	$1,095,900

Table 12.2.   Level 1 Reaction Data for ROI Calculations

improvement of $1,095,900. Because of the subjective nature of the process, the values were adjusted by a factor of two, an arbitrary number suggested by the retention coordinator and supported by the management group. This "adjusted" value was $547,050, rounded up to $548,000. The projected ROI, which was based on the feedback questionnaire at the end of the retention solution but before job application, was as follows.

$$\text{ROI} = \frac{\$548,000 - \$105,000}{\$105,000} \times 100 = 422\%$$

The retention coordinator communicated these projected values to the CEO, but cautioned that the data were very subjective, although they had twice been adjusted downward. The coordinator also emphasized that the forecasted results were generated by the managers involved in the culture, who should presumably be aware of what they could accomplish. In addition, the coordinator mentioned that a follow up was planned to determine the results actually delivered by the group.

A word of caution is in order when using forecasted ROI with reaction data: The calculations are highly subjective and may not reflect the extent to which managers will apply what they have learned to achieve results. A variety of influences in the work environment can enhance or inhibit the attainment of performance goals. Having high expectations after implementation is no guarantee that those expectations will be met. Disappointments are documented regularly with solutions throughout the world and reported in research findings.

While the process is subjective and possibly unreliable, it does have some usefulness. First, if evaluation must stop with the launch of the solution, this approach provides more insight into the value of the retention solution than data from typical reaction questionnaires. Unfortunately, there is evidence that a high percentage of evaluations stop at this first level of evaluation. Managers usually find these data more useful than a report stating, "Forty percent of participants rated the project above average." Reporting ROI data forecasted from reaction provides a more useful indication of the potential impact of the retention solution than the alternative, which is to report attitudes and feelings about the solution.

Second, these data can form a basis for comparing different projects of the same type. If one retention solution forecasts an ROI of 300 percent and another solution forecasts 30 percent, it would appear that one solution may be more effective than the other. The participants in the first retention solution have more confidence in the planned application of the second solution.

Third, collecting these data focuses increased attention on solution outcomes. Participants involved in the retention solution will have an understanding that specific behavior change is expected, which produces results for the organization. This issue becomes very clear to participants as they anticipate results and convert them to monetary values. Even if this projected improvement is ignored, the exercise is productive because of the important message sent to participants.

Fourth, if a follow-up is planned to pinpoint post-implementation results, the reaction data can be very helpful for comparison. The data collection helps participants plan the implementation of what they have learned. Incidentally, when a follow-up is planned, participants are usually more conservative with their projected estimates.

The calculation of the ROI with reaction data is increasing in use, and some organizations have based many of their ROI calculations at this level. Although they may be very subjective, the calculations do add value, particularly if they are included as part of a comprehensive evaluation system.

PROJECT COSTS FOR FORECASTING CALCULATIONS

In both of the previous scenarios, the costs for the proposed solution were developed to forecast ROI. The costs for the retention solution, whether projected or on a post-implementation basis, contains the same type of categories. The costs should be fully loaded to include both direct and indirect costs associated with the solution. In addition, some costs may be prorated if a particular cost for the solution may have residual value after implementation. Table 12.3 shows the typical cost categories that should be captured for retention solutions. These categories represent all significant costs associated with the solution. Additional information on cost categories is contained in the next chapter and in additional references (Phillips & Zuniga, 2008).

	Cost Item	Prorated	Expensed
A	Initial analysis and assessment		✓
B	Development of solutions		✓
C	Acquisition of solutions		✓
D	Implementation and application		✓
	Policy changes		✓
	Salaries/benefits for coordination time		✓
	Salaries/benefits for participant time		✓
	Materials		✓
	Hardware/software	✓	
	Travel/lodging/meals		✓
	Use of facilities		✓
	Capital expenditures	✓	
E	Maintenance and monitoring		✓
F	Administrative support and overhead	✓	
G	Evaluation and reporting		✓

Table 12.3.   Retention Solution Cost Categories

FINAL THOUGHTS

In this chapter we presented the techniques for forecasting ROI at four different time frames using different levels of evaluation data. Two of these techniques, pre-project forecasting and forecasting with reaction data, are useful for very simple and inexpensive projects. They may be helpful even in short-term, low-profile solutions. Forecasting using learning data and application data is rare and should be reserved only for large-scale projects involving significant learning events.

Pre-project forecasting may be necessary and actually desired, even if it is not required. Because business data are the drivers of the retention solution, business impact measures, such as turnover, should be identified up front. Estimating the actual change in these measures is a recommended and highly useful exercise, as it shows the sponsor the perceived value of the solution. This is a simple exercise that should take no more than one or two days. The result can be extremely valuable when communicating to the sponsor and provides some clear direction and focus for the retention solution coordinator.

In almost every retention solution, reaction data are collected from the participants. A worthwhile extension of reaction data is to include several questions that allow those individuals to project the actual success of the project. This approach is recommended as another simple tool for forecasting the actual ROI. This planned action provides additional insight into the potential worth of the solution and alerts the management team about potential problems or issue that may need attention as the remaining issues are addressed in the solution. The additional questions are very simple and can easily be obtained with fifteen to twenty minutes of the participants' time. For it to be successful and usable, participants must be committed to the process. This can usually be achieved by exploring ways to increase the response rate for the various instruments described in this book.

As expected, pre-project ROI calculations are the lowest in terms of credibility and accuracy, but have the advantage of being inexpensive and relatively easy to develop. ROI calculations using business impact are rich in credibility and accuracy, but are very expensive and difficult to develop. Although ROI calculations at this level are preferred, ROI development at other time frames with other levels of data is an important part of a comprehensive and systematic retention evaluation process.

References

Phillips, J.J., & Phillips, P.P. (2007). *Show me the money: How to determine the ROI of people, projects, and programs.* San Francisco, CA: Berrett-Koehler.

Phillips, J.J., & Zuniga, L. (2008). *Costs and ROI: Evaluating at the ultimate level.* San Francisco, CA: Pfeiffer.

Calculate ROI
of Retention Solutions

easuring the return on investment (ROI) in a retention solution is a topic of much interest. For clients, this process shows the ultimate payoff for retention strategies. For the HR staff and others involved in retention, it provides important insight into the strengths and weaknesses of solutions.

Understanding the drivers for the ROI process and the inherent weaknesses and advantages of ROI makes it possible to take a rational approach to this important issue. In this chapter we present the basic issues and steps needed to develop ROI measurement for retention.

KEY ROI ISSUES

The ROI process is a comprehensive methodology that provides a scorecard of six measures. These measures represent input from various sources during different time frames. The measures include: (1) reaction, (2) learning, (3) application and implementation, (4) business impact, (5) return on investment, and (6) intangible benefits. In addition, the ROI process uses at least one technique to isolate the effects of the retention solution from other influences. This comprehensive measurement system requires success with many issues and must become a routine part of the strategic accountability approach to turnover reduction.

Why ROI?

There are good reasons why return on investment is such a hot topic. Although the viewpoints and explanations may vary, some things are very clear. First, in most organizations, HR budgets have continued to grow year after year with a significant portion focusing on retention. Retention solutions are becoming more expensive with long-term commitments. As expenditures grow, accountability becomes a more critical issue. A growing budget creates a larger target for internal critics, often prompting the development of an ROI process.

Second, total quality management and continuous process improvement have brought increased attention to measurement issues. Today, organizations measure processes and outputs that were not previously measured, monitored, or reported. This focus has placed increased pressure on the HR function to develop measures of retention solution success.

Third, restructuring initiatives and the threat of outsourcing have caused HR to focus more directly on bottom-line issues. Many HR processes have been restructured so that programs are more closely aligned with business needs and maximum efficiencies are required in the HR cycle. These change processes have brought increased attention to evaluation issues and have resulted in measuring the contribution of specific solutions.

Fourth, the business management mindset of many current HR managers causes them to place more emphasis on economic issues within the HR function. Today's HR manager is more aware of bottom-line issues in the organization and more knowledgeable of operational and financial concerns. This new "enlightened" manager often takes a business approach to retention.

Fifth, a persistent trend of accountability has evolved in organizations all over the globe. Every support function is attempting to show its worth by capturing the value that it adds to the organization. From the accountability perspective, the HR function should be no different from the other functions—it must show its contribution to the organization.

Sixth, top executives are now demanding return on investment calculations from departments and functions where they were not previously required. For years, HR managers convinced top executives that programs couldn't be measured, at least at the monetary contribution level. Yet, many of these executives are now aware that it can and is being measured in many organizations, thanks in part to articles in publications aimed at top executives. Subsequently, top executives are demanding the same accountability from their HR functions. In some extremes, these functions are being asked to show the return on investment or face significant budget cuts. Others are just being asked for results.

Concerns with ROI

Although much progress has been made, the ROI Methodology is not without its share of problems and drawbacks. The mere presence of the process creates a dilemma for many organizations. When an organization embraces the concept and implements the process, the management team is usually anxiously waiting for results, only to be disappointed when they are not quantifiable. For an ROI process to be useful, it must balance many issues, including feasibility, simplicity, credibility, and soundness. More specifically, three major audiences must be pleased with the ROI process to accept and use it.

> *Practitioners.* For years, HR practitioners have assumed that ROI could not be measured. When examining a typical process, they found long formulas, complicated equations, and complex models that made the ROI process appear to be too confusing. With this perceived complexity, practitioners could visualize the tremendous efforts required for data collection and analysis, and more importantly, the increased cost necessary to make the process work. Because of these concerns, practitioners are seeking an ROI process that is simple and easy to understand so that they can easily implement the steps and strategies. Also, they need a process that will not take an excessive amount of time to implement. Finally, a process is needed that is not too expensive. In summary, from the perspective of the practitioners, the ROI process must be user friendly, time saving, and cost efficient.

Senior managers/sponsors/clients. Managers who must approve HR programs and retention solutions, and cope with the results of solutions, have a strong interest in developing the ROI. They want a process that provides quantifiable results, using a method similar to the ROI formula applied to other types of investments. Senior managers have a never-ending desire to have it all come down to an ROI calculation, reflected as a percentage. As with practitioners, they want a process that is simple and easy to understand. The assumptions made in the calculation and the methodology used in the process must reflect their frame of reference, experience, and level of understanding. They do not want, nor need, a string of formulas, charts, or complicated models. Instead, they want a process that they can explain to others, when necessary. More importantly, they need a process with which they can identify—one that is sound and realistic enough to earn their confidence.

Researchers. Finally, researchers will only support a process that measures up to close scrutiny. They usually insist that models, formulas, assumptions, and theories be sound and based on commonly accepted practices. Also, they want a process that produces accurate values and consistent outcomes. If estimates are necessary, researchers want a process that provides the most accuracy within the constraints of the situation, recognizing that adjustments need to be made when there is uncertainty in the process.

The challenge is to develop acceptable requirements for an ROI process that will satisfy researchers and, at the same time, please practitioners and senior managers. Sound impossible? Maybe not. The ROI process described here meets the requirements of these three groups (Phillips & Phillips, 2002).

BUILDING THE PROCESS

Building a comprehensive measurement and evaluation process is best represented as a puzzle where the pieces are developed and put in place over time. Figure 13.1 depicts the pieces necessary to build a comprehensive measurement and evaluation process. The first piece of the puzzle is the selection of an evaluation framework, which is a categorization of data.

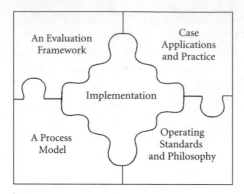

Figure 13.1.   ROI: The Pieces of the Puzzle

Next, the ROI process model must be developed showing how data is collected, processed, analyzed, and reported to various target audiences. This process model ensures that appropriate techniques and procedures are consistently utilized to address almost any situation. Also, there must be consistency as the process is implemented.

The third piece of the puzzle is the development of operating standards. These standards help ensure the results of the study are stable and not influenced by the individual conducting the study. Replication is critical for the credibility of an evaluation processes. Operating standards and guiding principles allow for replication, so that if more than one individual evaluates a specific solution, the results are the same.

Next, appropriate attention must be given to implementation issues, as the ROI process becomes a routine part of the HR function. Several issues must be addressed involving skills, communication, roles, responsibilities, plans, and strategies.

Finally, there must be successful case applications and practice describing the measurement of a turnover solution within the organization and the value a comprehensive measurement and evaluation process brings to the organization. While it is helpful to refer to case studies developed by other organizations, it is more useful and convincing to have studies developed directly within the organization.

The remainder of this chapter is focused on the individual pieces of the evaluation puzzle: developing a comprehensive ROI process.

AN EVALUATION FRAMEWORK

The ROI process described in this chapter is based on the five levels of evaluation (Phillips, 1994). The concept of different levels of evaluation is both helpful and instructive to understanding how the return on investment is developed for retention solutions. Table 13.1 shows the five-level framework used in the ROI process.

Level 1, *Reaction*, measures satisfaction first with the retention solution then from various stakeholders. This measurement is very important to retention solutions. Almost all organizations evaluate at Level 1, usually with generic questionnaires. While this level of evaluation is important as a customer-satisfaction measure, a favorable reaction does not ensure that stakeholders have learned new skills or knowledge that may be necessary to reduce turnover.

Level 2, *Learning*, focuses on what stakeholders have learned using tests, skill practices, role plays, simulations, group evaluations, and other assessment tools. Since training for supervisors and team leaders is critical as a retention solution, this measure is important. A learning check is helpful to ensure that stakeholders have absorbed the solution and know how to use it properly. However, a positive measure at this level is no guarantee that what is learned will be applied on the job. The literature is laced with studies showing how learning fails to be transferred to the job (for example, Broad, 2005).

At Level 3, *Application and Implementation*, a variety of follow-up methods are used to determine the progress with implementation. The frequency and use of skills are sometimes important measures at Level 3. Also, this level covers a variety of implementation issues

Level	Measurement Focus
1. Reaction and Satisfaction	Measures stakeholders' reaction to and satisfaction with the retention solution
2. Learning	Measures changes in knowledge, skills, and attitudes needed to implement the solution
3. Application and Implementation	Measures changes in on-the-job behavior and progress with the implementation of the solution
4. Business Impact	Measures changes in business impact variables related to the solution
5. Return on Investment	Compares monetary benefits of solution to the costs of the solution

Table 13.1.   Five Levels of Evaluation

such as new procedures, new policies, new steps, new actions, and new processes. While Level 3 evaluation is important to gauge the success of the implementation of a solution, it still does not guarantee that there will be a positive business impact in the organization, with turnover improvement.

The Level 4, *Business Impact*, measure focuses on the actual results achieved from the retention solutions efforts, as stakeholders successful implement the solution. In addition to turnover, typical Level 4 measures include output, quality, costs, time, job satisfaction, and customer satisfaction. Although the solution may produce a measurable business impact, there is still a concern that it may cost too much.

Level 5, *Return on Investment* (the ultimate level of evaluation), compares the monetary benefits from the solution with the solution costs. Although the ROI can be expressed in several ways, it is usually presented as a percentage or cost/benefit ratio. The evaluation chain is not complete until the Level 5 evaluation is conducted.

While almost all HR organizations conduct evaluations to measure satisfaction, very few actually conduct evaluations at the ROI level. Perhaps the best explanation for this situation is that ROI evaluation is often characterized as a difficult and expensive process. When business results and ROI are desired, it is also very important to evaluate the other levels. A chain of impact should occur through the levels as the skills and knowledge learned (Level 2) are applied on the job (Level 3) to produce business results (Level 4). If measurements are not taken at each level, it is difficult to conclude that the results achieved were actually caused by the retention solution. Because of this, it is recommended that evaluation be conducted at all levels when a Level 5 ROI evaluation is planned.

THE ROI PROCESS MODEL

The calculations of the return on investment for retention solutions begins with the model shown in Figure 13.2, where a potentially complicated process can be simplified with sequential steps (Phillips, 2003). The ROI process model provides a systematic approach to ROI calculations. A step-by-step approach helps keep the process manageable so users can address one issue at a time. Applying the model provides consistency between ROI calculations. Each major step of the model is briefly described below.

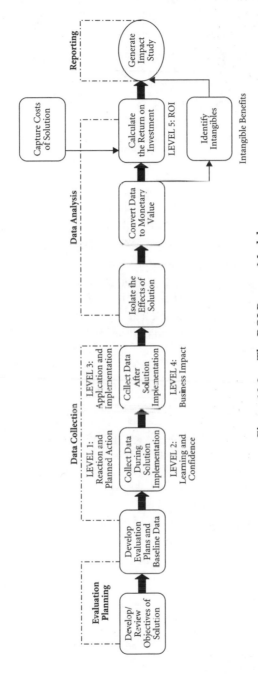

Figure 13.2.   The ROI Process Model

Evaluation Planning

One of the most important and cost-saving steps in the ROI process is developing evaluation plans. By considering key issues, the time, cost, and frustration involved in evaluation can be significantly reduced. Three specific plans should be considered.

The first step in planning the evaluation is to review the specific objectives for the retention solution using the same multiple level concept. For example, reaction and satisfaction objectives are established. Corresponding with the previous Level 1 evaluation. At this level, specific detail and requirements about the desired level of support and satisfaction for the solution is pinpointed. Learning objectives are established at the next level, particularly if the retention solution involves a significant amount of knowledge and skills enhancement. At this level, which corresponds with the learning evaluation, objectives are based on what each participant should know to make the solution successful.

Application and implementation objectives (Level 3) are established next to detail how the solution is implemented, covering time frames, progress, schedules, activities, and specific steps. These objectives profile precisely what will change as a result of the retention solution. The next level, impact (Level 4), details the specific business measures that should change as a result of the retention solution. While employee turnover is always one of the output measures of retention solution, others important measures may include job satisfaction, customer satisfaction, productivity, quality, and time savings. Finally, at Level 5, the ROI objectives are detailed, indicating the specific return on investment desired. For many retention programs in North America, Western Europe, Asia, Australia and New Zealand, 25 percent is typical; however, the client should specify the acceptable ROI level.

These objectives are directly linked to the evaluation and initial analysis levels. As Figure 13.3 illustrates, the five levels are helpful to see the direct linkages between the initial analysis of the problem and the evaluation. The objectives represent the transition from analysis to measurement and evaluation. It is particularly important to observe the actual direction of the arrow in Figure 13.3. The initial analysis often starts with the feasibility of solving the problem, driving to business needs and a detailed analysis of the job performance needs. Finally, skill and knowledge needs are identified and the preferences

Level	Initial Analysis	Solution Objectives	Measurement and Evaluation	Level

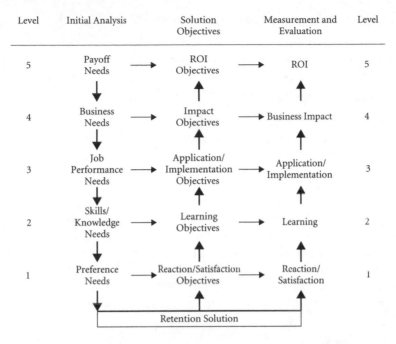

Figure 13.3.   The Linkage of Objectives, Evaluation, and Analysis

for the solution are outlined. Objectives are developed; the solution is implemented in the opposite direction of the analysis. From the measurement and evaluation perspective, the chain of impact is observed as reaction and satisfaction data is collected, followed by learning, application, and business impact. The ROI value is calculated from the process—benefits compared to costs. Consequently, this parallel alignment of levels and objectives, collected to levels of analysis and measurement and evaluation provides a very helpful and instructive tool to keep the process aligned and the retention solution on focus.

THE DATA COLLECTION PLAN. After the above elements have been considered and determined, the data collection plan is developed. The plan outlines in detail the steps to be taken to collect data for a comprehensive evaluation, and usually includes the following items:

- Broad areas for objectives of the solution are used;
- Specific measures or data descriptions are indicated when they are necessary to explain the measures linked to the objectives;

- Specific data collection methodologies for each objective are listed;
- Sources of data such as stakeholders, team leaders, and company records are identified;
- The time frame to collect the data is noted for each data collection method; and
- Responsibility for collecting data is assigned.

Table 13.2 shows an example of a data collection plan for a retention solution for nurses.

THE ROI ANALYSIS PLAN. The ROI analysis plan is a continuation of the data collection plan. This planning document captures information on several key issues necessary to develop the actual ROI calculation. These issues include:

- Significant business data items, usually turnover;
- The method for isolating the effects of the solution on the business measure;
- The method for converting data to monetary values;
- The solution cost categories, noting how certain costs should be prorated;
- The anticipated intangible benefits;
- The communication targets—those to receive the information; and
- Other issues or events that might influence solution implementation.

Table 13.3 shows an example of an ROI analysis plan for the retention solution for nurses.

PROJECT PLAN. A final planning document is the project plan. This document provides a time line of all the major events and milestones that must be completed in the project. It covers the timeline from the planning to the last communication or results. Almost any project planning software will fill this need. These three planning documents are necessary to successfully implement and manage the ROI process.

Solution: Reducing Talent Departure by Preventing Sexual Harassment

Responsibility: Jack J. Phillips   Date: _____

Level	Solution Objectives	Evaluation Method	Data Sources	Timing	Responsibilities
1. Reaction and Satisfaction	• Obtain a positive reaction to solution and materials • Obtain input for suggestions for improving solution	• Questionnaire	• Team leaders • Managers	• End of session	• Facilitator
2. Learning	• Knowledge of policy on sexual harassment • Knowledge of inappropriate and illegal behavior • Skills to investigate and discuss sexual harassment	• Pre- and post-test • Observation	• Team leaders • Supervisors	• Beginning of project and end of implementation • During session	• Meeting facilitator
3. Application and Implementation	• Administer policy • Conduct meeting with employees • Ensure that the workplace is free of sexual harassment	• Self-Assessment Questionnaire • Complete and submit meeting record • Employee survey	• Team leaders • Managers • HR records section • 25% sample of all non supervisory employees	• Six months after solution • One month after solution • Six months after solution	• Evaluator • HCMS staff • Employee communications
4. Business Impact	• Reduce employee turnover • Reduce internal complaints • Reduce external complaints	• Business performance monitoring • Questionnaire	• HR Records Section • Supervisors	• Monthly for one year before and after program	• Evaluator

Table 13.2.   Data Collection Plan

Project: Reducing Talent Departure by Preventing Sexual Harassment

Responsibility: Jack J. Phillips   Date: _____

Data Items	Methods of Isolating the Effects of the Solution	Methods of Converting Data	Cost Categories	Intangible Benefits	Communication Targets	Other Influences/Issues
Employee voluntary turnover	• Forecasting using percentage of turnover related to sexual harassment	• External studies within industry	• Needs assessment • Development/ acquisition • Coordination/ facilitation time • Materials • Food/ refreshments • Facilities • Participant salaries and benefits • Evaluation	• Job satisfaction • Absenteeism • Stress reduction • Public image • Recruiting	• All employees (condensed info.) • Senior executives (Summary of report with detailed backup) • All supervisors and managers (brief report) • HR/HRD staff (full report)	• Several initiatives to reduce turnover were implemented during this time period • Must not duplicate benefits from both internal and external complaints
Formal internal complaints of sexual harassment	• Trend-line analysis • Participant estimation (as a backup)	• Historical costs with estimation form EEO/AA staff (internal expert)				
External complaints of sexual harassment	• Trend-line analysis • Participant estimation (as a backup)	• Historical costs with estimation form EEO/AA staff (internal expert)				

Table 13.3.   ROI Analysis Plan

Collect Data

Following the planning process, implementation begins. Data collection is central to the ROI process. Both hard and soft data is collected. Data is usually collected during two time frames: during the initial launch of the solution and following implementation.

Retention (Level 1) and learning (Level 2) data are usually collected during initial sessions for the retention solution. For example, if a training program were presented as a solution, Level 1 and 2 data would be collected during that program. Several methods are appropriate for capturing the Level 1 and Level 2:

- Surveys and questionnaires are used to capture reaction and learning data;
- Interviews may be utilized to capture reaction and learning data;
- Focus groups can also capture reaction and, on some occasions, learning data; and
- Tests can be constructed to capture learning data. Informal methods are used in many applications, which include self assessment, facilitator assessment, and team assessment.

A variety of methods are available to collect post-implementation data for an ROI evaluation.

- Follow-up *surveys* are utilized to determine the degree to which participants have utilized various aspects of the retention solution, Level 3 data. Survey responses are often developed on a sliding scale and usually represent attitudinal data.
- Follow-up *questionnaires* are administered to uncover specific applications and implementation issues, as well as impact data (Level 3 and 4). Participants provide responses to a variety of open-ended and forced-response questions.
- One-the-job *observation* captures actual skill application and use (Level 3 data). Observations are particularly useful in retention solutions involving the team leader and are more effective when the observer is either invisible or transparent.
- Post-implementation *interviews* may determine the extent to which the solution has been implemented. Interviews allow for probing to uncover specific applications and are appropriate with Level 3 data.

- *Focus groups* are conducted to determine the degree to which behavior change and application has occurred. Focus groups are appropriate with qualitative data (Level 3).
- *Action plans* are developed by major stakeholders and implemented as part of the retention solution. A follow-up of the plans provides evidence of solution success. Level 3 and 4 data may be collected with action plans.
- *Business performance monitoring* is useful where various performance records and operational data (such as turnover data) are examined for improvement. This method is particularly useful for impact data (Level 4).

The important challenge is to select the data collection method or methods appropriate for the setting, stakeholders, and the specific solution, within the time and budget constraints of the organization.

Isolate the Effects of the Solution

An often-overlooked issue in most evaluations is the technique used to isolate the effects of retention solutions. In this step of the ROI process, specific strategies are explored to determine the amount of turnover improvement directly related to the solution. This step is essential because there are many factors that will usually influence turnover. The specific techniques utilized at this step will pinpoint the amount of improvement directly related to the solution. The result is increased accuracy and credibility of the ROI calculation. The following techniques have been used by organizations to address this important issue:

- A *control group* arrangement may be used to isolate the impact. With this technique, one group is involved in the solution while another similar group is not. The difference in the turnover of the two groups is attributed to the program. When properly set up and implemented, the control group arrangement is the most effective way to isolate effects of a retention solution.
- *Trend lines* are used to project the turnover rate based on pre-project data, as if the solution had not been undertaken. The projection is compared to the actual data after the solution is implemented and the difference represents an estimate of the

impact. Under certain conditions, this strategy can be an accurate way to isolate the impact of retention solutions.

- *Key stakeholders estimate* the amount of improvement related to the retention solution. Here, participants in retention solutions are provided with the total amount of improvement on a pre- and post-implementation basis, and asked to indicate the percent of the improvement that actually relates to the solution. These estimates should be adjusted for the error of the estimates.
- *Supervisors and managers estimate* the impact of retention solutions on turnover. Supervisors are presented with the total amount of turnover improvement and asked to indicate the percent related to the solution. Senior managers may estimate the impact of retention solutions. In these cases, managers provide an estimate or "adjustment" to reflect the portion of the improvement related to the solution. While these estimates might be inaccurate, there are some advantages to having senior management involved in this process, such as senior management ownership of the solution.
- *Experts provide estimates* of the impact of retention solution. Because the estimates are based on previous experience, the experts must be familiar with the type of solution and the specific situation.
- When feasible, *other influencing factors are identified and the impact estimated or calculated*, leaving the remaining unexplained improvement attributed to the solution. In this case, the influence of all other factors is developed and the solution remains the one variable not accounted for in the analysis. The unexplained portion of the turnover reduction is then attributed to the solution.

Collectively, these techniques provide a comprehensive set of tools to isolate the effects of retention solution.

Convert Data to Monetary Values

To calculate the return on investment, business impact data are converted to monetary values to compare with solution costs. This requires a value to be placed on each unit of data connected with the solution. For most retention solutions, the only output measure is turnover. However, some solutions will also drive other measures such as job satisfaction, productivity, quality, and customer service. Several approaches are available to convert data to monetary values where the specific technique selected usually depends on the type of data and the situation.

- *Output data is converted to profit contribution or cost savings.* With this approach, output increases are converted to monetary value based on their unit of contribution to profit or the unit of cost reduction. These values are standard values, readily available in most organizations.
- The *cost of quality is calculated* and quality improvements are directly converted to cost savings. These values are standard values, available in many organizations.
- For solutions where employee time is saved in addition to turnover, *wages and benefits are used for the value of time.* Because some solutions focus on improving the time required to complete projects, processes, or daily activities, the value of time becomes an important issue.
- *Historical costs and organizational records* are used when they are available for a specific measure. In this case, organization cost data is utilized to establish the specific value of an improvement. This approach is used by some organizations to develop the cost of turnover.
- When available, *internal and external experts* may be used to estimate a value for an improvement. In this situation, the credibility of the estimate hinges on the expertise and reputation of the individual. Consultants offering retention practices may be able to provide an estimate.
- *External databases* are sometimes available to estimate the value or cost of data items. Research, government, and industry databases can provide important information for these values. The difficulty lies in finding a specific database related to the situation. For turnover, a significant amount of research is available on the cost of turnover, precluding the development of internal cost value.
- *Participants in a retention solution estimate* the value of the data item. For this approach to be effective, participants must be capable of providing a value for the improvement.
- *Soft measures are linked, mathematically, to other measures* that are easier to measure and convert to value. This approach is

particularly helpful when establishing values for measures that are very difficult to convert to monetary values, such as customer satisfaction, employee satisfaction, stress, and employee complaints.

- *Supervisors and managers* provide estimates when they are both willing and capable of assigning values to the improvement. This approach is especially useful when participants are not fully capable of providing the input or in situations where supervisors need to confirm or adjust the participant's estimate.
- *HR staff estimates* may be used to determine a value of an output data item. In these cases, it is essential for the estimates to be provided on an unbiased basis.

This step in the ROI model is very important and is absolutely necessary to determine the monetary benefits from retention solutions. The process is challenging, particularly with soft data, but can be methodically accomplished using one or more of the above techniques.

Tabulate Costs of the Solution

The next step in the process is tabulating the costs of the retention solution. Tabulating the costs involves monitoring or developing all of the related costs of the solution. Among the components that should be included are

- The cost to design and develop the solution, possibly prorated over the expected life cycle of the solution;
- The cost of all materials provided to each stakeholder and team leader;
- The cost of the facilitator, coordinator, or leader, including preparation times as well as contact time;
- The cost of the use of facilities, if applicable;
- Travel, lodging, and meal costs for the participants, if applicable;
- Salaries plus employee benefits of the participants for the time they are involved in the solution, away from their normal job duties; and
- Administrative and overhead costs of the HR function allocated in some convenient way to retention solutions.

In addition, specific costs related to the diagnostic analysis and needs assessment should be included, if appropriate. The conservative approach is to include all of these costs so that the total is fully loaded.

Calculate the ROI

The return on investment is calculated using the benefits and costs. The cost/benefit ratio is the solution benefits divided by solution cost. In formula form it is as follows:

$$\text{BCR} = \frac{\text{Solution Benefits}}{\text{Solution Costs}}$$

The return on investment uses the net benefits divided by solution costs. The net benefits are the solution benefits minus the costs. In formula form, the ROI becomes

$$\text{ROI (\%)} = \frac{\text{Net Solution Benefits}}{\text{Costs}} \times 100$$

This is the same basic formula used in evaluating other investments where the ROI is traditionally reported as earnings divided by investment. The ROI from some solutions is high because of the huge savings generated when turnover is reduced.

ROI Calculation Example

To illustrate exactly how the calculation is developed, consider the following situation. In a hospital chain, a talent retention solution (for nurses) was implemented to reduce the number of sexual harassment complaints. The data collection and ROI analysis for this program is presented in Table 13.2 and Table 13.3. Exhibit 13.1 shows the calculation of the monetary benefits for this program. Only the calculation is shown. For additional information on this case study, please see the original publication (Phillips & Phillips, 2007).

As Exhibit 13.1 shows, most of the monetary benefit came directly from the turnover reduction, yielding a total value of $2.8 million. Sexual harassment complaints were another business impact measure directly connected with the program, yielding $360,000. Exhibit 13.2 show the actual solution costs. These are fully loaded costs that

Turnover Reduction

Unit of improvement = one turnover statistic (termination)

Turnover, preprogram = $6,651 \times 24.2\% = 1,610$

Turnover, preprogram, related to hostile environment: $1,610 \times 11\% = 177$

Turnover, post-program: $6,844 \times 19.9\% = 1,362$

Turnover, post-program related to hostile environment: $1,362 \times 3\% = 41$

Improvement related to program: $177 - 41 = 136$

Cost of one turnover: 75% of annual salary = $27,850 \times .75 = \$20,887$

Value of improvement: $136 \times \$20,887 = \$2,840,632$

Complaint Reduction

Unit of improvement = one internal complaint

Value of one internal complaint = $24,343

Total improvement: $55 - 35 = 20$

Improvement related to program: $20 \times 74\% = 14.8$

Value of improvement = $14.8 \times \$24,343 = \$360,276$

Total Benefits: $2,840,632 + $360,276 = $3,200,908

Exhibit 13.1. Calculation of Monetary Benefits

equate to $277,987. The calculations of the ROI for these values are as follows:

$$\text{CBR} = \frac{\text{Benefits}}{\text{Costs}} = \frac{\$360,276 + \$2,840,632}{\$277,987}$$

$$= \frac{\$3,200,908}{\$277,987} = 11.5\text{:}1$$

$$\text{ROI} = \frac{\text{Net Benefits}}{\text{Costs}} = \frac{\$4,300,908 - \$277,987}{\$277,987} = 1,052\%$$

Benefits based entirely on complaint and turnover reduction are used in the cost-benefit ratio to yield 11.5:1. Thus, for each dollar spent on the program, $11.50 was returned. The ROI calculation, which uses net benefits, shows a return of 1,052%, an impressive and staggering amount. The results were much greater than the evaluation team and senior management expected.

Cost Category	Total Cost
Assessment (estimated cost of time)	$9,000
Solution development/acquisition	$15,000
Coordination/facilitation time	$9,600
Travel and lodging for facilitation and coordinators	$1,520
Materials (655 @ $12)	$7,860
Food/refreshments (655 @ $30)	$19,650
Facilities (17 @ $150)	$2,550
Participant salaries and benefits ($130,797 × 1.39)	$181,807
Evaluation	$31,000
	$277,987

Exhibit 13.2.   Solution Costs

Identify Intangibles

In addition to tangible monetary benefits, most retention solutions will have intangible non-monetary benefits. Data items identified that are not converted to monetary values are considered intangible benefits. While many of these items can be converted to monetary values, for various reasons, they often are not. One reason is that the process used for conversion is too subjective and the resulting values lose credibility in the process.

These intangible benefits may include: increased job satisfaction, increased organizational commitment, improved teamwork, improved customer service, reduced complaints, and reduced conflicts. For some solutions, these intangible non-monetary benefits are extremely valuable, often carrying as much influence as the hard data items.

OPERATING STANDARDS AND PHILOSOPHY

To ensure consistency and replication of studies, operating standards must be developed and applied as the process model is utilized to develop ROI studies. It is extremely important for the results of a study to stand alone and be consistent, regardless of the individual conducting the study. The operating standards detail how each step and issue of the process will be handled. Exhibit 13.3 shows the guiding principles that form the basis for the operating standards.

1. When conducting a higher-level evaluation, collect data at lower levels.
2. When planning a higher level evaluation, the previous level of evaluation is not required to be comprehensive.
3. When collecting and analyzing data, use only the most credible sources.
4. When analyzing data, select the most conservative alternatives for calculations.
5. Use at least one method to isolate the effects of the program or project.
6. If no improvement data are available for a population or from a specific source, assume that little or no improvement has occurred.
7. Adjust estimates of improvements for the potential error of the estimates.
8. Avoid use of extreme data items and unsupported claims when calculating ROI calculations.
9. Use only the first year of annual benefits in the ROI analysis of short-term solutions.
10. Fully load all costs of the solution, project, or program when analyzing ROI.
11. Intangible measures are defined as measures that are purposely not converted to monetary values.
12. Communicate the results of the ROI Methodology to all key stakeholders.

Exhibit 13.3.   Guiding Principles

The guiding principles not only serve as a way to consistently address each step, but also provide a much-needed conservative approach to the analysis. A conservative approach may lower the actual ROI calculation, but it will also build credibility with the target audience for communicating results, especially senior executives. For additional information on calculating return on investment, see other resources (Phillips & Zuniga, 2008).

FINAL THOUGHTS

ROI calculations for retention solutions are being developed by many organizations to meet the demands of influential stakeholders. The result is a process that shows the value-added contribution of a retention strategy in a format desired by many senior executives and administrators. In this chapter we demonstrated that the ROI process represents significant and challenging progress for most organizations. The process must be based on a sound framework, using a process model that provides step-by-step procedures and credible methodologies. Through careful planning, methodical procedures, and logical and practical analysis, ROI calculations can be developed reliably and accurately for any type of retention solution.

References

Broad, M.L. (2005). *Beyond transfer of training: Engaging systems to improve performance.* San Francisco, CA: Pfeiffer.

Phillips, J.J. (Ed.). (1994). *In action: Measuring return on investment, vol. 1.* Alexandria, VA: American Society for Training and Development.

Phillips, J.J. (2003). *Return on investment in training and performance improvement programs* (2nd ed.). Boston, MA: Butterworth-Heinemann.

Phillips, J.J., & Phillips, P.P. (2002, May/June). How to measure the return on your HR investment. *Strategic HR Review, 1*(4), 16–21.

Phillips, J.J., & Zuniga, L. (2008). *Cost and ROI: Evaluating at the ultimate level.* San Francisco, CA: Pfeiffer.

Phillips, P.P., & Phillips, J.J. (2007). *Proving the value of HR: ROI case studies,* Birmingham, AL: ROI Institute.

CHAPTER FOURTEEN

Make Adjustments and Continue

W ith data in hand, what's next? Should the data be used to modify the retention solution, change the solution, show the contribution of the solution, justify new solutions, gain additional support for managing retention solutions, or build goodwill? How should the data be presented? The worst course of action is to do nothing. Making adjustments is as important as achieving results. This chapter provides useful information to help present data to the various audiences and drive important actions. We discuss how to communicate to, and build relationships with, the senior management team. The chapter concludes with a discussion of how to overcome the resistance to implementing solutions and how to take a long view of maintaining workforce stability.

THE IMPORTANCE OF COMMUNICATING RESULTS

Communicating results is a critical issue when implementing retention solutions. Constant communication throughout the process, and at specific follow-up times, ensures that information is flowing so that adjustments can be made and all stakeholders are aware of the success of the solution. Several issues underscore the importance of communicating results of a retention solution.

Communication Is Necessary to Make Improvements

Because information is collected at different points during the process, the feedback to the various stakeholder groups is the only way for adjustments to be made. Thus, the quality and timeliness of communication become critical issues for making necessary improvements. Even after the project is completed, communication is necessary to make sure the target audience fully understands the results achieved and how the results could either be enhanced in future programs or in the current program, if it is still operational.

Communication Is Necessary to Explain Contributions

Communication must be planned and executed to ensure that the audiences understand the contribution of the retention solution using six types of measures. The different target audiences will need thorough explanations of the results. Communicating business impact and ROI data can quickly become confusing for even the most sophisticated target audiences. A communication strategy including techniques, media, and the overall process will determine the extent to which the audiences understand the contribution.

Communication Is a Sensitive Issue

Communication is one of those important issues that can cause major problems. Because the results of an initiative can be closely linked to the political issues in an organization, communication can upset some individuals while pleasing others. At times, the reputation of an individual or group is at stake. If certain individuals do not receive the information or if the information is unfavorable, problems can quickly surface. Not only is it an issue of understanding, but it is also a fairness, quality, and political correctness issue to make sure that information is presented effectively to all key individuals who need it.

A Variety of Target Audiences Need Different Information

Because there are so many potential target audiences for data, it is important for the communication to be tailored to their needs. A varied audience will have varied needs. Some groups, such as sponsors and executives, need information on the outcome of the project, measured in reduced turnover and ROI. Team leaders and managers need to know whether they are implementing the solution properly. Project developers and solutions coordinators need to know whether the solution was on track. Employees need to be convinced that the organization is addressing the issue. Here are a few questions that should be addressed for each audience:

1. Who are the target audiences? Identify specific target audiences that should always receive information and others that will receive information when appropriate.
2. What will actually be communicated?
3. When will the data be communicated?
4. How will the information be communicated?
5. Where should the communication take place?
6. Who will communicate the information?
7. What specific actions are required or desired?

Collectively, these questions make communication critical, although it is often overlooked or underestimated in retention solutions. In this chapter we build on this important issue and shows a variety of techniques for communicating to various target audiences.

PRINCIPLES OF COMMUNICATING RESULTS

The skills required to communicate results effectively are almost as delicate and sophisticated as those needed to obtain results. The style is as important as the substance. Regardless of the message, audience, or medium, a few general principles apply and are explored next.

Communication Must Be Timely

Usually, results should be communicated as soon as they are known. From a practical standpoint, it may be best to delay the communicationuntil a convenient time, such as the publication of the next newsletter or the next general management meeting. Several issues about timing must be addressed. Is the audience ready for the results when considering other pressing issues? Is the audience expecting results? When is the best time to have the maximum effect on the audience? Are there circumstances that dictate a change in the timing of the communication?

Selecting the Audience Is Crucial to Success

When approaching a particular audience, the following questions should be asked about each potential group:

- Are they interested in the initiative?
- Do they really want to receive the information?
- Has someone already made a commitment to them regarding communication?
- Is the timing right for this audience?
- Are they familiar with the retention solution?
- How do they prefer to have results communicated?
- Do they know the HR staff members?
- Are they likely to find the results threatening?
- Which presentation medium will be most convincing to this group?

The potential target audiences to receive information about HR results are varied in terms of job levels and responsibilities. Determining which groups will receive a particular communication requires careful thought, as problems can arise when a particular group receives inappropriate information or when another is omitted altogether. A sound way to select the proper audience is to analyze the reason for communication. Table 14.1 shows common target audiences and the rationale for selecting that audience.

While this list shows the most common target audiences, there can be others. For instance, management or employees can be subdivided into different departments, divisions, or even subsidiaries of the organization. The number of audiences can be large in a complex organization. At a minimum, four target audiences are recommended:

Reason for Communication	Primary Target Audiences
Secure Approval for the Retention Solution	Client, Top Executives
Gain Support for the Retention Solution	Immediate Managers, Team Leaders
Secure Agreement with the Issues	Participants, Team Leaders
Build Credibility for the HR Department	Top Executives
Enhance Reinforcement of the Processes	Immediate Managers
Drive Action for Improvement	HR Staff Members
Prepare Participants for the Retention Solution	Team Leaders
Show the Complete Results of the Retention Solution	Client Team
Underscore the Importance of Measuring Results	Client, HR Staff Members
Explain Techniques Used to Measure Results	Client, Support Staff
Create Desire for Stakeholders to Be Involved	Team Leaders
Stimulate Interest in the HR Department's Services	Top Executives
Demonstrate Accountability for Client Expenditures	All Employees
Market Future HR Programs	Prospective Clients

Table 14.1.   Common Target Audiences

a senior management group, the participants' immediate manager or team leader, the project participants, and the HR staff.

Communication Should Be Targeted to Specific Audiences

Communication will be more effective if it is designed for a particular group. A single report for all audiences may not be appropriate. The scope, size, media, and actual information will vary from one group to another. The message should be specifically tailored to the interests, needs, and expectations of the target audience. The results of a retention solution include the six types of data developed in this book. Some of the data are developed earlier in the project and may be communicated during implementation. Other data are collected after implementation and communicated in a follow-up study. Thus, the results, in the broadest sense, may range from early feedback in qualitative terms to ROI values in a follow-up impact study.

To the greatest extent possible, the HR staff should know and understand the target audience. They should try to understand audience bias, as each will have a particular bias or opinion. Some will quickly support the results, whereas others may be against them or be neutral. The staff should be empathetic and try to understand differing views. This is especially critical when the potential exists for the audience to react negatively to the results.

Media Should Be Carefully Selected

Some types of communication media may be more effective than others with certain audiences. Face-to-face meetings with key managers may be better than special bulletins. A memo distributed exclusively to top management may be more effective than the company newsletter. A downloadable report on the web may be appropriate for other audiences. Determining the appropriate method of communication can improve the effectiveness of the process.

Communication Should Be Unbiased and Modest

It is important to separate fact from fiction and accurate statements from opinions. Some audiences may accept communication from HR staff members with skepticism, anticipating biased opinions. Boastful statements sometimes turn off audiences, and most of the content is lost. Although sensational claims may get audience attention, they often detract from the importance of the results. Observable, believable facts carry far more weight.

Communication Must Be Consistent

The timing and content of the communication should be consistent with past practices. A special communication at an unusual time during the project may provoke suspicion. Also, if a particular group, such as top management, regularly receives communication on HR outcomes, it should continue receiving communication—even if the results are not positive. If some results are omitted, it might leave the impression that only positive results are reported.

Testimonials Can Be Effective

The value of opinions is strongly influenced by the source— particularly those who are respected and trusted. Testimonials about HR results, when solicited from respected individuals, can influence the effectiveness of the message. This respect may be related to leadership ability, role, position, special skills, or expert knowledge. A testimonial from an individual who commands little respect or is regarded as a substandard performer can have a negative impact on the message.

HR's Reputation Will Influence the Communication Strategy

Opinions are difficult to change. For example, and a negative opinion of HR may not change because new data is being presented. Conversely, the presentation of facts alone may strengthen the good opinions held by some. It helps to reinforce their position and provides a defense in discussions with others. An HR department with a high level of credibility and respect may have a relatively easy time communicating results. Low credibility can create problems when trying to persuade employees or management of a new approach. The reputation of the department always must be an important consideration in developing the overall strategy.

Planning the Communication Is a Critical Step

Any successful activity must be carefully planned for maximum results. Planning is important to ensure that each audience receives the proper information at the right time and that appropriate actions are taken. The questions presented earlier must be addressed when developing any plan.

It is especially important to have a plan for presenting the results of an impact study. This is more specialized than the plan for communicating a progress report because it involves an impact study from a major retention solution. Table 14.2 shows the communication plan for a major retention project with a stress-reduction solution. (Excessive stress was causing high burnout and, consequently, high turnover.)

In this example, five different communication pieces were developed, each for a different audience. The complete report of the ROI impact study, a seventy-five-page document, served as the historical account of the project. It was prepared for the client, the HR staff, and the managers of each of the teams involved in the studies. An

Communication Document	Communication Target(s)	Distribution Method
Complete Report with Appendices (75 pages)	Client Team/HR Staff/Intact Team Manager	Distribute and Discuss in a Special Meeting
Executive Summary (8 pages)	Senior Management in the Business Units/Senior Corporate Management	Distribute and Discuss in a Routine Meeting
General Interest Overview and Summary Without the Actual ROI Calculation (10 pages)	Participants	Mail with Letter
General Interest Article (1 page)	All Employees	Publish in Company Publication
Brochure Highlighting Program, Objectives, and Specific Results	Team Leaders with an Interest in the Project	Include with Other Marketing Materials

Table 14.2.   Retention Solution Communication Plan

executive summary, a much smaller document, was designed for a select group of higher-level executives. A general-interest overview and summary without the ROI calculation went to the participants. A third document, a general-interest article, was developed for company publications, and a brochure was developed to show the success of the retention solution. The brochure was used in marketing the same solution internally to other teams.

Following these general principles for communication are important to the overall success of the effort. They should serve as a checklist for the HR team.

DEVELOPING THE IMPACT STUDY REPORT

The type of formal evaluation report to present depends on the extent of detailed information you want to present to the various target audiences. Brief summaries of project results with appropriate charts may be sufficient for some. In other situations, particularly with significant HR interventions requiring extensive funding, the amount of detail in the evaluation report is more crucial. A complete and comprehensive impact study report may be necessary.

Content of the Report

This report can then be used as the basis of information for specific audiences and various groups. The report may contain any or all of the following sections:

Management/executive summary. The management summary is a brief overview of the entire report, explaining the basis for the evaluation and the significant conclusions and recommendations. It is designed for individuals who are too busy to read a detailed report. It is usually written last but appears first in the report for easy access.

Background information. The background information provides a general description of the retention solution. If applicable, the analysis and events that led to the implementation of the retention solution are summarized. The solution is fully described. The extent of detailed information depends on the amount of information the audience needs.

Objectives. The objectives for the retention solution are outlined. These objectives provide the framework from which the different types or levels of data will be collected.

Evaluation strategy/methodology. The evaluation strategy identifies all the components that make up the total evaluation process. Several components of the ROI Methodology, presented in this book, are discussed in this section of the report. The specific purposes of evaluation are outlined, and the evaluation design and methodology are explained. The instruments used in data collection are also described and usually presented as exhibits. Any unusual issues in the evaluation design are discussed. Finally, other useful information related to the design, timing, and execution of the evaluation is included.

Data collection and analysis. This section explains the methods used to collect data, as outlined in earlier chapters. The data collected are usually presented in the report in summary form. Next, the methods used to analyze data are presented with interpretations.

Project costs. Costs of the retention solution are presented in this section, by category. For example, analysis, development, implementation, operation, and evaluation costs are recommended categories for cost presentation. The assumptions made in developing and classifying costs are presented here.

Reaction and satisfaction. This section details the data collected from key stakeholders, particularly the participants involved in the retention solution, to measure the reaction and satisfaction with the solution.

Learning. This section shows a brief summary of the improvement in knowledge and skills related to the retention solution. It explains how much participants have learned new processes, skills, tasks, procedures, and practices needed to make the retention solution successful.

Application and implementation. This section shows how the retention solution was implemented and the success of the application of new skills and knowledge. Key implementation issues are addressed, including any major success and/or lack of success.

Business impact. This section shows the changes in turnover and retention and other business impact measures that initially influenced the need for the project. This shows the extent to which performance has changed because of the implementation of the retention solution.

Return on investment. This section actually shows the ROI calculation along with the benefits/cost ratio. It compares the calculated value with the expected value and provides an interpretation of the actual calculation.

Intangible measures. This section shows the various intangible measures directly linked to the retention solution. Intangibles are those measures not converted to monetary values or included in the actual ROI calculation. They are reported only if there is evidence of linkage to the solution.

Barriers and enablers. The various problems and obstacles affecting the success of the retention solution are detailed and presented as barriers to implementation. Also, those factors or influences that had a positive effect on the solution are included as enablers. Together, they provide important insight into the factors that can hinder or enhance projects in the future.

Conclusions and recommendations. This section presents conclusions based on all the results. If appropriate, brief explanations are presented on how each conclusion was reached. A list of recommendations or changes in the solution, if appropriate, is provided with brief explanations for each recommendation. It is important that the conclusions and recommendations be consistent with one another and with the findings described in the previous section.

Developing the Report

Exhibit 14.1 shows the table of contents from a typical evaluation report for an ROI evaluation. This specific study was conducted for a large chemical company and involved an ROI analysis on a retention solution. The typical report provides background information, explains the processes used and, more important, presents the results.

General Information
- Background Information on Retention Solution
- Objectives of Study

Methodology for Impact Study
- Levels of Evaluation
- The ROI Methodology
- Collecting Data
- Isolating the Effects of the Retention Solution
- Converting Data to Monetary Values

Data Analysis Issues
Cost of Retention Solution
Results: General Information
- Response Profile
- Success with Objectives

Results: Reaction and Satisfaction with Retention Solution
- Data Sources
- Data Summary
- Key Issues

Exhibit 14.1. Format of an ROI Impact Study Report

Results: Learning for Solution Success

- Data Sources
- Data Summary
- Key Issues

Results: Application and Implementation of Solution

- Data Sources
- Data Summary
- Key Issues

Results: Turnover Reduction (or Prevention)

- General Comments
- Linkage with Other Business Measures
- Key Issues

Results: ROI and Its Meaning
Results: Intangible Measures Linked to Solution
Barriers and Enablers

- Barriers to Solution Success
- Enablers for Solution Success

Conclusions and Recommendations

- Conclusions
- Recommendations

Exhibits

Exhibit 14.1.   (*continued*)

While this report is an effective, professional way to present ROI data, several cautions must be noted. Because this document reports the success of an HR-initiated retention solution involving a group of employees, complete credit for the success must go to the stakeholders who made the difference and their immediate leaders. Their performance generated the success. Another important caution is to avoid boasting about results. Although the ROI process may be accurate and credible, it may still contain subjective assessment. Huge claims of success can quickly turn off an audience and interfere with the delivery of the desired message.

A final caution concerns the structure of the report. The methodology should be clearly explained, along with assumptions made in the analysis. The reader should easily see how the values were developed and how the specific steps were followed to make the process more conservative, credible, and accurate. Detailed statistical analyses should be placed in an appendix.

COMMUNICATING INFORMATION ON RETENTION SOLUTIONS

Perhaps the biggest challenge of communication is the actual delivery of the message. This can be accomplished in a variety of ways and settings, based on the target audience and the media selected for the message. Several approaches deserve additional coverage and are presented here.

Providing Ongoing Feedback

One of the most important reasons for collecting reaction, satisfaction, and learning data is to provide feedback so adjustments or changes can be made throughout the project. In most retention solutions, data are routinely collected and quickly communicated to a variety of groups. Exhibit 14.2 shows the typical areas of feedback provided to several feedback audiences using a variety of media.

Data are collected during the project at four specific time intervals and communicated to at least four audiences—sometimes six. Some of these feedback sessions result in identifying specific actions that need to be taken. This process becomes comprehensive and must be managed in a very proactive way. The following steps are recommended for providing feedback and managing the feedback process (Block, 2001):

Communicate quickly. Whether the results are good or bad, it is important to let individuals involved in the project have the information as soon as possible. The recommended time for providing feedback is usually a matter of days and certainly no longer than a week or two after the results are known.

Simplify the data. Condense data into an understandable, concise presentation. This is not the forum for detailed explanations and analysis.

Appropriateness of objectives	Project coordination
Appropriateness of plans	Project communication
Appropriateness of schedule	Motivation of project participants
Progress made with plans	Cooperation of project participants
Importance of project	Capability of project participants
Support for project	Likelihood of project success
Resources for project	Barriers to project success
Integration of project with other systems	Enablers to project success
Project leadership	

Exhibit 14.2.   Areas of Feedback for Retention Solutions

Examine the role of the solution team and the client in the feedback situation. Sometimes the solution team (or HR executive) is the judge, jury, prosecutor, defendant, or witness. On the other hand, sometimes the client is the judge, jury, prosecutor, defendant, or witness. It is important to examine the respective roles in terms of reactions to the data and the actions that need to be taken.

Use negative data in a constructive way. Some of the data will show that things are not going so well, and the fault may rest with the HR department or the client. In that case, the story basically changes from "Let's look at the success we've made" to "Now we know which areas to change."

Use positive data in a cautious way. Positive data can be misleading, and if it is communicated too enthusiastically, expectations may be created that may be realized.

Choose the language of the meeting and communication very carefully. Use language that is descriptive, focused, specific, short, and simple. Avoid language that is too judgmental, macro, stereotypical, lengthy, or complex.

Ask the client for reactions to the data. After all, the client is the number 1 customer, and the client's reaction is critical because it is most important that the client be pleased with the program.

Ask the client for recommendations. The client may have some good recommendations of what needs to be changed to keep the solution on track or put it back on track if it derails.

Use support and confrontation carefully. These two issues are not mutually exclusive. There may be times when support and confrontation are needed for the same group. The client may need support and yet be confronted for lack of improvement or sponsorship. The solution team may need to be confronted about the problem areas that are developed but may need support as well.

React and act on the data. Weigh the different alternatives and possibilities to arrive at the adjustments and changes that will be necessary.

Secure agreement from all key stakeholders. This is essential to make sure everyone is willing to make adjustments and changes that seem necessary.

Keep the feedback process short. Don't let it become bogged down in long, drawn out meetings or lengthy documents. If this occurs, stakeholders will avoid the process instead of being willing to participate in the future.

Following these twelve steps will help move the program forward and provide important feedback, often ensuring that adjustments are supported and made.

As briefly mentioned earlier in the chapter, the timing of communication is extremely important. The communication must be routine and continuous to make changes and drive improvement. Figure 14.1 shows an example of communication from a six-month retention solution project. As the figure illustrates, data is collected prior to the project and at different intervals during the project. Finally, after a six-month follow-up is completed, it is presented to a variety of target audiences as described earlier. The important issue in

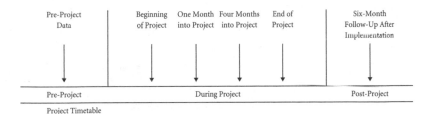

Figure 14.1. Timing of Feedback for a Six-Month Retention Project

the planning stage is to address the timing issue along with audiences and information.

PRESENTING IMPACT STUDY DATA TO SENIOR MANAGEMENT

Perhaps one of the most challenging and potentially stressful communications is presenting an impact study to the senior management team—the client seeking a retention solution. The challenge is convincing this highly skeptical and critical group that outstanding results have been achieved (assuming they have), in a reasonable time frame, addressing the salient points, and making sure the managers understand the process used to measure success. Two particular issues can create challenges. If the results are impressive, it may be difficult to make the managers believe the data. On the other extreme, if the data are negative, it will be a challenge to make sure managers don't overreact to the negative results and look for someone to blame. Several guidelines can help make sure this process is planned and executed properly:

- Plan a face-to-face meeting with senior team members for the first one or two major impact studies. If they are unfamiliar with the complete ROI process, a face-to-face meeting is necessary to make sure they understand the process. The good news is that they will probably attend the meeting because they have not seen ROI data developed for this type of project. The bad news is that it takes some of their precious time, usually one to two hours for this presentation.

- After the group has experienced a face-to-face meeting with a couple of presentations, an executive summary may suffice. At this point they understand the process, so a shortened version may be appropriate.

- After the group is familiar with the process, a brief version may suffice. A one- to two-page summary with charts and graphs showing all six types of measures will usually work.

- When making the initial presentation, the results should not be distributed in advance, or even during the session, but saved until the end of the session. This will allow enough time to present the process and react to it before the target audience sees the actual ROI number.

- Present the process step-by-step, showing how the data were collected, when they were collected, who provided the data, how the data were isolated from other influences, and how they were converted to monetary values. The various assumptions, adjustments, and conservative approaches are presented along with the total cost of the initiative. The costs are fully loaded so that the target audience will begin to buy into the process of developing the actual ROI.

- When the data are actually presented, reveal results step-by-step, starting with reaction, moving through to ROI, and ending with the intangibles. This allows the audience to see the chain of impact with reaction, learning, application, business impact, and ROI. After some discussion about the meaning of the ROI, present the intangible measures. Allocate adequate time to each level of data, as needed for the audience. This helps overcome the potentially negative reactions to a very positive or negative ROI.

- Show the costs of additional accuracy, if it is an issue. The tradeoff for more accuracy and validity often means more time and direct expense. Address this issue whenever necessary, agreeing to collect more data if required.

- Solicit concerns, reactions, and issues for the process and make adjustments accordingly for the next presentation.

Collectively, following these steps will help you prepare for and present one of the most critical meetings for the human resources staff.

CONDUCTING A RETENTION REVIEW MEETING

No group is more important than top executives when it comes to building support for managing retention. In many situations, this group is also the client for retention solutions. Improving communications with this group requires developing an overall strategy and building informal and formal relationship with the senior team.

A retention review meeting is an effective time to communicate to top executives about managing retention. While such a review can be conducted more frequently, an annual review is common. The primary purpose is to show top management what has been accomplished in retention management and what is planned for the future. Also, the review provides an opportunity for input and advice to the HR staff about retention issues, including needs, problems with the present solutions, and evaluation issues. The meeting can last from two hours to two days, depending on its scope and the amount of information. This meeting is best suited for situations in which retention is a critical issue, long-term strategies for managing retention are in place, and multiple solutions are being implemented in the same firm. A typical agenda for a half-day version of this review meeting is shown in Exhibit 14.3.

This meeting may be the single most important event on the HR department's calendar during the year. It must be planned carefully, executed in a timely manner, and controlled to accomplish its purpose. This approach described here has been used in many organizations, and the reaction has been extremely favorable. Executives and managers want to know what the organization is accomplishing with retention, what results have been achieved and,

Time	Annual Review Meeting Topic
8:00 a.m.	Review of retention issues and strategies
8:30	Review of turnover data and analysis
9:00	Description of each retention solution and the results achieved
10:30	Significant deviations from the expected results (both positive and negative)
11:00	Basis for determining retention needs for the next year
11:15	Anticipated solutions for the coming year (secure support and approval)
11:30	Proposed evaluation strategy and potential payoffs
12:00	Problem areas for managing retention (lack of support, where management involvement is needed or other potential problems that can be corrected by executive management)
12:30	Concerns of executive management
1:00	Adjourn

Exhibit 14.3.   Annual Review Agenda

most of all, they want to have input on the decisions for retention solutions.

USING THE ORGANIZATION'S PUBLICATIONS AND STANDARD COMMUNICATION TOOLS

To reach a wide audience, the HR department can use in-house publications to communicate information about retention solutions. Whether a newsletter, magazine, newspaper, e-mail, intranet, or websites, these types of media usually reach all employees. The information can be quite effective if communicated appropriately. The scope should be limited to general interest articles, announcements, and interviews.

Project results. Results communicated through these types of media must be significant enough to arouse general interest. For example, a story with the headline, "New Flex Time Project Reduces Turnover by 10 Percent," will catch the attention of many people because they may have participated in the solution and can appreciate the significance of the results. Reports on the accomplishments of a subgroup of participants may not create interest unless the audience relates to the accomplishments.

For many retention solutions, results are achieved weeks or even months after the project is completed. Participants need reinforcement from many sources. If results are communicated to a general audience, including the participant's subordinates or peers, there is additional pressure to continue the project or similar ones in the future.

Building interest. Stories about managing retention and the results achieved creates a favorable image. Employees are made aware that the organization is investing time and money to improve performance and prepare for the future. This type of story provides information about projects that employees otherwise may not have known about and sometimes creates a desire to participate, if given the opportunity.

Stakeholder recognition. General audience communication can bring recognition to participants, particularly those who excel in some aspect of the project. When participants deliver unusually high performance, public recognition can enhance their self-esteem.

Human-interest stories. Many human-interest stories can come out of retention solutions. In one organization, the editor of the company newsletter participated in a comprehensive leadership development project and wrote a stimulating article about what it was like to be a participant. The article gave the readers a view of the entire course and its effectiveness in terms of the results achieved, including a reduction in turnover. It was an interesting and effective way to communicate about a challenging activity.

Case studies. Case studies represent an effective way to communicate the results of a retention solution. A typical case study describes the situation, provides appropriate background information (including the issues that led to the solution), presents the techniques and strategies used to develop the solution, and highlights the key issues in the project. Case studies tell an interesting story of how the solution was developed and the problems and concerns identified along the way. In one fast-food company, the new employee orientation was redesigned to reduce turnover in the first sixty days of employment. The success was reported in the company newsletter.

Case studies have many useful applications in an organization. They can offer different perspectives and draw conclusions about approaches or techniques. A case study can serve as a self-teaching guide for individuals trying to understand how retention is managed. Case studies provide appropriate recognition for those involved in the actual case. More importantly, they recognize the stakeholders who achieved the results. The case study format is an effective way to learn about managing retention.

DRIVING ACTION FROM RETENTION SOLUTIONS

The primary reason for collecting and communicating data is to drive improvement. Any type of measurement and evaluation process will yield important data to enable changes or to provide assurance that solutions are working as planned.

Sources of Data for Action

Essentially, all collection methods have the potential of yielding data that can drive actions for improvement. When stakeholders provide input into the success (or lack of success) of a particular solution, they almost always include information, comments, and suggestions that can lead to improvements in the process. This is particularly true with interviews and questionnaires when specific questions focus on the barriers to success. A series of questions can be used to explore reasons for lack of success, uncovering obstacles, inhibiters, and specific barriers that need to change, be minimized, or removed to drive the necessary results.

On the flip side, it is helpful to examine the enablers to success. In a series of questions, the issues that have helped make the project successful can be uncovered so that what is going well can remain in place, be supported, and perhaps even enhanced. A comprehensive analysis of barriers and enablers is always recommended for any major project.

Other tactics can also uncover data that suggest improvement. Sometimes management support is a critical issue. The degree to which managers are supporting (or not supporting) a retention solution is important. Specific questions about the level of support can uncover dysfunctional situations or, on the positive side, excellent management support practices. Answers to such questions help improve the process when presented to the management team for action. Also, items such as "Recommendations for Improvement," "Suggestions for Changes," and "Other Comments" may provide rich data. Sometimes, unsolicited comments deposited in the organization's feedback system provide valuable data (labeled "sound off," "feedback," "speak up," etc.). These suggestion/comment systems often provide an avenue for stakeholders to voice opinions about retention issues and the effectiveness of particular solutions aimed at reducing turnover.

Potential Actions from Retention Solution

Essentially, one of four actions can develop after data is collected about the success of the retention program. The first option is to accept the status quo—leave the solution in place without change. This is rarely the case, and would only be true if all of the data suggest maximum success and that nothing needs to be changed to improve the program.

It is more likely that some adjustments need to be made in the retention solution. The results often suggest minor adjustments are needed to fine-tune the process or system.

A third option is to redesign the solution. This action is appropriate when the data show that the solution is not successful. The solution in place may have been an appropriate response to the need, but it was improperly designed or unsuccessfully implemented.

A fourth option is to discontinue the solution. In this case, the data most likely shows that the solution is not matching the need and there is no way that this solution will drive turnover down or prevent it in the future. The best course of action is to kill it. This action is rare.

Finding which of these options is important. Timely data must be collected so that actions can be taken quickly, before time and resources are wasted or diverted.

Developing the Action Plan

After it is determined that adjustments or redesign is needed for a major improvement, an action plan should be developed detailing the specific steps that will be taken to adjust, refocus, or redesign the retention solution. Any format will do as long as it follows the SMART requirements (specific, measurable, achievable, realistic, and time-based). The action planning process brings organization, structure, discipline, and follow-through.

Not Every Project Needs an ROI Calculation

As mentioned in earlier chapters, a comprehensive evaluation system that includes ROI is not necessarily appropriate for every retention solution. Minor solutions representing minimal investments and small amounts of time may not be appropriate to evaluate at the ROI level. Exhibit 14.4 lists the issues that must be considered when deciding to take a project to this level of accountability. Solutions that are very expensive, time-consuming, highly visible, and very strategic may require a comprehensive evaluation to include all six types of data, with ROI being one of the measures.

MAINTAINING A LOW TURNOVER RATE

The ultimate goal of the strategic accountability approach to managing retention is to develop a very low turnover rate, which translates

- The life cycle of the solution
- The link between the solution and operational goals and issues
- The importance of the solution to strategic objectives
- The cost of the solution
- Visibility of the solution
- The size of the target audience
- The investment of time
- Top executives' interest in the solution

**Exhibit 14.4.   Criteria for Selecting Retention Solutions
for ROI Evaluation**

into high retention. The starting point in the cycle may vary. This process could be developed in response to a high turnover issue and, as the process develops, causes are identified, solutions are implemented, and results are realized. Ultimately, turnover should be reduced. The process could start with the challenge of maintaining a current low turnover rate. The process is the same, but the payoffs are often based on what turnover rate would be realized if the solution were not implemented. Several steps should be taken when attempting to maintain a low turnover rate.

Revisit the Targets

A low turnover rate is only meaningful relative to what is expected or accepted. In Chapter 4, the concept of setting targets for turnover for a particular group was introduced. Three specific targets were identified: acceptable, employer of choice, and a stretch goal, usually in the top 10 to 25 percent of organizations in the same industry. These targets must be operational to maintain a low turnover. As turnover increases to one of these levels, specific actions will be triggered, with some actions more substantial than others. Targets become the trigger points for action.

Look at Special Challenges

Maintaining a low turnover presents special challenges. The first is to resist over-investing in prevention programs. While this may seem like unnecessary advice, some organizations spend large amounts of money developing new programs and projects and solving problems that do not necessarily exist. Consider, for example, a major automobile manufacturer who built an on-site fitness center with the primary objectives to increase the attraction of prospective employees and help retain current employees. While these are noble objectives consistent with many attraction and retention goals, the solution was not needed in this case. The employer enjoyed an excellent reputation in the community with a lucrative benefits package and hourly wage rates almost double that of the state's average. When the company announced a new assembly line opening up on the third shift, for example, it was flooded with thousands of applicants, many of them very high-quality candidates. Further investigation revealed an *extremely* low turnover—almost too low. Employees were already staying because of the excellent work environment and the generous pay and benefits package. The addition of the fitness center could be a positive contribution to the organization, but not for the purpose of attracting and retaining employees.

Another challenge is to consider using leading indicators to spot turnover problems before they become serious issues. As mentioned in Chapter 3, intention to quit is an important leading indicator, along with organizational commitment and job satisfaction data. These leading indicators can be crucial for early analysis and action before turnover develops into a serious problem.

A very important challenge is to take immediate action when a problem is uncovered. Quick action requires a rapid analysis of the turnover issue, the development an appropriate solution, and an efficient implementation and feedback of the results. The ability to take quick action can prevent a turnover problem from becoming disastrous.

A final special challenge is the notion of complacency. It is sometimes tempting to consider the retention issue as unimportant and move on to other challenges. While it *is* important to move to other critical issues in the organization, turnover should always be monitored, on a leading indicator basis, if possible, to ensure that retention is not becoming an issue. It is counterproductive to wait until turnover becomes an issue to tackle it again. Complacency can cause serious problems, eroding the good things that have been developed previously.

Monitor Outside the HR Area

Peripheral vision provides an awareness of impending trouble. For example, the economy and the measures associated with it (described earlier) often become leading indicators of more serious problems to come. If jobs are being created at a faster rate than the local market can handle, a potential turnover issue is developing.

Another idea is to monitor the competition. Very aggressive competitors sometimes feed off the success of others (that is, employees are recruited within an industry because of the quality, skills, and expertise of the employee in another company). Essentially, competitors are buying capable employees rather than investing in resources to develop them. This can happen unexpectedly as competition becomes more aggressive (or desperate) and searching for quick-fix approaches.

The health of the business must also be monitored—analyzing back orders, revenue, and projections—making sure that the organization is healthy financially and has adequate back orders and resources to withstand a potential dip in the economy.

OVERCOMING RESISTANCE TO MANAGING RETENTION

The Resistance

Logically, it would appear obvious that the management team would want to support solutions designed to lower turnover. After all, if turnover is the cause of many of the operational issues, most managers would welcome a lower turnover rate. The problem arises from the fact that some managers may not understand the reasoning for a particular solution, or do not have time to invest in supporting and reinforcing the solution.

Most of the solutions described in this book require management involvement. Frequently, the role of the management team and their influence on the retention issue has been underscored. The manager is the key. Managers have to be involved in the solution and devote serious time to making it work. In exasperation, some managers ask, "Don't we have enough to manage without having to manage retention?" Retention solutions may be an unwelcome addition to

1. It costs too much.
2. It takes too much time.
3. Who is asking for this?
4. It is not in my job description.
5. I did not have input on this.
6. I do not understand this.
7. What happens if the solutions are ineffective?
8. How can we be consistent with this?
9. The process is too subjective.
10. Our upper management will not support this.

Exhibit 14.5.   Open Resistance to Retention Solutions

their mix of responsibilities. Some managers have accepted high turnover as a cost of doing business.

The result of this frustration might be a display of open resistance to managing retention. Exhibit 14.5 shows some typical management resistance to retention solutions. Some of these are based on myths, while others may be realistic. Managers may not understand what they should be doing and have many questions about the data and the process. Management resistance alone can make many of the retention solutions ineffective.

Actions to Overcome Resistance

It is important to take specific steps to overcome resistance to a retention solution. The strategic accountability approach, which forms a basis for this book, is client-focused. While retention solutions are usually orchestrated by the human resources staff, they are designed for the management team. It requires constant communication with managers to make them aware of how retention impacts the organization, explain their role in the solution, and keep them involved in the process. Figure 14.2 shows the building blocks to overcome resistance of retention programs. For large organizations with a variety of retention solutions, it may be helpful to focus on many of these building blocks. A special retention function or retention task force may be developed to address these issues. More information on implementation of this kind of process is available in other works (Phillips & Tush, 2008).

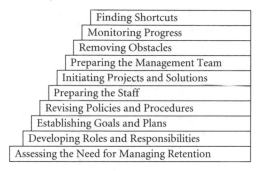

Figure 14.2.   Building Blocks for Overcoming Resistance

Taking the Long View

It is important to take a long view when managing retention. Look at the workforce from a long-term perspective, anticipating downturns in the business so that recruiting can stop when needed. For the most part, it is unnecessary to have abrupt shifts in employment levels. For example, Cisco Systems halted a tremendous recruiting effort, followed immediately by massive layoffs. This illustrates that someone was not anticipating or understanding the issues.

Long term, problems should be anticipated and recruiting channels adjusted to prepare for downturns or major upturns of employment. For example, a major government organization with thousands of research scientists is facing a shortfall of these scientists in the future, as the majority of the workforce in those job categories will retire in the next five years. Consequently, the tremendous challenge for the organization is to ensure that staffing is appropriate. In another scenario, a company completing a major government contract to assemble weapon systems knew in advance when the assembly line would phase out. The HR function, in concert with the management team, redirected staff, retrained staff, and even helped with outplacement opportunities. The employees who were destined for layoff were trained in other careers that were desperately needed in their local area. Engineers became building contractors, technicians became heating and air conditioning specialists, and flight line mechanics became diesel mechanics. This required extensive training, but served as an orderly outplacement for these employees to redirect their careers.

Still another technology organization looked to the future and saw a major shortfall of people available for their jobs in their field. Anticipating that this could lead to high turnover rates (as current job holders may leave for "better" opportunities). the company embarked on an internal training program to prepare employees for the shortage of skills, choosing to upgrade their own employees rather than trying to recruit trained professionals. This extensive training, combined with a service commitment in exchange for the training, kept a stable workforce in place during what otherwise might have been an extremely volatile period of time.

These are only a few of the many examples of organizations that take the long view in terms of their human resource staffing issues. While the focus on the book is on retention, it is important to make sure that *all* the staffing issues are addressed in a consistent, coherent manner.

FINAL THOUGHTS

In this chapter we presented the final step in the strategic accountability approach for managing retention. Communicating results to drive action and make adjustments is a crucial final step. At the completion of this step, the process continues until turnover is at acceptable levels and maintained at those levels. If this step in the process is not taken seriously, the full positive impact of changes will not be realized. The chapter began with the principles of communicating results, with discussions on communication issues and processes. The various target audiences were detailed and, because of its importance, emphasis was placed on communicating with the executive group. A suggested format for a detailed evaluation report was provided, and much of the remainder of the chapter included ways in which data can be used to drive improvement and maintain a low turnover, particularly taking the long view.

References

Block, P. (2001). *Flawless consulting fieldbook and companion: A guide to understanding your expertise*. San Francisco, CA: Pfeiffer.

Phillips, J.J., & Tush, W.F. (2008). *Communication and implementation: Sustaining the practice*. San Francisco, CA: Pfeiffer.

CHAPTER FIFTEEN

Case Study: A Master's Degree for High-Potential Employees

Federal Information Agency

Jack J. Phillips

~~~

T his case illustrates how the high turnover rate of high-potential information specialists was drastically reduced by offering a free master's degree in information science. The program, while expensive, had a dual impact of upgrading skills and stemming turnover—with an impressive ROI.

BACKGROUND

The Federal Information Agency (FIA)provides various types of information to other government agencies and businesses as well as state and local organizations, agencies, and interested groups. Operating through a network across the United States, the work is performed by several hundred communication specialists with backgrounds in systems, computer science, electrical engineering, and information science. These are the critical talent in the agency. Almost all the specialists have bachelor's degrees in one of these fields. The headquarters and operation center is in the Washington, D.C., area, where 1,500 of these specialists are employed.

The FIA has recently experienced two problems that have senior agency officials concerned. The first problem is an unacceptable rate of employee turnover for this group of specialists—averaging 38 percent in the past year alone. This has placed a strain on the agency to recruit and train replacements. An analysis of exit interviews indicated that employees leave primarily for higher salaries. Because the FIA is somewhat constrained in providing competitive salaries, it has become extremely difficult to compete with private sector for salaries and benefits. Although salary increases and adjustments in pay levels will be necessary to lower turnover, the FIA is exploring other options in the interim.

The second problem concerns the need to continuously update the technical skills of the staff. While the vast majority of the 1,500 specialists have degrees in various fields, only a few have master's degrees in their specialties. In this field, formal education is quickly outdated. The annual feedback survey with employees reflected a strong interest in an internal master's degree program in information science. Consequently, FIA explored the implementation of an in-house master's degree in information science conducted by the School of Engineering and Science at Regional State University (RSU). The master's degree program would be implemented at no cost to the participating employee and conducted on the agency's time during routine work hours. Designed to address both employee turnover and skill updates, the program would normally take three years for participants to complete.

This case study shows a unique retention solution in a government agency that was losing critical talent, communication specialist. These critical employees were leaving at a high rate, about 35 percent annually, because of higher salaries in the private sector. The solution focused on career development with a master's degree program offered by the agency. In addition, the solution was tackling another issue as often as the case with the retention solutions. This case study is intriguing and shows the power of matching the right solution to the problem.

PROGRAM DESCRIPTION

RSU was selected for the master's program because if its reputation and the match of their curriculum to FIA needs. The program allows participants to take one or two courses per semester. A two-course per semester schedule (with one course in the summer session) would take three years to complete. Both morning and afternoon classes were available, each representing three hours per week of class time. Participants were discouraged from taking more than two courses per term. Although a thesis option was normally available, FIA requested a graduate project be required for six hours of credit as a substitute for the thesis. A professor would supervise the project. Designed to add value to the FIA, the project would be applied in the agency and would not be as rigorous as the thesis. Participants signed up for three hours in the second and third year of the program.

Classes were usually offered live with professors visiting the agency's center. Occasionally, classes were offered through video-conference or independent study. Participants were asked to prepare for classroom activities on their own time, but were allowed to attend classes on the agency's time. A typical three-year schedule is shown in Exhibit 15.1.

Senior management approved the M.S. curriculum, which represented a mix of courses normally offered in the program and others specially selected for FIA staff. Two new courses were designed by university faculty to be included in the curriculum. These two represented a slight modification of existing courses and were tailored to the communication requirements of the agency. Elective courses were not allowed for two reasons. First, it would complicate the offering to a certain extent, requiring additional courses, facilities, and professors—essentially adding cost to the program. Second, the FIA wanted a prescribed, customized curriculum that would add value to the agency while still meeting the requirements of the University.

	Year 1	Year 2	Year 3
Fall	2 courses – 6 hours	2 courses – 6 hours	2 courses – 6 hours
Spring	2 courses – 6 hours	2 courses – 6 hours	2 courses – 6 hours
Summer	1 course – 3 hours	1 course – 3 hours	1 course – 3 hours

Graduate Project – 6 hours (3 hours Year 2, 3 hours Year 3)
Total semester hours – 48

Exhibit 15.1.   Typical Three-Year Schedule

SELECTION CRITERIA

An important issue involved the selection of employees to attend the program. Most employees who voluntarily left the agency resigned within the first four years, and were often considered to have high potential. With this in mind, the following criteria were established for identifying and selecting the employees to enroll in the program:

1. A candidate should have at least one year of service prior to beginning classes.
2. A candidate must meet the normal requirements to be accepted into the graduate school at the university.
3. A candidate must be willing to sign a commitment to stay with the agency for two years beyond program completion.
4. A candidate's immediate manager must nominate the employee for consideration.
5. A candidate must be considered "high potential" as rated by the immediate manager.

The management team was provided initial information on the program, kept informed of its development and progress prior to actual launch, and briefed as the program was described and selection criteria were finalized. It was emphasized that the selection should be based on objective criteria, following the guidelines offered. At the same time, managers were asked to provide feedback as to the level of interest and specific issues surrounding the nomination of candidates.

A limit of one hundred participants entering the program each year was established. This limit was based on two key issues:

1. The capability of the university in terms of staffing for the program—RSU could not effectively teach over one hundred participants each semester.
2. This was an experiment that, if successful, could be modified or enhanced in the future.

PROGRAM ADMINISTRATION

Because of the magnitude of the anticipated enrollment, the FIA appointed a full-time program administrator who was responsible for organizing and coordinating the program. The duties included registration of the participants, all correspondence and communication with the university and participants, facilities and logistics (including materials and books), and resolving problems as they occur. The FIA absorbed the total cost of the coordinator. The university assigned an individual to serve as liaison with the agency. This individual was not additional staff; the university absorbed the cost as part of the tuition.

The Drivers for Evaluation

This program was selected for a comprehensive evaluation to show its impact on the agency using a four-year time frame. Several influences created the need for this detailed level of accountability.

1. Senior administrators have requested detailed evaluations for certain programs considered to be strategic, highly visible, and designed to add value to the agency.

2. This program was perceived to be very expensive, demanding a higher level of accountability, including return on investment.

3. Because retention is such a critical issue for this agency, it was important to determine if this solution was the appropriate one. A detailed measurement and evaluation should reflect the success of the program.

4. The passage of federal legislation and other initiatives in the United States, aimed at bringing more accountability for taxpayers' funds, has created a shift in increased public sector accountability.

Consequently, the implementation team planned a detailed evaluation of this program beyond the traditional program evaluation processes. Along with tracking costs, the monetary payoff would be developed, including the return on investment (ROI) in the program. Because this is a very complex and comprehensive solution, other important measures would be monitored to present an overall, balanced approach to the measurement.

Recognizing the shift toward public sector accountability, the human resources staff had developed the necessary skills to implement the ROI process. A small group of HR staff members had been certified to implement the ROI process within the agency. The ROI process is a comprehensive measurement and evaluation process that develops six types of data and always includes a method to isolate the effects of the program.

The evaluation of the MS program was conducted by several of these team members with the assistance of the original developer of the ROI process, Dr. Jack J. Phillips.

Objectives of the Program

From the various meetings, memos, and documents related to the program, the objectives evolved. Most of the objectives were linked to the original analysis; the others were fined-tuned during the process. The following is a comprehensive set of objectives for the program. The participants should:

1. Have a positive reaction to the program, content, quality, and administration.
2. Achieve an above-average grade point average for the program (3.0 out of a possible 4.0).
3. Understand their role in making the program successful.
4. Use the knowledge and skills learned in the program directly on the job.
5. Develop and apply innovative projects to add operational value to the agency.

The program should:

1. Have a very high completion rate, with at least 80 percent of the participants obtaining their degrees.
2. Reduce avoidable turnover to no more than 10 percent for the target audience.
3. Enhance job satisfaction, commitment to the organization, and career development.
4. Upgrade technology and capability of the agency.
5. Generate operational results through direct value-added projects.
6. Improve recruiting success as more job applicants apply to future opportunities.

7. Generate a return on investment of at least 25 percent when benefits are spread over a four-year period.

These objectives frame the direction and focus of the program and become important information to develop the data collection plan and ROI analysis plan.

Program Costs

The cost of the program was tabulated and monitored and reflected a fully loaded cost profile, which included all direct and indirect costs. One of the major costs was the tuition for the participants. The university charged the customary tuition, plus $100 per semester course per participant to offset the additional travel, faculty expense, books, and handouts. The tuition per semester hour was $200 ($600 per three-hour course).

The full-time administrator was an FIA employee, receiving a base salary of $37,000/year, with a 45 percent employee benefits upload factor. The administrator had expenses of approximately $15,000 per year. Salaries for the participants represented another significant cost category. The average salary of the job categories of the employees involved in the program was $47,800, with a 45 percent employee benefits factor. Salaries usually increase approximately 4 percent per year. Participants attended class a total of eighteen hours for each semester hour of credit. Thus, a three-hour course represented fifty-four hours of off-the-job time in the classroom. The total hours needed for one participant to complete the program for one participant was 756 hours (14 × 54).

Classroom facilities was another significant cost category. For the one hundred participants, four different courses were offered each semester and each course was repeated at a different time slot. With a class size of twenty-five, eight separate semester courses were presented each regular semester. Half that schedule was offered in the summer. Although the classrooms used for this program were those normally used for other training and education programs offered at the agency, the cost for providing the facilities was included. (Because of the unusual demand, an additional conference room was built to provide ample meeting space.) The estimate for the average cost of all meeting rooms was $40 per hour of use.

	Program Costs			
	Year 1	Year 2	Year 3	Total
Initial Analysis (Prorated)	$ 1,667	$ 1,667	$ 1,666	$ 5,000
Development (Prorated)	$ 3,333	$ 3,333	$ 3,334	$ 10,000
Tuition – Regular	$ 300,000	$ 342,000	$ 273,000	$ 915,000
Tuition – Premium	$ 50,000	$ 57,000	$ 45,500	$ 152,500
Salaries/Benefits (Participants)	$ 899,697	$ 888,900	$ 708,426	$2,497,023
Salaries/Benefits (Program Administrator)	$ 53,650	$ 55,796	$ 58,028	$ 167,474
Program Coordination	$ 15,000	$ 15,000	$ 15,000	$ 45,000
Facilities	$ 43,200	$ 43,200	$ 34,560	$ 120,960
Management Time	$ 3,000	$ 3,000	$ 3,000	$ 9,000
Evaluation	$ 3,333	$ 3,333	$ 3,334	$ 10,000
Total	$1,372,880	$1,413,229	$1,145,848	$3,931,957

Exhibit 15.2.   Total Fully Loaded Costs of MS Program for One Hundred Participants

The cost for the initial assessment was also included in the cost profile. This charge, estimated to be approximately $5,000, included the turnover analysis and was prorated for the first the years. The FIA's development costs for the program were estimated to be approximately $10,000 and were prorated for three years. Management time involved in the program was minimal, but estimated to be approximately $9,000 over the three-year period. This consisted primarily of meetings and memos regarding the program. Finally, the evaluation costs, representing the cost to actually track the success of the program and report the results to management, was estimated to be $10,000.

Exhibit 15.2 represents the total costs of the initial group in the program for three years using a fully loaded cost profile. All of the cost categories mentioned earlier are included. This value is necessary for the ROI calculation.

DATA COLLECTION
Data Collection Issues

To understand the success of the project from a balanced perspective, a variety of types of data had to be collected throughout program implementation. During the initial enrollment process, meetings were conducted with participants to obtain their commitment to provide data at different time frames. The program administrator had regular access to participants who were willing to provide data about their reactions to the program, detail the extent of knowledge and skill enhancement, and describe the successes they achieved on the job. Measures were taken at four distinct levels:

1. Reaction to individual courses and the program, including the administrative and coordination issues.
2. The knowledge and skills obtained from the individual courses and learning about the program.
3. Application and implementation of the program as learning is applied on the job and the program is coordinated effectively.
4. Changes in business measures in the agency, directly related to the program.

In addition to these data items, program costs were monitored so that the return on investment could be calculated.

Collecting different types of data required measures to be taken at different time frames. From the beginning of the program, it was planned that some data categories would be collected at the end of each semester. Reaction would be measured and learning would be monitored with individual grade point averages. At periodic intervals, follow-up data was collected to reflect the progress of the program and its application on the job. Finally, business impact data directly linked to the program was measured during the program as well as at the conclusion. While this program was perceived to have a long-term impact, data had to be collected throughout the process with an early impact developed.

Data Collection Plan

The program administrator was responsible for the initial data collection and semester feedback sections. Individual faculty members were asked to collect reaction and learning measures at the end of each course. While most of the data would come directly from the participants, the records from the agency were monitored for certain business measures, such as turnover. In addition, immediate managers of participants provided input concerning the actual use of the program on the job. Table 15.1 shows the data collection plan for this program.

Reaction

Reaction to the program was collected at specific time periods. A few issues involving reaction and satisfaction were collected from prospective participants at an information briefing when the program was announced. Perceived value, anticipated difficulty of the courses, and usefulness of the program on the job were captured in initial meetings. Next, reaction measures were collected for each individual course as the participants rated the course material, instructor, delivery style, and learning environment. Also, at the end of each semester, a brief reaction questionnaire was collected to provide constant feedback of perceptions and satisfaction with the program. Upon completion of the program, an overall reaction questionnaire was distributed.

Learning

The initial meeting with the participants provided an opportunity to collect information about their understanding of how the program works and their role in making the program successful. Most of the learning took place in individual courses. The faculty member assigned grades based on formal and informal testing and assessment. These grades reflected individual learning, skills, and knowledge. Professors used a variety of testing methodology such as special projects, demonstrations, discussion questions, case studies, simulations, and objective tests. The overall grade point average (GPA) provided an ongoing assessment of the degree to which the participants were learning the content of the courses.

APPLICATION AND IMPLEMENTATION

Application and implementation measures were assessed at several different time intervals. At the end of each year, a questionnaire was distributed where the participants indicated the success of the program in three areas:

1. The opportunities to use the skills and knowledge learned in the program.

Program: Fedeal Information Agency   Responsibility: Jack Phillips   Date: _____

Level	Broad Program Objective(s)	Measures	Data Collection Method/Instruments	Data Sources	Timing	Responsibilities
1	REACTION/SATISFACTION • Positive reaction to program, content, quality, and administration	• 4.0 on a scale from 1 to 5	• Reaction questionnaire	• Participants	• At the intro of the program • End of course • End of semester	• Program administrator • Faculty • Program administrator
2	LEARNING • Maintain above-average grades • Understand the purpose and the participant's role of the program	• 3.0 grade point average out of a possible 4.0 • 4.0 on a scale from 1 to 5	• Formal and informal testing in each course • Questionnaire at the end of initial meeting	• Participants • Participants	• End of each course • At the introduction of the program	• Faculty • Faculty
3	APPLICATION/IMPLEMENTATION • Use of the knowledge and skills on the job • Develop and apply innovative projects to add operational value • Enjoy a very high completion rate	• Various measures on a scale of 1 to 5 • Completion of project • Completion rate of 90%	• Questionnaires • Action plans • Monitoring records	• Participants • Participants • Agency records	• End of each year • One-year follow-up • End of program	• Program administrator • Program administrator • Program administrator
4	BUSINESS IMPACT • Reduce avoidable turnover • Improve job satisfaction/commitment • Career enhancement • Upgrade technology and agency capability • Improve operational results • Recruiting success	• Number of avoidable exits each month divided by the average number each month • 4.0 on a scale of 1 to 5 • Monetary values • Number of candidates	• Monitoring records • Questionnaires • Action plans • Monitoring records	• Agency records • Participants • Managers • Participants • Agency records	• Monthly • End of each year • End of program • one-year follow-up	• HR staff • Program administrator • Program administrator • Program administrator
5	ROI • Achieve a 25 percent return on investment					

Comments: _____

Table 15.1.   Data Collection Plan for MS Program

2. The extent to which the skills have actually been used on the job.

3. The effectiveness in the use of the skills.

In addition, several questions focused on the progress with (and barriers to) the implementation of the program. At this level of analysis, it was important to determine whether the program material was actually being used on the job. Program statistics were collected, including dropout and completion rates of the participants.

Business Measures

Because the program was implemented to focus on retention of specialists, the primary business measure was turnover. Turnover rates for the participants in the program were compared directly with individuals not involved in the program to determine whether the rates were significantly reduced. In addition to avoidable turnover, tenure of employees was tracked, which reflected the average length of service of the target job group. It was anticipated that the program would have an impact on a variety of other business measures as well, including the following:

1. Productivity (from projects)

2. Quality (from projects)

3. Enhanced agency capability

4. Technology upgrade

5. Job satisfaction

6. Employee commitment

7. Recruiting success

8. Career enhancement

In the planning process, it was decided that these measures would be explored to the extent feasible to identify improvements. If this was not feasible, the perceived changes in these business measures would be collected directly from the participants.

Graduate Projects

An important part of the program was a graduate work-study project required to complete the master's degree. The project involved at least two semesters of work and provided six hours of credit. It was supervised be a faculty member and approved by the participants' immediate manager. The project had to add value to the agency in some way as well as improve agency capability, operations, or technology upgrade. At the same time, it should be rigorous enough to meet the requirements of the university. In a sense it was a master's thesis, although the participants were enrolled in a non-thesis option. Through this project, the participants were able to apply what they had learned. The project was identified during the first year, approved and implemented during the second year, and completed in the third year.

This project provided an excellent opportunity for participants to support the agency and add value to agency operations. As part of the project, participants developed an action plan detailing how their project is (will be) being utilized on the job. The action plan, built into the graduate project, provided the timetable and detail for application of the project. A part of the action plan is a detail of the monetary contribution to the agency (or forecast of the contribution). This was required as part of the project and ultimately became evidence of contribution of the project. Follow-up on the action plan provided the monetary amount of contribution from the graduate project.

Data Collection Summary

Table 15.2 shows a summary of the various instruments used to collect data, along with the level of evaluation data. As this table reveals, data collection was comprehensive, continuous, and necessary for a program with this much exposure and expense. Data collected at Levels 1, 2, and 3 were used to make adjustments in the program. Adjustments were made throughout the program as feedback was obtained. This action is particularly important for administrative and faculty related issues.

ANALYSIS
ROI Analysis Plan

Table 15.3 presents a completed planning document for the ROI analysis. This plan, which was completed prior to the beginning of the program, addresses key issues of isolating the influence of the program, converting the data to monetary values, and costing

Type of Instrument	Reaction/ Satisfaction	Learning	Application/ Implementation	Business Impact
1. Questionnaire after intro to program	X	X		
2. End of course instructor evaluation	X			
3. End of semester evaluation questionnaire	X			
4. Individual course tests		X		
5. Annual evaluation questionnaire			X	
6. Action plans with follow-up			X	X
7. One-year follow-up questionnaire			X	X
8. Monitoring records				X

Table 15.2.   Data Summary by Evaluation Level

the program. As the table shows, avoidable turnover, the key data item, is listed along with the technology and operations improvement expected from individual graduate projects. It was anticipated that the program would pay off on turnover and improvements from projects.

Recruiting success is also listed as a measure for potential isolation and conversion. An increase in the number of applicants interested in employment with the FIA was anticipated as the communication and publicity surrounding the program became known in various recruiting channels. Other business impact measures were considered to be intangible and listed in the intangible benefits column. (Intangible benefits are defined as those measures purposely not converted to monetary values.) During the planning stage, it was anticipated that measures such as improved job satisfaction, enhanced agency capability, and improved organizational commitment would not be converted to monetary value. Although very important, these measures would be listed as intangible benefits—only if they were linked to the program.

The cost categories discussed earlier were detailed in this planning document. Costs are fully loaded and include both direct and indirect categories. The communication targets were comprehensive. Seven groups were identified as needing specific information from this study.

Program: <u>MS Information Science</u>   Responsibility: _____   Date: _____

Data Items (Usually) Level 4	Methods for Isolating the Effects of the Program/Process	Methods of Converting Data to Monetary Values	Cost Categories	Intangible Benefits	Communication Targets for Final Report	Other Influences/Issues During Application	Comments
Avoidable Turnover	• Comparison group • Participants' estimates • Manager estimates	• External studies	• Initial analysis • Program development • Tuition • Participant salaries/benefits • Program coordination costs • Facilities • Management time • Evaluation	• Improved job satisfaction • Improved operational commitment • Career enhancement • Enhanced agency capability • Technology upgrade	• Participants • Immediate managers of participants • Program sponsor • Senior agency administrators • Agency HR staff • RSU administrators • All agency employees	• Need to monitor external employment conditions • Need to identify other potential internal influences on turnover reductions	Payoff of program will probably rest on turnover reduction and improvements from projects
Technology and Operating Improvements	• Participants' estimates	• Standard values • Historical costs • Expert input • Participant estimates					
Recruiting Success	• Participants' estimates	• Internal expert estimates					

Table 15.3.   ROI Analysis Plan for MS Program

The ROI analysis and data collection plans provide all the key decisions about the project prior to the actual data collection and analysis.

Isolating the Effects of the Program

Several methods were utilized to isolate the effects of the program, depending on the specific business impact measure. For avoidable turnover, three methods were initially planned. A comparison group was identified, which would serve as the control group in a traditional control group experiment. The individuals selected for the M.S. program would be matched with others not in the program, using the same tenure and job status characteristics. Recognizing the difficulty of success with a control group arrangement, both the participants and managers were asked to indicate the percent of the turnover reduction they believed to be directly related to this program. A questionnaire was provided to obtain this input.

For the technology and operations improvement data, participants' estimates were utilized as a method for isolating the effects of the program using data from action plans for the projects. The same approach was planned for isolating the effects of the program on recruiting success.

Converting Data to Monetary Values

The methods used to convert data to monetary values varied as well. For avoidable turnover, external studies were used to pinpoint the approximate value. From various databases, studies in similar job categories had revealed that the cost of turnover for these specialized job groups was somewhere between two and three times the average annual salary. This was considerably higher than the HR staff at the FIA anticipated. As a compromise, a value of 1.75 times the annual salary was used. While this value is probably lower than the actual fully loaded cost of turnover, it is conservative to assign this value. It is much better to use a conservative estimate for this value than to calculate the fully loaded cost for turnover. Most retention specialists would agree that 175 percent of annual pay is a conservative, fully loaded cost of turnover for information specialists.

To obtain the monetary values of project improvements, participants were asked to use one of four specific methods to identify the value:

1. Standard values were available for many items throughout the agency and their use was encouraged when placing monetary values on a specific improvement.

2. Historical costs could be utilized, capturing the various costs of a specific data item as it is improved by the project. These cost savings values are taken directly from general ledger accounts and provide a very credible cost value.

3. If neither of the above methods was feasible, expert input, using internal sources, was suggested.

4. Finally, if the other methods failed to produce a value, participants were instructed to place their own estimates for the value. In those cases, the confidence of the estimate would be obtained.

For recruiting success, internal expert estimates would be utilized, directly from the recruiting staff. Collectively, these techniques provided an appropriate array of strategies to convert data to monetary values.

RESULTS
Reaction and Satisfaction Measurements

Reaction measurements, taken during the initial program introductions, were informal and confirmed that the participants recognized the value of the program and its usefulness to them as well as the agency. Also, any concerns about the difficulty of the program were addressed during that meeting.

Two opportunities to collect reaction and satisfaction data occurred at the end of each semester. For each course, the instructor obtained direct feedback using standard instrumentation. Exhibit 15.3 shows the faculty evaluation selected for this program. It was a slightly modified version of what RSU normally collects for their instructors. In addition to providing feedback to various RSU department heads, this information was provided to the program

Issue	Average Rating*
Knowledge of Topic	4.35
Preparation for Classes	4.25
Delivery/Presentation	3.64
Level of Involvement	4.09
Learning Environment	4.21
Responsiveness to Participants	4.31
Ability to Relate to Agency Needs	3.77

*On a 1 to 5 scale, with 5 = exceptional

Exhibit 15.3.   Reaction and Satisfaction with Faculty

administrator as well as the major sponsor for this project. This constant data flow was an attempt to make adjustments if the faculty was perceived to be unresponsive and ineffective in delivering the desired courses. As Exhibit 15.3 shows, on a scale from 1 to 5, the responses were extremely effective. The only concerns expressed were with the presentation and ability to relate to agency needs. At several different times, adjustments were made in an attempt to improve these two areas. The ratings presented in Exhibit 15.4 were the cumulative ratings over the three-year project for the one hundred participants who initially began the program.

At the end of each semester, a brief scannable questionnaire was collected to measure satisfaction with, and reaction to, the program. Exhibit 15.4 shows the various items rated on this questionnaire. The goal was to have a composite of at least 4 out of 5 for this program,

Issue	Average Rating*
Value of Program	4.7
Difficulty of Program	4.1
Usefulness of Program	4.5
Quality of Faculty	3.8
Appropriateness of Course Materials	3.9
Intent to Use Course Material	4.2
Amount of New Information	3.7
Recommendation to Others	4.6

*On a 1 to 5 scale, with 5 = exceptional

Exhibit 15.4.   Measures of Reaction to, and Satisfaction with, the Program

Year	Cumulative Grade Point Average*
Year 1	3.31
Year 2	3.25
Year 3	3.18

*Out of a possible 4.0

Exhibit 15.5.   Cumulative Grade Point Averages

and it was achieved. The only areas of concern were the quality of the faculty, the amount of new information, and the appropriateness of the course material. Adjustments were made to improve these areas.

Learning Measurements

Learning was primarily measured through formal testing processes utilized by individual faculty members. As stated earlier, a variety of methods were used ranging from objective testing to simulations. The tests yielded an individual grade that translated into a grade point average. The grade objective for the overall program was to maintain a 3.0 grade point average out of a possible 4.0. Exhibit 15.5 shows the cumulative grade point average through the three-year period ending with an average of 3.18, exceeding the target for the overall program.

Application and Implementation Measures

Application and implementation was measured with three instruments: the annual questionnaire at the end of each program year, the follow-up on the action plans, and a one-year follow-up questionnaire. The two questionnaires (annual and follow-up) provided information about overall application and utilization of the program and course material. Exhibit 15.6 shows the categories of data for the annual questionnaire, which, for the most part, was duplicated in the follow-up questionnaire. As this exhibit reveals, nine topical areas were explored with the focus on the extent to which the participants were utilizing the program and the skills and knowledge learned. It also explored improvements and accomplishments over and above the individual project improvement. Barriers and enablers to implementation were detailed in addition to input on the management support for the program along with recommendations for improvement.

Topics for Annual Questionnaire

Course Sequencing/Availability	Barriers to Implementation
Use of Skills/Knowledge	Enablers to Implementation
Linkage with Impact Measures	Management Support for Program
Improvements/Accomplishments	Recommendations for Improvement
Project Selection and Application	

Exhibit 15.6.   Categories of Data for Annual Questionnaire

Issue	Average Rating*
Opportunity to use skills/knowledge	3.9
Appropriateness of skills/knowledge	4.1
Frequency of use of skills/knowledge	3.2
Effectiveness of use of skills/knowledge	4.3

*On a 1 to 5 scale, with 5 = exceptional

Exhibit 15.7.   Application Data: Use of Knowledge and Skills

Several questions were devoted to each of these categories. For example, Exhibit 15.7 presents application data for knowledge and skills, showing four specific areas and the ratings obtained for each. While these ratings reveal success, there was some concern about the frequency of use and opportunity to use skills. The input scale for these items was adjusted to job context. For example, in the frequency of skills, the range of potential responses was adjusted to reflect anticipated responses and, consequently, in some cases it may have missed the mark. Some skills should be infrequently used because of the nature of the skill and the opportunity to use them. Thus, low marks on these two categories were not particularly disturbing considering the varied nature of program application.

Business Impact

Although business data was monitored in several ways, the annual and follow-up questionnaire obtained input on the perceived linkage with impact measures. As shown in Exhibit 15.6, one category of data provided the opportunity for participants to determine the extent to which this program influenced several impact measures. As far as

Annualized Avoidable Turnover	1 Year Prior to Program	1st Year Sept to Aug	2nd Year Sept to Aug	3rd Year Sept to Aug	1 Year Post-Program
Total Group 1,500	38%	39%	36%	35%	34%
Program Participants Group	N/A	5% (5)	4% (4)	3% (3)	3% (3)
Similar Group	N/A	34%	35%	33%	36%

Table 15.4.   Turnover Data

Four-Year Expected Turnover Statistics = 138

Four-Year Actual Turnover Statistics = 15

Four-Year Total Group Turnover Statistics = 144 (with a base of 100)

actual business improvement value, two data items were converted to monetary values: turnover and project application.

Turnover Reduction

The primary value of the program would stem from annual turnover reduction of the target group. Table 15.4 shows the annualized, avoidable turnover rates for three different groups. The first is the total group of 1,500 specialists in this job category. The next group is the program participants, indicating that of the one hundred initial participants, twelve left during the program (5 percent, 4 percent, 3 percent), and three left in the first year following completion, for a total of fifteen in the four-year time span. For the similar comparison group, one hundred individuals were identified and the numbers were replenished as turnover occurred. As the numbers revealed, essentially the entire comparison group had left the agency by the end of the third year. This comparison underscores the cumulative effect of an excessive turnover rate. Using the comparison group as the expected turnover rate yields a total expected turnover of 138 in the four-year period (34 percent, 35 percent, 33 percent, 36 percent). The actual, however, was fifteen for the same period. Thus, the difference in the two groups (138 compared with 15) equals 123 turnover statistics prevented with this program, using the control group arrangement to isolate the results of the program.

The participants and managers provided insight into the percent of the turnover reduction attributed to the program. For their estimate, the process starts with the difference measured in the total group compared to the actual. Using a base of one hundred, the total group was expected to have 144 turnover statistics (39 percent, 36 percent, 35 percent, 34 percent). One hundred twenty-nine (144 −15 = 129) is the difference between the total group and the actual turnover statistic. Since there were other contributing factors, participants were asked to indicate what percentage of this reduction they attributed to the program. The participants' and managers' estimates were combined (using a simple average to reflect equal weight) to yield a 93 percent allocation to this program. The confidence estimate for this value is 83 percent (the average of the two). Obviously, both groups realized that this program was accomplishing its major goal of reducing turnover. Thus, if 129 are adjusted by 93 percent and 83 percent, the yield is one hundred turnover statistics. Given the choice of using 123 or 100, the lower number is used, although it might not be as credible as the actual control group comparisons. It is conservative to indicate that at least one hundred turnover statistics were prevented in the four-year time frame for this analysis.

The value for the turnover reduction is rather straightforward, with 1.75 times the annual earnings used as a compromised value. The total value of the turnover improvement is 100 × $47,800 × 1.75 = $8,365,000. This is a significant, yet conservative, value for the turnover reduction.

Project Values

The participants developed projects that were designed to add value to the agency by improving capability and operations. Exhibit 15.8 shows the summary of the data from the projects. Eighty-eight individuals graduated from the program and all had approved and implemented projects. Of that number, seventy-four actually provided data on their project completion in the one-year follow-up on their action plan. Of that number, fifty-three were able to convert the project to a monetary value. The participants were asked to estimate the amount of improvement that was directly related to the project (%), recognizing that other factors could have influenced the results. The values are reported as adjusted values in the table. Only forty-six of those were useable values, as unsupported claims

Number of Projects Approved and Implanted	88
Number of Projects Reporting Completion	74
Number of Projects Reporting Monetary Values	53
Number of Project with Usable Monetary Values	46
Average Value of Project – Adjusted	$55,480
Highest Value of Project – Adjusted	$1,429,000*
Lowest Value of Project – Adjusted	$1,235
Average Confidence Estimate	62%
Total Value (Adjusted twice)	$1,580,000

*Discarded in the analysis

Exhibit 15.8.   Monetary Values from Project

and unrealistic values were omitted from the analysis. For example, the highest value ($1,429,000) was eliminated because of the shock value of this number and the possibility of error or exaggeration. The average confidence estimate was 62 percent. When each project value is multiplied by the individual confidence estimate, the total adjusted usable value is $1,580,000.

Intangibles

The intangible benefits were impressive with this program. Recruiting success was not converted to monetary value, but included instead as a subjective intangible value. All of the intangible measures listed in the initial data collection plan were linked to the program, according to participants or managers. A measure was listed as an intangible if at least 25 percent of either group perceived it as linked to the program. Thus, the intangibles were not included in the monetary analysis but were considered to be important and included in the final report.

BCR and ROI Calculations for Turnover Reduction

The benefits/cost ratio (BCR) is the total monetary benefits divided by the total program costs. For turnover reduction, the BCR calculation becomes:

$$\text{BCR} = \frac{\text{Monetary Benefits}}{\text{Total Program Costs}} = \frac{\$8,365,000}{\$3,931,957} = 2.13$$

The ROI calculation for the turnover reduction is the net program benefit divided by the cost. In formula form it becomes:

$$\text{ROI} = \frac{\text{Monetary Benefits} - \text{Total Program Costs}}{\text{Total Program Costs}}$$

$$= \frac{\$4,433,043}{\$3,931,957} \times 100 = 113\%$$

BCR and ROI Calculations for Total Improvement

The BCR for the value obtained on turnover reduction and project completion yields the following:

$$\text{BCR} = \frac{\$8,365,000 + \$1,580,000}{\$3,931,957} = \frac{\$9,945,000}{\$3,931,957} = 2.53$$

The ROI, using program benefits for the two improvements, is as follows:

$$\text{ROI} = \frac{\$9,945,000 - \$3,931,957}{\$3,931,957} \times 100 = 153\%$$

COMMUNICATING RESULTS

Because these are large values, it was a challenge to communicate them convincingly to the senior team. The conservative nature of this approach helps defend the analysis and make the results more credible and believable. The step-by-step results were presented to the senior team using the following sequence:

1. A brief review of the project and its objectives
2. Overview of the methodology
3. Assumptions used in the analysis
4. Reaction and satisfaction measures
5. Learning measures
6. Application and implementation measures
7. Business impact measures
8. ROI
9. Intangibles

10. Barriers and enablers

11. Interpretation and conclusions

12. Recommendations

This information was presented to the senior team in a one-hour meeting and provided an opportunity to present the methodology and results. This meeting had a three-fold purpose.

1. To present the methodology and assumptions for capturing the ROI, building credibility with the process and analysis;

2. Using a balanced approach, to how the impact of a major initiative and how it provides a payoff for the agency and taxpayers; and

3. To show how the same type of solution can be implemented and evaluated in the future.

The project was considered a success.

Jack J. Phillips, Ph.D., is chairman of the ROI Institute, Inc. A world-renowned expert on measurement and evaluation, Dr. Phillips provides consulting services for Fortune 500 companies and workshops for major conference providers around the world. He is the author or editor of more than thirty books and more than one hundred articles.

CHAPTER SIXTEEN

Case Study: Skill-Based Pay

Southeast Corridor Bank (SCB)

Patricia Pulliam Phillips

T his study demonstrates how a retention improvement program generated extremely high impact, including an impressive return on investment. This case, which analyzes a turnover problem in branch operations, focuses on how the specific causes of turnover were determined, how the solutions were matched to the special causes, and how the actual calculation of the impact of the turnover reduction is developed. In this organization, branch employees were considered to be critical talent, because of their contact with, and relationship to, the customer. The strength of the case lies in the techniques utilized to ensure that the solutions are appropriate and that the turnover reduction represented a high payoff solution.

BACKGROUND

Southeast Corridor Bank (SCB), a regional bank operating in four states with sixty branches, had grown from a single-state operation to a multi-state network through a progressive and strategic campaign of acquisitions. As with many organizations, SCB faced merger and integration problems, including excessive employee turnover. SCB's annual turnover rate was 57 percent, compared to an industry average of 26 percent. The new senior vice president for human resources faced several important challenges when he joined SCB, among them the need to reduce turnover. Although management was not aware of the full impact of turnover, they knew it was causing operational problems, taking up much staff and supervisor time, and creating disruptive situations with customers.

MEASURING AND MONITORING TURNOVER

SCB monitored turnover by various categories and defined them as either voluntary separations or terminations for performance. Departures due to retirement and/or disability were not included in the definition. A turnover for performance was an important issue that could be rectified if the performance deficiency could be recognized or prevented early.

The turnover rate was monitored by job group, region, and branch. Branches had the highest turnover rate, averaging some 71 percent in the previous year—far exceeding any expectations and industry averages (turnover compared with other financial institutions and data from the American Bankers Association). In addition to branches, turnover was considered to be excessive in a few entry-level, clerical job classifications in regional and corporate offices.

IMPACT OF TURNOVER

The impact of turnover was developed at the beginning of the study. External turnover studies in the banking industry had revealed that the cost of turnover for bank employees was 110 percent to 125 percent of annual pay. Using the categories listed in Chapter 5, this fully loaded cost was published in several trade publications. When reviewing the proposed program and the proposed method for calculating the payoff, the senior executive team suggested a lower value. In essence, the senior team thought that turnover wasn't quite that expensive and suggested only 90 percent (0.9 times an annual pay).

DETERMINING THE CAUSE OF TURNOVER

Three basic techniques were used to pinpoint the actual cause of turnover. First, as described briefly above, the analysis of individual job groups and tenure within job groups gave insight into where turnover was occurring, the magnitude of the problem, and some indication of the cause. Much of the turnover occurred in the early stages of employment (in the six- to eighteen-month category).

Second, exit interviews from departing employees were examined to see whether specific reasons for departure could be pinpointed. As with most exit data, accuracy was a concern as the departing employees may have been biased when reporting the reason for leaving. The stigma of individuals not wanting to burn bridges left the data incomplete and inaccurate.

Recognizing this problem, the HR team used the nominal group technique to determine more precisely the causes of turnover. A highly structured and unbiased focus group, this process is described next.

NOMINAL GROUP TECHNIQUE

The nominal group technique was selected because it allowed unbiased input to be collected efficiently and accurately across the organization. A focus group was planned with twelve employees in each region for a total of six groups representing all six regions. In addition, two focus groups were planned for the clerical staff in corporate headquarters. This approach provided approximately a 10 percent sample and was considered to be a sufficient number to pinpoint the problem.

Participants for focus groups represented areas where turnover was highest. They described why their colleagues were leaving—not why *they* would leave. Input was solicited from participants in a carefully structured format, using third-party facilitators. The data were integrated and weighted so that the most important reasons were clearly identified. This process has the advantages of low cost, high reliability, and being unbiased. Data were captured in a two-hour meeting in each regional location. Only two days of external facilitator time was necessary to collect and summarize data for review.

The nominal group technique unfolds quickly in ten easy steps.

1. The process is briefly described along with a statement of confidentiality. The importance of participant input is underscored and participants understand what they must do and what it means to SCB.

2. On a piece of paper, participants are asked to make a list of specific reasons why they feel their colleagues have left SCB or why others may leave in the future. It is very important for the question to reflect the actions or potential actions of *others*, although their comments will probably reflect their own views (and that is what is actually needed).

3. In a round-robin format, each person reveals one reason at a time and the reasons are recorded on a flip chart. At this point, no attempts are made to integrate the issues, but just to record the data on paper. It is important to understand the issue and fully described it on paper. The lists are placed on the walls so that when this step is complete, as many as fifty or sixty items are listed and visible.

4. The next step is to consolidate and integrate the lists. Some of the integration is easy because the items may contain the same words and meaning. For others, it is important to ensure that the meanings for the cause of the turnover are the same before they are consolidated. When integrated, the remaining list may contain thirty or forty different reasons for turnover.

5. Participants are asked to review all of the items and to carefully select which ten items they consider to be the most important causes and list them individually on index cards. At first, participants are not concerned about which cause is number one, but are instructed to simply list the ten most important ones on the cards. Participants usually realize that their original list was not complete or accurate, and they will pick up other issues for this list.

6. Participants sort the ten items by order of importance, the number one item being the most important, and number ten the least important.

7. In a round-robin format, each participant reveals a cause of turnover, starting from the top. Each participant reveals his or her number-one item, and 10 points are recorded on the flip chart next to the item. The next participant reveals the number-one issue and so on until the entire group has offered one top cause for turnover. Next, the number-two reason is identified, and 9 points are recorded on the flip chart next to the item. This process continues until all cards have been revealed and points recorded.

8. The numbers next to each item are totaled. The item with the most points becomes the number-one cause of turnover. The one with the second-most points becomes the second cause of turnover and so on. The top fifteen causes are then captured from the group and are reported as the weighted average cause of turnover from *that* group.

9. This process was completed for all six regional groups and the clerical staff groups. Trends began to emerge quickly from one group to the other. The actual raw scores from each group were combined for the integration of the six regional focus groups.

10. The top fifteen scores indicate the top fifteen reasons for turnover in the branches and clerical groups.

SPECIFIC NEEDS

Exhibit 16.1 shows the top ten reasons only for employees leaving the bank branches. A similar list was developed for the clerical staff, but the remainder of this case study will focus directly on the efforts to reduce turnover in the branch network. Branch turnover is the most critical issue with the highest turnover rates and representing the largest number of employees. The results of the focus groups were a clear pattern of specific needs. Recognizing that not all of the causes of turnover could be addressed immediately, the bank set out to work on the top five while a variety of options for solutions were considered. Eventually, a skill-based pay system was implemented.

SOLUTION: SKILL-BASED PAY

The skill-based pay system addressed the top five issues. The program was designed to expand the scope of the jobs with increases in pay for the acquisition of skills and provide a clear path for advancement

1. Lack of opportunity for advancement
2. Lack of opportunity to learn new skills and new product knowledge
3. Pay level not adequate
4. Not enough responsibility and empowerment
5. Lack of recognition and appreciation of work
6. Lack of teamwork in the branch
7. Lack of preparation for customer service problems
8. Unfair and unsupportive supervisor
9. Too much stress at peak times
10. Not enough flexibility in work schedules

Exhibit 16.1.   Top Ten Reasons Why Branch Employees Leave the Bank

Banking Representative Level	Job Duties
I	Basic teller transactions (deposits, check cashing, etc.)
II	Same as above plus opening and closing accounts, CDs, savings bonds, special transactions, etc.
III	Same as above plus limited liability consumer loans, applications for all consumer loans, home equity loans, referrals for mortgage loans, etc.

Table 16.1.   Proposed Job Levels

and job growth. Jobs were redesigned from narrowly focused teller duties to an expanded job, "banking representative." The teller job title was eliminated, and the tellers became Banking Representative I, II, or III. Table 16.1 shows the basic descriptions of the jobs with new initial wage rates. A branch employee would be considered a Banking Representative I if he or she could perform one or two simple tasks such as processing deposits and cashing checks.

As Banking Representatives I took on additional responsibilities and performed different functions, they would be eligible for a promotion to Banking Representatives II. If they performed all the basic functions of the bank branch, including consumer loan applications, promotions to Banking Representatives III was appropriate. Branch employees could progress as they developed job-related skills. Centralized training opportunities were available to develop the needed skills while structured on-the-job training was provided through the branch manager, assistant manager, and teller supervisor. Self-study, videos, and distance learning were also available to help learn new skills. The concept of multiple tasks was aimed at broadening responsibilities and empowering employees to perform a variety of tasks needed to provide excellent customer service. Pay increased following skill acquisition and demonstrated accomplishment, recognized accomplishments, and increased responsibility.

Although the skill-based system had some definite benefits from the employee perspective, there were also some benefits for the bank. Not only was turnover expected to be lower, but actual staffing levels could be reduced in larger branches. In theory, if all employees in a branch could perform all the duties, fewer employees would be needed. Previously, minimum staffing levels were required in certain critical jobs and those employees were not always available for other job duties.

In addition, improved customer service was anticipated. This new approach would prevent customers from having to wait in long lines for specialized services. For example, in the typical branch bank, it is not unusual to see long lines for special functions (opening a checking account, closing out a CD, or taking a consumer loan application) while teller functions (paying and receiving) often have little or no waiting. With each employee performing all the tasks, shorter waiting lines would not only be feasible, but expected.

To support this new arrangement, the marketing department referenced the concept in their promotion of the branch staff and products and services. Included with the checking account statements was a promotional piece labeled, "In Our Branches There Are No Tellers." This document described the process and explained that all the branch employees could perform all branch functions and consequently provide faster, more efficient service.

MEASURING SUCCESS

Measuring the success of the new solution required collecting data at four levels. At the first level, reaction and satisfaction was measured during meetings with the employees and during regularly scheduled training sessions. This measurement provided input on employee acceptance of the new arrangement and different elements of the program. Using brief surveys, data were collected on a 5-point scale. As expected, the results were positive, averaging a 4.2 composite rating, with 5 representing exceptional.

At the second level, learning is measured in two different ways. For each training and learning opportunity, skill acquisition and knowledge increase is measured. Informal self-assessments are taken for many of the programs. A few critical skills required actual demonstration to show that employees could perform the skill (for example, documentation, compliance, and customer services). When learning measurements revealed unacceptable performance, participants were provided an opportunity to repeat training sessions or take more time to practice. In limited cases, a third opportunity was provided. After one year of operation, only two employees were denied a promotional opportunity due to their performance in training programs.

At the third level, application and implementation was measured by collecting four types of data as shown in Table 16.2. Actual participation in the program reflected the willingness for individuals to pursue skill acquisition through a variety of efforts. The results were impressive.

In all, 95 percent of the branch employees wanted to participate in the program. The remaining 5 percent were content with the Banking Representative I classification and were not interested in learning new skills. Requests for training and learning opportunities were a critical part of the formal processes. Employees had to map out their own developmental efforts, which were approved by the branch manager. In all, some eighty-six requests per month were logged, almost taxing the system for providing training and learning opportunities. Reviews of the status and progress—to be considered for the promotion for the next level—were significant, with a total of 138. This review was the formal way of demonstrating skills for promotion. Promotions increased quickly; as much as double that of previous promotions in the branch network. As the table shows, actual promotions one year prior to the program was 139, increasing to 257 one year after the program was initiated.

	1 Year Prior	1 Year Post
Participation in Program	N/A	95%
Requests for Training	45 per month	86 per month
Review Situations	N/A	138
Actual Promotions	139	257

Table 16.2. Selected Application and Implementation Data

Branch Employee Turnover (Monthly)	Avoidable turnover. Total number of employees leaving voluntarily and for performance reasons divided by the average number of employees in the branch for the month. This number is multiplied by 12 to develop the annual turnover rate.
Staffing Level	The total number of employees in the branch, reported monthly.
Customer Satisfaction	Customer reaction to the job changes (faster service, fewer lines) measured on a 1 to 5 scale.
Job Satisfaction	Employee feedback on selected measures on the annual feedback survey process.
Deposits	Savings, checking, and securities deposits by type and product.
Loan Volume	Consumer loan volume by loan type.
New Accounts	New accounts opened for new customers.
Transaction Volume	Number of face-to-face transactions, paying and receiving, by major category.
Cross-Selling	New products sold to existing customers.

Table 16.3.   Business Measures Influenced by the Project

Nine categories of business impact measures were monitored and are shown in Table 16.3, along with the definitions. In all, nine categories of data were expected to be influenced to some degree by this project, although the first four were considered to be the primary measures.

The most important expected benefit was a reduction in turnover. The major thrust of the project was to reduce the total of avoidable turnover. The second measure was staffing levels. With more highly skilled employees, fewer staff should be necessary, at least for the larger branches. The third measure was customer service. With fewer customers waiting in line and less need to move from one line to another, customers should be more satisfied. The fourth measure is job satisfaction; employees should be more satisfied with their work, their jobs, and career possibilities. Finally, there was an expected increase in volume attributed to the project because there were fewer customers waiting in line. Consequently, customers would visit more often or would not leave in frustration because of delays. This should result in increases in deposits, consumer loan volume, new accounts, transaction volume, and cross-selling measures. Additionally, these last five categories were operational measures of each branch and were expected to move very little because of this project.

ISOLATING THE EFFECTS OF THE SKILL-BASED PAY PROJECT

An important issue was to isolate the actual impact of the skill-based pay project from other influences. In almost any type of situation, multiple influences drive specific business measures. To add credibility and validity to the analysis, a specific method was used to isolate the effects of the project for each data item used in the ROI calculation. As shown in Table 16.4, the method used for isolating the effect of the project on turnover reduction was to obtain estimates directly from branch managers and the branch staff. In brief group meetings, the branch staffs were provided the results of the turnover reduction and were asked to allocate the percentage linked directly to the skill-based pay effort. Each branch provided this information.

As a first step in the process, branch team members would discuss the other factors that could have contributed to turnover reduction (only two were identified). They were asked to discuss the linkage between each factor and the actual turnover reduction. This discussion, in a focus group format, improved the accuracy of this estimation. However, since it is estimation, an error adjustment was made. Individuals were asked to indicate the level of confidence in their allocation of turnover improvement to the skill-based pay project using a scale of 0 to 100 percent. With this scale, 0 percent means no confidence and 100 percent means absolute certainty. The confidence percentage was used as a discount for the allocation. For example, if an individual allocated 60 percent of the turnover

Data Item	Method of Isolating the Effects	Method of Converting Data
Employee Turnover	Branch Manager Estimation Staff Estimation	External Studies
Staffing Levels	Branch Manager Estimation	Company Payroll Records
Customer Service	Customer Input	N/A
Job Satisfaction	Staff Input	N/A
Deposits, Loan Volume, New Accounts	Branch Manager Estimation	Standard Value (% Margin)
Transaction Volume	Branch Manager Estimation	Standard Value (% Margin)
Cross-Selling	Staff Estimation	Standard (Average % Margin)

Table 16.4. **Business Measures and Planned Analysis**

reduction to this specific project and was 80 percent confident in that allocation, the adjusted value would be 48 percent (60 percent times 80 percent). When collected properly, this method of isolation provides a conservative estimate for the effect of skill-based pay on turnover reduction. In this example, the branch manager input was combined with the staff employees on equal weighting. Essentially, the results were averaged.

For staffing levels, actual improvements were adjusted with the branch manager estimation. In essence, using the process described above, branch managers indicated the degree to which the new project resulted in actual staff reduction. Staff reductions only occurred in 30 percent of the branches (the larger ones), and this estimate only involved those branch managers. Since no other factors contributed to this staff reduction, branch managers gave the entire reduction amount to the skill-based project.

Table 16.4 shows the planned method for isolation for each measure that is a part of the planning for the study. Increases in deposits, loan volume, new accounts, transactions, and cross-selling were minimal and were influenced by many other variables. Consequently, no attempt was made to isolate the effect on them or use the monetary improvements in the ROI analysis. However, they are listed as intangibles, providing evidence that they have been driven with the turnover reduction program.

Survey cards completed at the end of a transaction and deposited at the entrance to the branch provided a sample of customer service reactions. The customers appreciated the new approach, liked the service delivered, and indicated that they would continue to use the branch. The annual employee job satisfaction survey showed improvements in advancement opportunities, a chance to use skills, pay for performance, and other related issues. Customer service and job satisfaction measures were not isolated or converted to monetary volume and consequently not used in the ROI calculation. However, these measures are very important and influential in the final evaluation and listed as intangible benefits.

CONVERTING DATA TO MONEY

Table 16.4 also shows the method used (or planned) to convert data to monetary value. Turnover was converted to monetary value using a value from external studies. The specific amount was calculated using .9 times the annual salary as the cost of one turnover. This value was considered a conservative amount since several studies had values ranging from 1.1 to 1.25 times annual earnings. More importantly, the value was developed and agreed to in a meeting with the senior management prior to the actual calculation of values. The average annual salary of the branch staff below the branch manager level was $18,500. Collectively, the staffing reductions translated into significant savings far exceeding expectations. For each turnover reduction, a $16,650 (18,500 × .9) savings was realized. Table 16.5 shows the turnover reduction of 174. The contribution factor (the percent of the reduction linked to the solution) and confidence estimate error adjustment is multiplied by the 174 to yield 120 prevented turnovers. The contribution factor and confidence estimates were obtained in branch meetings, described earlier. The cost of a turnover ($16,650) is multiplied by 120 to yield an annual value of almost $2 million. That amount is doubled for a two-year savings. At this point in data collection, the second-year value is not known and a second-year forecast is needed.

The method for converting staffing levels to monetary value was to use the actual salaries for those job levels eliminated. Only a few branches were affected. The actual number was multiplied times the average salary of the branch staff. The value was captured for one year and projected for another year assuming the same level. A two-year time frame was used because it was considered a conservative way to evaluate (one year of actual data and the forecast of one year). Although the program should provide extended value, additional benefits beyond the two years were excluded. This is the conservative basis of the ROI Methodology.

ANALYSIS

The turnover reduction at the branches was significant, moving from 71 percent to 35 percent in one year. Although some of the smaller branches had no staffing changes, the larger branches had fewer staff members. In all, 30 percent of the branches were able to employee at least one less staff member either part-time or full-time. Also, 10 percent of the branches were able to reduce their staff by two individuals.

Table 16.6 shows the calculations of the annual and projected values for the total benefits for the two-year period. Different scenarios could have been considered such as capturing the first-year value

	Prior Year	One-Year Post	Actual Difference	Contribution Factor	Confidence Estimate	Adjusted Amount	Unit Amount	Annual Benefits	Two-Year Benefits
Turnover	71% (336)	35% (162)	174	84%	82%	120	$16,650	$1,998,000	$3,996,000
Staffing Levels	480 (Average)	463 (End of Year)	17	100%	100%	17	$18,500	$ 314,500	$ 629,000

Table 16.5.   Calculation of Business Results

Project Costs	Year 1	Year 2
Initial Analysis	$14,000	–
Program Development	$2,500	–
Participant Time	$345,600	$195,000
Branch Manager Time	$40,800	$30,200
Salary Increases	$446,696	$203,900
Administration/Operation	$4,600	$4,100
Evaluation	$3,000	–
	$857,196	$433,200

Table 16.6. Fully Loaded Project Costs

only. Benefits had to be captured or projected for the same two-year period as the costs. The total two-year benefit was $4,625,000.

PROJECT COST

Table 16.6 shows the fully loaded project cost of the skill-based project. The initial analysis costs were included and included time, direct costs, and travel expenses for focus groups. The development of the program included the time and materials. The next two categories were the branch staff time and represented an estimate of all the time away from normal work to understand the program and learn new skills. The next category is the actual salary increases, that is, the additional salary in the branch as a result of a potential early promotion. The total amount of first-year promotions ($977,600) was reduced by the rate of promotions in the year before the solution was implemented.

Administration and operation was ongoing and involved the time required from the HR staff to administer the program. Finally, the evaluation costs were included and represented the costs related to developing the impact study project. The total cost presented in this table contains several of the items in a one-year actual and one-year forecast while the other items are the total cost of the project. The total two-year cost was $1,290,396.

ROI AND ITS MEANING

The two-year monetary benefits are combined with costs to develop the benefit-cost ratio (BCR) and the return on investment (ROI) using the following formulae.

$$\text{BCR} = \frac{\text{Solution Benefits}}{\text{Solution Cost}} = \frac{\$4,625,000}{\$1,290,396} = 3.58$$

$$\begin{aligned} \text{ROI} &= \frac{\text{Net Solution Benefits}}{\text{Solution Cost}} \\ &= \frac{\$4,625,000 - \$1,290,396}{\$1,290,396} \times 100 = 258\% \end{aligned}$$

This BCR value indicates that for every $1 invested in the project, $3.58 is returned. In terms of ROI, for every $1 invested, $2.58 is returned after the costs are captured. These results are excellent, since most of the ROI studies have target (expected) values in the 25 percent range. The ROI is only one measure and should be considered in conjunction with the other measures. It is an estimate that is developed utilizing a conservative approach. It probably underestimates the actual return from this project.

COMMUNICATION OF RESULTS

The results were communicated to the senior management team in an executive staff meeting where approximately thirty minutes were allocated to the project. The communications were very critical, and three points were made:

- The project was quickly reviewed, including the description of the solution.
- The methodology used for evaluating the project was described.
- The results were revealed one level at a time presenting the following six types of data:
  - Reaction to, and satisfaction with, the skill-based pay system
  - Learning the system and how to use it
  - Application/implementation of the system
  - Business impact of skill-based pay
  - Return on the investment in skill-based pay
  - Intangible measures linked to skill-based pay

This presentation provided a balanced profile of the project and was convincing to the senior management team. The intangibles were important, particularly the customer service improvement. Overall, the senior team was very pleased with the success of the project and impressed with the analysis. This was the first time that a human resources solution had been evaluated using a balanced measurement approach, including ROI.

LESSONS LEARNED

Although this study was on track with the right solution, a few lessons were learned. Perhaps it would have been safer to forecast the ROI at the time the solution was implemented. Forecasting is an important step in the strategic accountability approach to managing retention. It was considered, but not pursued. However, increasing the branch salaries to the extent planned for this solution is a risky scheme. It would be difficult to retract this program if it did not show enough value to make it worthwhile. A forecasted ROI could provide more confidence at the time of implementation.

Also, branch managers and regional managers were not entirely convinced that skill-based pay would add value. Additional effort was needed to capture their buy-in and help them understand the full cost of turnover. They needed to see how this system could alleviate many of their problems as well as add monetary value to the branches.

Finally, branch manager time was underestimated, as these managers had to deal with numerous requests for training and juggle schedules to ensure the staff maintained the training they needed. Also, managers had to provide additional training and spend the time necessary to confirm that bank representatives had obtained the skills necessary for promotion.

Patricia Pulliam Phillips, Ph.D., is an internationally recognized author, consultant, and president and CEO of the ROI Institute, Inc. She provides consulting services to organizations worldwide and helps organizations build capacity in the ROI Methodology through teaching workshops and graduate-level courses.

CHAPTER SEVENTEEN

Case Study: Coaching for New Employees

Global Media Company

Lisa Ann Edwards and Christina Lounsberry

T his case illustrates how a pilot study generated a return on investment for a coaching program targeted to new-hires. By pinpointing a turnover problem with new employees who voluntarily terminate their employment prior to their first-year anniversary, this study focuses on how the specific causes of turnover were determined, how the solution was matched to the special causes, and how a calculation of the actual impact of the turnover reduction was developed. The strength in this case lies in the success in gaining support for the ROI approach in an organization that does not see the benefit of the ROI method.

BACKGROUND

Ruche Media Company (RMC) is a global media company with twenty-four offices located around the world. The corporate headquarters of this $260M organization is based in a major metropolitan city in North America. Most of the 1,100 employees are based at the corporate headquarters, while the remaining workforce is located in sales offices in major metropolitan cities throughout the world. As with many organizations, RMC has faced industry consolidation problems, competitive pricing pressures and employee turnover. In 2005, RMC's annual voluntary turnover rate was 22 percent worldwide compared to an industry average of 19 percent; or 9 percent for companies listed in *Fortune* 100 Great Places to Work. Although management was not concerned with addressing the turnover problem, it suspected it was causing operational problems, taking up much staff and manager time, and creating disruptive situations with customers. This pilot study represents a way to build support for addressing retention in an organization that needs to see turnover as a real business issue and better understand the value in a methodical, strategic approach that links the solution to business impact and ROI.

MEASURING AND MONITORING TURNOVER AT RMC

RMC monitored turnover by various categories and defined them as either voluntary or involuntary separations. Reasons for voluntary separations included career opportunities, dissatisfaction with pay/benefits/policies, dissatisfaction with working conditions, and personal reasons. Involuntary separations included reductions in workforce, disciplinary action, and termination for failure to meet performance expectations. No one terminated employment as a result of a disability or because of retirement during the period reviewed, so these categories were not considered in the analysis.

After creating a common definition of turnover, RMC analyzed the turnover rates by various demographics such as location, business group and years of service. Through this analysis, it was discovered that turnover was highest among employees who were employed for less than one year at RMC in the corporate office. In fact, RMC discovered that turnover in the corporate office was 30 percent, and 12 percent of all new-hires departed prior to their one-year anniversary.

DEVELOP FULLY LOADED COSTS OF TURNOVER

After reviewing where turnover was the greatest, RMC then calculated the turnover costs. It was agreed that existing studies would be utilized

Middle Managers (e.g., Department Managers)	125 to 200%
Type/Category	Turnover Cost Ranges as a Percent of Annual Wage/Salary
Entry Level – Hourly, Non-Skilled (e.g., Fast-Food Worker)	30 to 50%
Service/Production Workers – Hourly (e.g., Courier)	40 to 70%
Skilled Hourly (e.g., Machinist)	75 to 100%
Clerical/Administrative (e.g., Scheduler)	50 to 80%
Professional (e.g., Sales Representative, Nurse, Accountant)	75 to 125%
Technical (e.g., Computer Technician)	100 to 150%
Engineers (e.g., Chemical Engineer)	200 to 300%
Specialists (e.g., Computer Software Designer)	200 to 400%
Supervisor/Team Leaders (e.g., Section Supervisor)	100 to 150%

Table 17.1.   Turnover Costs Summary

Source: ROI Institute (www.roiinstitute.net)

for turnover costs. Table 17.1 contains a list of turnover cost ranges as a percent of annual wage or salary as captured from dozens of impact studies. The data are arranged by job category, ranging from non-skilled, entry-level positions to middle managers. The ranges listed represent the cost of turnover as a percent of annual wage/salary and are rounded off for ease of use and communication. The costs represented in these studies are fully loaded and include the exit cost of the previous employee, recruiting, selection, orientation, initial training, wages and salaries while in training, lost productivity, quality problems, customer dissatisfaction, loss of expertise/knowledge, supervisor's time for turnover, and temporary replacement costs. The data in this table reflects studies in industry and trade magazines as well as practitioner publications, academic research, and independent studies conducted by professional organizations and associations.

In order to obtain an average cost of turnover that could be used per turnover, RMC calculated the cost of turnover for each individual who left the organization during a twelve-month period by multiplying that individual's wage/salary by the median percent of annual wage/salary for the job category appropriate for that individual. The cost of each turnover during that period was then totaled and divided by the total number of individuals during that period to arrive at an average turnover cost of $116,927.09 per employee. Using this average cost of turnover, the total cost of turnover company-wide was calculated at $28.3M— $8.7M in the corporate office and $2.8M for first-year employees in the corporate office. More importantly, $116,927.09 became the commonly agreed-up average cost of one turnover.

DETERMINING THE CAUSE OF TURNOVER

Two basic techniques were used to pinpoint the actual cause of turnover. First, a review of the turnover causes as recorded in the human resource information system (HRIS) database indicated that 46 percent of those individuals leaving prior to their first-year anniversary listed "career" as the reason they were leaving the organization. It was surprising that an individual who had not yet met his or her first-year anniversary would leave for career reasons, so RMC reviewed the exit interview forms to pinpoint the actual cause of turnover. It was believed that a review of the exit interviews would illuminate any hidden causes of the turnover that would better explain why individuals were leaving for career reasons prior to their first-year anniversary. Exhibit 17.1 shows the most frequently mentioned causes of turnover as uncovered and recorded during the exit interview.

Since this program was a pilot study and involved a relatively small number of participants, it was decided that it was unnecessary to do a more thorough investigation of the cause of turnover. Ideally, RMC would have conducted focus groups with new-hires and utilized the nominal group technique to gain a more comprehensive understanding of the cause of turnover; however, given the size of the study, it was decided that step was unnecessary.

1. General chaos, confusion and disorganization
2. Unclear job expectations
3. Unsure what responsibilities were from one day to the next
4. Doing a different job than hired for

Exhibit 17.1.   Stated Reasons for Voluntary Separation

SOLUTION: NEW-HIRE COACHING PILOT STUDY

Recognizing that not all of the causes of turnover could be addressed immediately, a solution was designed to help new-hires navigate the stated chaos, confusion, and disorganization frequently mentioned and recorded in the exit interviews. RMC created a new-hire coaching pilot study, "The Inside Track." The Inside Track was designed to ensure a new-hire's success, retain the new-hire through to his or her first-year anniversary, improve new-hire commitment, and better understand challenges new-hires face.

Participant Selection

The program was intended for new-hires located in the corporate office who had joined the company within the last two months of the start date of the pilot study. E-mails marketing the new program were sent to a group of new-hires, who were later invited to an information session to learn more about the program before committing to it. Participants were informed that this was a pilot study to improve new-hire on-boarding and ensure success and the importance of staying in the program for the its duration was communicated to the participants during the information session. More than 90 percent of participants who attended the information sessions enrolled in the program, making a total of thirteen participants. Of those participants, two individuals dropped out within the first two-weeks. One of those participants decided he/she did not need the program. That individual is still at RMC. The other participant dropped out due to termination; however, it was later discovered that the individual should not have been included in the program at the start, as the individual's manager was in the process of exiting the employee from the organization and the individual's tenure far exceeded the selection criteria of the program.

Program Design

Participants attended a one-hour group coaching session each month for four consecutive months. They were also able to participate in a maximum of eight individual coaching sessions with a professional internal coach. At the start of the study, participants completed a pre-assessment survey that was designed to measure their level of engagement and commitment to the organization, and all participants took the survey at the conclusion of the study as well. The final survey also asked for Level 1 data, including participants' reactions to the program and specific open-ended questions related to their perceptions of the impact of the study.

GROUP COACHING. Participants were invited to a one-hour monthly group coaching session for four consecutive months. Each session utilized an appreciative inquiry approach, and sessions were designed around the fundamental belief that the power to be successful in a new job lies within the individual.

The topic of Session I was strengths—how new-hires were using their strengths in their job and how their new roles mapped to the hopes and dreams they had for themselves prior to beginning their work at RMC. Session II was designed to help new-hires understand their development level within the framework of a learning model and how to ask for what they needed from their managers based on that framework. Session III concerned successful career management strategies and helping new-hires to prepare for their performance evaluation later in the year. Finally, Session IV covered career development tactics and a discussion was held about how to avoid common career derailers.

INDIVIDUAL COACHING. All participants had the opportunity to participate in a maximum of eight individual coaching sessions. All participants were required to define a coachable issue and worked with a professionally trained, internal coach. Research by Posner and Schmidt (1993). has shown that people who have clarity about their personal values have higher levels of commitment to the organization than those who do not regardless of the organization's values. With this understanding, the context of the coaching work included the whole person and sometimes addressed personal values, personal mission as well as the cycle of renewal of adult development, especially as it related to the individual's new role at RMC. Again, the fundamental assumption underlying the coaching philosophy and style was that the power for career success lies within the individual.

Measuring Success

There were four primary objectives of this program:

1. Ensure new-hires' success;

2. Improve new-hire engagement and commitment;

3. Better understand challenges new-hires face; and

4. Retain new-hires through to their first-year anniversaries.

ENSURE NEW-HIRES' SUCCESS. Measuring success of the solution for new-hires' success was measured by asking for the participants' reactions to and satisfaction with the program. Measurement at this level provided input from the participants on their reactions to the solution, their perspectives on the different elements of the program, and whether or not they accomplished the goals they set for themselves at the start of the program. Using the post-assessment survey to collect this information, data was collected on a 5-point scale. As expected, the results were positive, averaging a 5.0 composite rating. Figure 17.1 represents participants' responses to the five questions related to participant reaction to and satisfaction with the program:

In addition to asking participants' reactions to the program, the post-assessment survey also provided participants the opportunity to re-state their goals from the start of the coaching program and indicate whether they accomplished their goals by the end of the program. Table 17.2 lists participants' goals at the start of the program and outcome at the conclusion of the program.

IMPROVE NEW-HIRE ENGAGEMENT AND COMMITMENT. RMC also measured participants' level of engagement and commitment to the organization before and after the program. Overall, there was an 11 percent improvement on all items related to engagement. Further, each of the items used in the survey are believed to be correlated to specific bottom-line measurables such as retention, profitability, productivity and customer satisfaction. Figure 17.2 represents participants' percent agreement to questions as related to retention, profitability, productivity, and customer satisfaction at the start of the program and at the conclusion of the program.

BETTER UNDERSTAND CHALLENGES NEW-HIRES FACE. Another objective of this study was to better understand the challenges that new-hires face

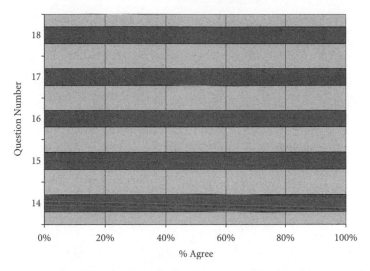

Q14. Overall, I am satisfied with *The Inside Track* (New-Hire Coaching Pilot Study) program.
Q15. Overall, this program was relevant in helping me to be successful in my job.
Q16. Overall, this program was a good use of my time.
Q17. I have used the information from the program and insight gained from the coaching in my job.
Q18. I would recommend this program to other new-hires.

Figure 17.1. Participants' Reactions to Pilot Study

and why they might choose to leave RMC prior to their first-year anniversaries. To gather this data, the internal coach recorded notes at the end of each coaching session and was able to extract common themes heard about the various challenges and barriers they faced at RMC. Exhibit 17.2 lists the most common challenges faced by new-hires that emerged out of the individual coaching sessions.

RETAIN NEW-HIRES THROUGH TO THEIR FIRST-YEAR ANNIVERSARIES. Finally, a fourth objective of this study was to retain new-hires throughout their first-year. Voluntary turnover of first-year employees at RMC is 12 percent. Given this statistic, it would be normal for one individual from the study to terminate employment prior to the first-year anniversary. Instead, not one individual terminated employment prior to his or her first-year anniversary. As a result, RMC saved $116,927.09. Interestingly, at the conclusion of the study, three participants confided to the coach that had the program not been in place to support them throughout their first year, they would

Participant Number	Stated Goal	Outcome: Do You Believe You Made Progress in Reaching Your Goals?
1	Career development	Definitely
2	Focus on goals and responsibilities	I was able to work on a plan of attack for addressing areas that need change and how I can be instrumental in that process.
3	I wanted to learn effective methods for voicing my ideas and opinions, and understand the management philosophy at RMC.	I'm getting there; have been given the proper tools and techniques.
4	Learning RMC business operations developing leadership capabilities	Yes
5	Managing employees	Yes
6	To learn more about RMC as a whole	Yes
7	How to obtain training	Yes
8	Improving the working relationship with my manager and clarifying my role and responsibilities	Yes
9	Career focus, organizational skills, work/life balance, time management	Yes
10	Mostly items from my personal life	Yes
11	Time management and stress management	Absolutely

Table 17.2.   Participants' Goals and Outcomes

likely have voluntarily terminated their employment. While this was an interesting insight, RMC chose a conservative approach to evaluating the program and only acknowledged a savings of one turnover.

CONVERTING DATA
Solution Benefit

It was agreed that the solution benefit would be 50 percent of the average cost of one turnover. RMC acknowledged that there might be other factors influencing retention in addition to this program. While it might have been ideal to run a control group or to ask the participants for their evaluations of the effect of this program on their decision to stay with the organization for the full year, it was

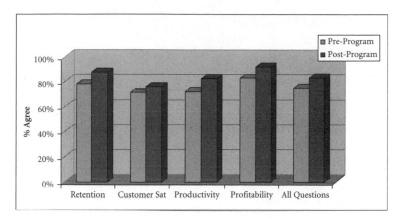

Figure 17.2.   Percent Agreement Pre-Program vs. Post-Program

1. Manager unavailable for direction and support;
2. Available manager, but poor direction and support;
3. Chaotic, disorganized workflow; and
4. Lack of training for tools specific to the job.

Exhibit 17.2.   Common Challenges Faced by New-Hires

agreed that one-half of the impact, or $58,463.45, would be utilized to calculate ROI. Table 17.3 shows costs for the program.

Project Cost

Cost Category	Cost
Internal Coach's Salary and Benefits	
Group Coaching	$450.00
Individual Coaching	$3,898.13
Materials	$55.00
Facilities	$7,730.00
Participants' Salary and Benefits	
Group Coaching	$1,760.00
Individual Coaching	$2,772.00
Total	**$16,665.13**

Table 17.3.   Cost of the Program

Calculating ROI

In effect the ROI was calculated as follows:

$$\text{ROI} = \text{Net Solution Benefits}$$
$$= \$58,463.45 - \$16,665.13 \times 100$$
$$= 251\% \text{ROI}$$

Solution Cost $16,665.13

In terms of ROI, for every $1 RMC invested, $2.51 was returned after the costs were captured. These results are excellent; however, ROI is only one measure and should be considered in consideration of other measures. It should be remembered that this is an estimate that is developed utilizing a conservative approach and it probably underestimates the actual return from this project.

As a result of this study, the recommendation was made that this program be adopted for full implementation.

LESSONS LEARNED

This study is a good example of how to implement a pilot study in an organization that may not yet be ready to take on a full ROI study. By conducting a smaller study and demonstrating to management how an ROI study may be useful, individuals may be able to garner greater support for conducting a full-scale ROI study in the future.

Had the organization been in greater support of an ROI study, several elements would have been conducted differently. For example, the cause of turnover would have been more thoroughly investigated. While the program was effective in reducing turnover, it is likely that there are other causes and perhaps better solutions that would have had a more significant and broader impact. Additionally, the effects of the program could have been isolated by asking for participants' estimation of the impact, or better yet, running a control group that received the pre- and post-assessment, but not the solution.

In conclusion, this pilot study did positively demonstrate the impact of coaching on new-hire retention, and the organization was satisfied with the result.

COMMUNICATION STRATEGY

Because this pilot study only had support for the solution, and not the ROI aspect of the study, it was a challenge to communicate the study to a senior-level and broader audience. The approach of the study helped to defend the analysis and make the results more believable and credible at the middle-management level. The results were presented to the vice president of human resources as well as two directors of human resources in the following sequence:

1. Brief review of the project and its objectives;
2. Overview of the methodology;
3. Assumptions used in the analysis;
4. Reaction and satisfaction measures;
5. Engagement and commitment measures;
6. Business impact;
7. ROI; and
8. Recommendations

This information was presented in a one-hour meeting that provided an opportunity to present the methodology and results. This meeting had two purposes:

1. Present the methodology, assumptions, solution and results and
2. Gain support to implement the solution on a broader scale.

The project was considered a success.

Questions for Discussion

1. Can the value of this program be forecast? If so, how?
2. Most of the costs are estimated or rounded off. Is this appropriate? Explain.
3. What issues surface when developing cost data? How can they be addressed?
4. Are the ROI values realistic? Explain.
5. Is this study credible? Explain.

REFERENCE

Posner, B.Z., & Schmidt, W.H. (1993). Values congruence and differences between the interplay of personal and organizational value systems. *Journal of Business Ethics, 12,* 171–177.

Lisa Ann Edwards is the director, Global Learning and Development, with a global media company and is the founder of Bloom Consulting, Inc., a consulting firm specializing in employee engagement and retention. She holds a master's degree in psychology and a coaching certification from The Hudson Institute. She may be contacted at Lisa@BloomWhereYouArePlanted.com.

Christina Lounsberry is a learning and development specialist with a global media company and is an experienced facilitator, classroom instructor and human resources specialist.

⟞ Index

~~ About the Authors

Jack J. Phillips, Ph.D., is a world-renowned expert on accountability, measurement, and evaluation. Phillips provides consulting services for Fortune 500 companies and major global organizations. The author or editor of more than fifty books, he conducts workshops and presents at conferences throughout the world.

Phillips has received several awards for his books and work. On two occasions, *Meeting News* named him one of the twenty-five Most Influential People in the Meetings and Events Industry, based on his work on ROI. The Society for Human Resource Management presented him an award for one of his books and honored a Phillips' ROI study with its highest award for creativity. The American Society for Training and Development gave him its highest award, Distinguished Contribution to Workplace Learning and Development, for his work on ROI.

His expertise in measurement and evaluation is based on more than twenty-seven years of corporate experience in the aerospace, textile, metals, construction materials, and banking industries. Dr. Phillips has served as training and development manager at two Fortune 500 firms, as senior human resource officer at two firms, as president of a regional bank, and as management professor at a major state university.

This background led Dr. Phillips to develop the ROI Methodology—a revolutionary process that provides bottom-line figures and accountability for all types of learning, performance improvement, human resources, technology, and public policy programs.

Dr. Phillips regularly consults with clients in manufacturing, service, and government organizations in forty-four countries in North and South America, Europe, Africa, Australia, and Asia.

Phillips and his wife, Dr. Patti P. Phillips, recently served as authors and series editors for the *Measurement and Evaluation Series* published by Pfeiffer (2008), which includes a six-book series on the ROI Methodology and a companion book of fourteen best-practice case studies. Other books recently authored by Phillips include *ROI for Technology Projects: Measuring and Delivering Value* (Butterworth-Heinemann, 2008); *Return on Investment in Meetings and Events: Tools and Techniques to Measure the Success of All Types of Meetings and Events* (Butterworth-Heinemann, 2008); *Show Me the Money: How to Determine ROI in People, Projects, and Programs* (Berrett-Koehler, 2007); *The Value of Learning* (Pfeiffer, 2007); *How to Build a Successful Consulting Practice* (McGraw-Hill, 2006); *Investing in Your Company's Human Capital: Strategies to Avoid Spending Too Much or Too Little* (Amacom, 2005); *Proving the Value of HR: How and Why to Measure ROI* (SHRM, 2005); *The Leadership Scorecard* (Elsevier Butterworth-Heinemann, 2004); *Managing Employee Retention* (Elsevier Butterworth-Heinemann, 2003); *Return on Investment in Training and Performance Improvement Programs*, 2nd ed. (Elsevier Butterworth-Heinemann, 2003); *The Project Management Scorecard*, (Elsevier Butterworth-Heinemann, 2002); *How to Measure Training Results* (McGraw-Hill, 2002); *The Human Resources Scorecard: Measuring the Return on Investment* (Elsevier Butterworth-Heinemann, 2001); *The Consultant's Scorecard* (McGraw-Hill, 2000); and *Performance Analysis and Consulting* (ASTD, 2000). Phillips served as series editor for ASTD's In Action casebook series, an ambitious publishing project featuring thirty titles. He currently serves as series editor for Elsevier Butterworth-Heinemann's Improving Human Performance series.

Dr. Phillips has undergraduate degrees in electrical engineering, physics, and mathematics; a master's degree in decision sciences from Georgia State University; and a Ph.D. in human resource management from the University of Alabama. He has served on the boards of several private businesses—including two NASDAQ companies—and several nonprofits and associations, including the American Society for Training and Development and the National Management Association. He is chairman of the ROI Institute, Inc., and can be reached at (205) 678-8101, or by e-mail at jack@roiinstitute.net.

Lisa Ann Edwards, M.S., specializes in talent management, specifically as it relates to accountability and business impact. In her role as director, Global Learning and Development, for Corbis, a global media company with offices across the world, Edwards is responsible for designing and implementing effective solutions around performance management, career development, learning and development, talent review, and succession planning.

In addition to her work as an internal consultant, Edwards is also the founder of Bloom; a company that specializes in helping companies keep their best employees. She has worked with mid-sized and Fortune 500 companies to help them re-engage their employees and has conducted many workshops and presented at conferences throughout the world. Prior to founding Bloom, Edwards was a strategic business consultant and worked with young, high-growth-oriented businesses. Her consulting work focused on business development and included market research, strategic market development, and implementation of marketing tactics.

Prior to consulting, Lisa co-founded a poster publishing company in 1994 that repositioned her family's printing firm, where she had worked in human resources for twelve years. She successfully created strategic alliances and facilitated the development of the business to a position of stability and growth.

Edwards' formal education includes a bachelor's degree in psychology from St. Mary's College in Notre Dame, Indiana, and a master of science degree in psychology from Southern Methodist University. She may be contacted by email at: Lisa@BloomWhereYou ArePlanted.com.

Pfeiffer Publications Guide

This guide is designed to familiarize you with the various types of Pfeiffer publications. The formats section describes the various types of products that we publish; the methodologies section describes the many different ways that content might be provided within a product. We also provide a list of the topic areas in which we publish.

FORMATS

In addition to its extensive book-publishing program, Pfeiffer offers content in an array of formats, from fieldbooks for the practitioner to complete, ready-to-use training packages that support group learning.

FIELDBOOK Designed to provide information and guidance to practitioners in the midst of action. Most fieldbooks are companions to another, sometimes earlier, work, from which its ideas are derived; the fieldbook makes practical what was theoretical in the original text. Fieldbooks can certainly be read from cover to cover. More likely, though, you'll find yourself bouncing around following a particular theme, or dipping in as the mood, and the situation, dictate.

HANDBOOK A contributed volume of work on a single topic, comprising an eclectic mix of ideas, case studies, and best practices sourced by practitioners and experts in the field.

An editor or team of editors usually is appointed to seek out contributors and to evaluate content for relevance to the topic. Think of a handbook not as a ready-to-eat meal, but as a cookbook of ingredients that enables you to create the most fitting experience for the occasion.

RESOURCE Materials designed to support group learning. They come in many forms: a complete, ready-to-use exercise (such as a game); a comprehensive resource on one topic (such as conflict management) containing a variety of methods and approaches; or a collection of like-minded activities (such as icebreakers) on multiple subjects and situations.

TRAINING PACKAGE An entire, ready-to-use learning program that focuses on a particular topic or skill. All packages comprise a guide for the facilitator/trainer and a workbook for the participants. Some packages are supported with additional media—such as video—or learning aids, instruments, or other devices to help participants understand concepts or practice and develop skills.

- *Facilitator/trainer's guide* Contains an introduction to the program, advice on how to organize and facilitate the learning event, and step-by-step instructor notes. The guide also contains copies of presentation materials—handouts, presentations, and overhead designs, for example—used in the program.

- *Participant's workbook* Contains exercises and reading materials that support the learning goal and serves as a valuable reference and support guide for participants in the weeks and months that follow the learning event. Typically, each participant will require his or her own workbook.

ELECTRONIC CD-ROMs and web-based products transform static Pfeiffer content into dynamic, interactive experiences. Designed to take advantage of the searchability, automation, and ease-of-use that technology provides, our e-products bring convenience and immediate accessibility to your workspace.

METHODOLOGIES

CASE STUDY A presentation, in narrative form, of an actual event that has occurred inside an organization. Case studies are not prescriptive, nor are they used to prove a point; they are designed to develop critical analysis and decision-making skills. A case study has a specific time frame, specifies a sequence of events, is narrative in structure, and contains a plot structure—an issue (what should be/have been done?). Use case studies when the goal is to enable participants to apply previously learned theories to the circumstances in the case, decide what is pertinent, identify the real issues, decide what should have been done, and develop a plan of action.

ENERGIZER A short activity that develops readiness for the next session or learning event. Energizers are most commonly used after a break or lunch to stimulate or refocus the group. Many involve some form of physical activity, so they are a useful way to counter post-lunch lethargy. Other uses include transitioning from one topic to another, where "mental" distancing is important.

EXPERIENTIAL LEARNING ACTIVITY (ELA) A facilitator-led intervention that moves participants through the learning cycle from experience to application (also known as a Structured Experience). ELAs are carefully thought-out designs in which there is a definite learning purpose and intended outcome. Each step—everything that participants do during the activity—facilitates the accomplishment of the stated goal. Each ELA includes complete instructions for facilitating the intervention and a clear statement of goals, suggested group size and timing, materials required, an explanation of the process, and, where appropriate, possible variations to the activity. (For more detail on Experiential Learning Activities, see the Introduction to the *Reference Guide to Handbooks and Annuals*, 1999 edition, Pfeiffer, San Francisco.)

GAME A group activity that has the purpose of fostering team spirit and togetherness in addition to the achievement of a pre-stated goal. Usually contrived—undertaking a desert expedition, for example—this type of learning method offers an engaging means for participants to demonstrate and practice business and interpersonal skills. Games are effective for team building and personal development mainly because the goal is subordinate to the process—the means through which participants reach decisions, collaborate, communicate, and generate trust and understanding. Games often engage teams in "friendly" competition.

ICEBREAKER A (usually) short activity designed to help participants overcome initial anxiety in a training session and/or to acquaint the participants with one another. An icebreaker can be a fun activity or can be tied to specific topics or training goals. While a useful tool in itself, the icebreaker comes into its own in situations where tension or resistance exists within a group.

INSTRUMENT A device used to assess, appraise, evaluate, describe, classify, and summarize various aspects of human behavior. The term used to describe an instrument depends primarily on its format and purpose. These terms include survey, questionnaire, inventory, diagnostic, survey, and poll. Some uses of instruments include providing instrumental feedback to group members, studying here-and-now processes or functioning within a group, manipulating group composition, and evaluating outcomes of training and other interventions.

Instruments are popular in the training and HR field because, in general, more growth can occur if an individual is provided with a method for focusing specifically on his or her own behavior. Instruments also are used to obtain information that will serve as a basis for change and to assist in workforce planning efforts.

Paper-and-pencil tests still dominate the instrument landscape with a typical package comprising a facilitator's guide, which offers advice on administering the instrument and interpreting the collected data, and an initial set of instruments. Additional instruments are available separately. Pfeiffer, though, is investing heavily in e-instruments. Electronic instrumentation provides effortless distribution and, for larger groups particularly, offers advantages over paper-and-pencil tests in the time it takes to analyze data and provide feedback.

LECTURETTE A short talk that provides an explanation of a principle, model, or process that is pertinent to the participants' current learning needs. A lecturette is intended to establish a common language bond between the trainer and the participants by providing a mutual frame of reference. Use a lecturette as an introduction to a group activity or event, as an interjection during an event, or as a handout.

MODEL A graphic depiction of a system or process and the relationship among its elements. Models provide a frame of reference and something more tangible, and more easily remembered, than a verbal explanation. They also give participants something to "go on," enabling them to track their own progress as they experience the dynamics, processes, and relationships being depicted in the model.

ROLE PLAY A technique in which people assume a role in a situation/ scenario: a customer service rep in an angry-customer exchange, for example. The way in which the role is approached is then discussed and feedback is offered. The role play is often repeated using a different approach and/or incorporating changes made based on feedback received. In other words, role playing is a spontaneous interaction involving realistic behavior under artificial (and safe) conditions.

SIMULATION A methodology for understanding the interrelationships among components of a system or process. Simulations differ from games in that they test or use a model that depicts or mirrors some aspect of reality in form, if not necessarily in content. Learning occurs by studying the effects of change on one or more factors of the model. Simulations are commonly used to test hypotheses about what happens in a system—often referred to as "what if?" analysis—or to examine best-case/worst-case scenarios.

THEORY A presentation of an idea from a conjectural perspective. Theories are useful because they encourage us to examine behavior and phenomena through a different lens.

TOPICS

The twin goals of providing effective and practical solutions for workforce training and organization development and meeting the educational needs of training and human resource professionals shape Pfeiffer's publishing program. Core topics include the following:

Leadership & Management

Communication & Presentation

Coaching & Mentoring

Training & Development

E-Learning

Teams & Collaboration

OD & Strategic Planning

Human Resources

Consulting

What will you find on pfeiffer.com?

- The best in workplace performance solutions for training and HR professionals

- Downloadable training tools, exercises, and content

- Web-exclusive offers

- Training tips, articles, and news

- Seamless on-line ordering

- Author guidelines, information on becoming a Pfeiffer Affiliate, and much more

Discover more at www.pfeiffer.com